PEOPLE TYPES & TIGER STRIPES

PEOPLE TYPES & TIGER STRIPES

Using Psychological Type to Help Students Discover their Unique Potential

GORDON LAWRENCE

CAPT®
Center for Applications of Psychological Type, Inc. | 2815 NW 13th St., Suite 401 | Gainesville, FL 32609 | www.capt.org

First Edition 1979. Second Edition 1982. Third Edition 1993. Fourth Edition 2009

Published by
Center for Applications of Psychological Type, Inc.
2815 N.W. 13th Street, Suite 401
Gainesville, Florida 32609
352.375.0160
www.capt.org

Printed in the United States of America.

Library of Congress Cataloging-in-Publication Data

Lawrence, Gordon, 1930-
[People types & tiger stripes]
People types and tiger stripes : using psychological type to help students discover their unique potential / Gordon Lawrence. -- 4th ed.
p. cm.
Previously published under title: People types & tiger stripes.
ISBN 978-0-935652-87-1 (pbk.)
1. Teaching. 2. Individualized instruction. I. Title.

LB1025.3.L38 2009
371.102--dc22

2009031451

TABLE OF CONTENTS

2

PART TWO: ADVANCED APPLICATIONS

PREFACE

THIS BOOK HAS tripled in content since I wrote the first edition in 1979, reflecting the growth of my own understanding and uses of Carl Jung's and Isabel Myers' ideas about psychological types. The first edition was mostly about types of learning styles and was addressed specifically to teachers and others concerned with planning instruction. The second edition (1982) kept the same focus and had double the content. During the 1980s, there were few books about the psychological types, and many people besides educators were reading this one. During the same years, Myers' self-report instrument for identifying people's type preferences—the Myers-Briggs Type Indicator® (MBTI®) assessment—became the most widely used instrument of its kind in career guidance, personal counseling, management and organizational development, and many other applications besides those in schools and colleges where I worked. So in the 1992 edition I included new material for users of type concepts in all settings. The new topics included:

- introducing type effectively into an organization
- ethical pitfalls in using type and how to avoid them
- stereotyping: how to spot it and give it up
- practical ways of introducing type to individuals and small groups
- an understanding of deeper layers of type theory
- type development and how to foster it
- consideration of the types as sixteen distinct kinds of mind

And more new content related to education:

- type and curriculum reform
- exercises on adapting teaching styles
- more case examples of using type in colleges and schools
- summaries of research involving the MBTI assessment in studies of learning styles

In this edition, I have added to the book the text of my booklet, *Descriptions of the Sixteen Types.* As I was going through the book to update it with resources and references for this 2009 edition, I was delighted to see—as I had hoped to find—that the content remains timely and sound after all these years.

It has been a joy to work with and be one steward of the timeless contributions of Jung and Myers, as well as Mary McCaulley, CAPT's president from its founding in 1975 until her death in 2003. Being her colleague through those years was an honor and an education for me. My work builds on theirs, and I feel privileged to extend what they accomplished.

I have been so fortunate to have many colleagues who contributed to my knowledge and skills, and to the content of this book—too many to mention by name. Thank you. I would like though to thank my editor, Eleanor K. Sommer, who did thoughtful and careful editorial work on this edition. And finally I am deeply grateful to my wife, Carolyn, for her partnership in exploring type concepts. Her influence is in every chapter.

Gordon Lawrence

PROLOGUE

THIRTEEN-YEAR-OLD LISA is a problem for her teachers. She's bright enough, but she seems to value popularity above everything else. Talkative, friendly, and gregarious, she relies on her friends to make decisions for her, and she patterns her behavior after theirs. Adults see her as flighty and unsure of herself and her own point of view. Her work and conversations are often trite and shallow. While she is conscientious and wants to please, sometimes her classmates and teachers are annoyed by her "helpfulness," and they wish she would mind her own business. When criticized by a teacher or her friends, she seems deeply hurt and resentful. Lisa frustrates her teachers; this is not because she disrupts class or resists assignments. The problem is that they realize her personal development is not going well, and they feel powerless to do anything about it. Perhaps, through their planning meetings, they can focus on a strategy to help Lisa develop some perspective and "a mind of her own." But at least fifty more of the students they see every day need attention as much as Lisa does, and there is no time to work out a strategy for each of them.

THIRTY-THREE-YEAR-OLD LISA is a problem for her boss. She's bright enough for her job, but she seems to value popularity above everything else. Talkative, friendly, and gregarious, she relies on her co-workers and friends to make decisions for her, and she patterns her behavior after theirs. They see her as flighty and unsure of herself and her own point of view. Her work and conversations are often trite and shallow. While she is conscientious and wants to please, sometimes her co-workers and boss are annoyed by her "helpfulness," and they wish she would mind her own business. Whenever they criticize her work, she seems deeply hurt and resentful.

Lisa frustrates her boss but not because she slacks off or resists assignments. The boss realizes her personal development problems are interfering with her work and feels powerless to do anything about it. Improvement on those problems would certainly benefit her work performance, but helping her with them is outside the boss's responsibility.

Do you see in Lisa's behavior a pattern you recognize? Probably every classroom has a "Lisa," as do many workplaces. All of us in the helping professions have encountered her. As you might suppose, I wrote the two descriptions to make the point that personal development problems not dealt with in childhood and youth can follow a person into adult life.

This book presents ways to recognize the basic ingredients in behavior that make up a motivation pattern, and then it explains how to make an educated, shortcut prediction about what strategy will work best with the students and people we teach and supervise. The information in this book can help a variety of people identify their resources, not just the ones who might be struggling or in trouble. The focus of the book is on a system for identifying mind-sets, learning styles, and motivation patterns, and on how to use these patterns to plan instruction, facilitate teams, and coordinate activities among various students and adults. The objective is to help people find and enhance their strengths and use them to deal with their weak spots.

Behind this book lies a long, personal search by me to find practical and effective means of matching work assignments to people's different kinds of mental processing. A variety of approaches exist. Many of them merit attention. The approach presented here is based on Carl G. Jung's ideas about psychological types, as made practical through the work of Isabel Briggs Myers (Jung 1923/1971; Myers 1980). Theirs is a remarkable theory that offers a fresh perspective on people's mental patterns of dealing with their world—including their learning styles.

This book includes readings and instructions for activities that explain the essential ideas and that guide you in applications of the ideas. The activities that are designed for small groups also can be used by individuals with the occasional assistance of a colleague. Although this book is addressed to teachers and others in helping professions, many others—including parents and bosses—will be able to translate the ideas and activities to their own framework. Because most of my own work has been in education, the examples I use are mainly from school and college settings.

The book is divided into two parts. Part one has seven chapters on basic applications of the concepts, including the beginning theory needed for guiding sound uses of the ideas. Part two has five chapters, one on the deeper aspects of the Jung/Myers theory and four on advanced applications. My purpose was to provide materials useful to all readers, whatever their applications or prior knowledge of the work of Jung and Myers. Chapters 2, 3, and 9 deal specifically with education applications. All the others address uses of the ideas in any setting.

1

Part One: Basic Applications

1

People Types & Tiger Stripes

PEOPLE'S HABITS TELL a lot about them. Not just their "good" and "bad" habits, but also habits such as what they pay attention to, what they care about, and how they decide things. These are mental habits. Do you know any people with mental habits like these?

> Chris is quick to notice people's feelings, and tries to stay out of arguments. Jan likes to argue, likes to explain things, and sometimes doesn't notice people's feelings. John's father wants him to have a budget and keep a record of how he spends his weekly allowance. John says record keeping isn't important to him. Pat wishes her mother would watch the clock more and get to places on time. Pat's mother wishes Pat would relax and not get an ulcer over being late five minutes.

Some mental habits are very deep in a person. Trying to change them is like trying to change the stripes on a tiger—like trying to change the grain in a piece of wood. What we will look at here are the kinds of *mental* habits that we probably can't change but can learn to use better.

For instance, in the previously mentioned examples Chris will always have the mental habit, or mental filter, that makes him alert to people's feelings. It is just part of his basic nature. He can't change that, but he can learn to use it in ways that help him rather than hurt him or others. If he grows to use it well, he'll be good at building relations with people and helping them. If he doesn't develop that way, the weight of other people's dark emotions might drag him down, or he could use the knowledge of their emotions to hurt them.

Or consider the contrasting example of Jan who likes to argue, to explain things, and is less alert to people's feelings. Most likely her path for growth will be learning to know when to argue and when to keep quiet. Her instinct to argue isn't likely to change, but she could learn to shape it to her advantage by recognizing that people's feelings are facts to be aware of, to be taken into account to improve her arguments, and to make her explanations more persuasive and helpful.

If there are deep habits of mind that shape our development and learning, as suggested in the examples, then we need to find out at least three things:

What are the most important deep habits?

How do we spot them in people?

How do we work with them to get the best outcomes?

That's what this book is about!

Patterns of Mental Habits

The deep mental habits come in patterns, in combinations. Described below are eight patterns you can use to study yourself, your friends, and your family. Pick out your own patterns. There are no better or worse patterns. Think carefully and try to pick the patterns that really describe you best—just as you are. This exercise is not a test. It is simply a way for you to start looking at the patterns in yourself. After you have completed the exercise, you will be able to see how the eight sets form into patterns of people types, and you can get an idea of which type may be yours.

EXERCISE

IDENTIFYING MENTAL HABITS

(Read through the set of descriptions and then follow the instructions below. Repeat this procedure for all four sets of descriptions on pages 3–6.)

Table 1.1 Which pattern describes you better: E or I?

E	I
E likes action and variety	**I** likes quiet and time to consider things
E likes to do mental work by talking to people	**I** likes to do mental work privately before talking
E acts quickly, sometimes without much reflection	**I** may be slow to try something without understanding it first
E likes to see how other people do a job and to see results	**I** likes to understand the idea of a job and to work alone or with just a few people
E wants to know what other people expect of him or her	**I** wants to set his or her own standards

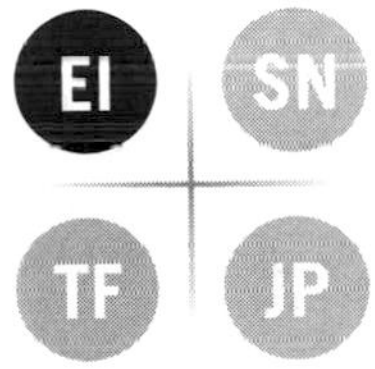

E's interest turns mostly outward to the world of action, people, and things. **I**'s interest turns more often to the inner world of ideas and private things. Everyone turns outward to act and inward to reflect. You must do both, but you are more comfortable doing one or the other, just as right-handers are more comfortable with the right hand but do use the left one. **E** stands for Extraversion, which means outward turning. **I** stands for Introversion, which means inward turning.

Circle the E or the I to show which pattern fits you better.

Table 1.2 Which pattern describes you better: S or N?

S	N
S pays most attention to solid facts	**N** pays most attention to the meanings of facts and how they fit together
S trusts eyes and ears and other senses to find out what's really true	**N** likes to use imagination to find new ways to do things, new possibilities
S likes to work on things that are useful right now	**N** likes solving new problems, and dislikes using the same thing over and over
S likes first-hand experience that gives practice in familiar skills and new ones	**N** likes using new skills more than practicing old ones
S is patient with details but impatient when the details get complicated	**N** is impatient with details but doesn't mind complicated situations

S pays most attention to the facts that come from personal experience. **S** can more easily see the details, while N can more easily see the "big picture" and is comfortable using imagination. **S** and **N** are two kinds of perception, that is, two ways of finding out or giving attention to experiences. **S** stands for Sensing perception, and **N** stands for Intuition perception. Everybody uses both their Sensing and their Intuition to find out things. You use both, but you prefer one and use it more than the other.

Circle the S or the N to show which pattern fits you better.

Table 1.3 Which pattern describes you better: T or F?

T	F
T likes to decide things using logic	**F** likes to decide things using personal feelings and values
T likes to keep emotions out of making decisions	**F** likes praise and likes to please people, even in small matters
T may neglect or hurt other people's feelings without knowing it	**F** is usually very aware of other people's emotions
T gives more attention to things or ideas than to human relationships	**F** can predict how other people will feel
T likes to analyze and argue	**F** values harmony, feels unsettled by arguments and conflicts

T makes decisions by examining data, staying impersonal and cool. **T** stands for Thinking judgment. **F** makes decisions by paying attention to personal feelings and values. **F** stands for Feeling judgment. You make **T** and **F** decisions every day, but you use one kind of judgment more than the other.

Circle the **T** or the **F** to show which pattern fits you better.

Table 1.4 Which pattern describes you better: J or P?

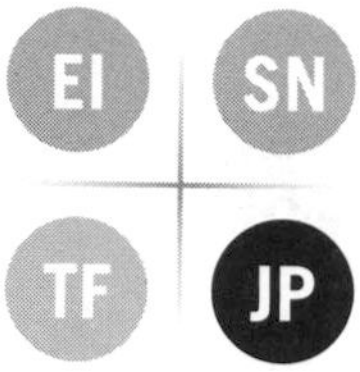

J	P
J likes to make a plan, to have things settled and decided ahead	**P** likes to stay flexible and avoid fixed plans
J tries to make things come out the way they "ought to be"	**P** deals easily with unplanned and unexpected happenings
J likes to finish one project before starting another	**P** likes to start many projects but may have trouble finishing them all
J usually has mind made up	**P** usually is looking for new information
J may decide things too quickly	**P** may decide things too slowly
J wants to be right	**P** wants to miss nothing
J lives by standards and schedules	**P** lives by making changes to deal with problems as they come along

J stands for Judging and **P** stands for Perceiving. **J** people run their outer life with settled judgments. **P** people run their outer life in an open, perceiving way.

Circle the **J** or the **P** to show which pattern fits you better.

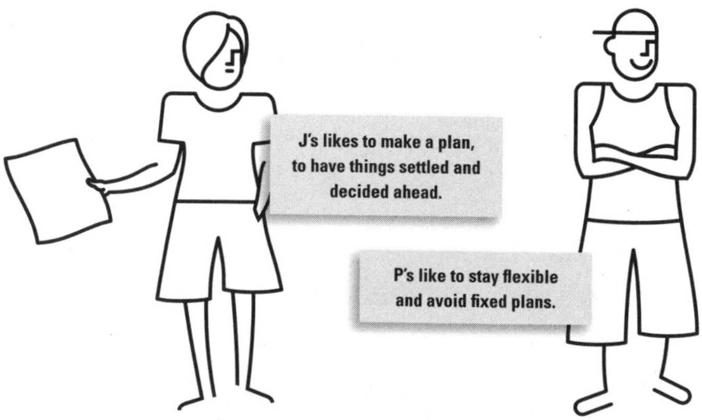

People Types Come from the Four Sets of Choices

Now you can put together the four letters of the patterns that describe you best.

Draw a circle around the same letters you circled in the previous pages.

E I   S N   T F   J P

Write your four circled letters here: ____ ____ ____ ____

These four letters together make up a whole pattern called a type.

It may be your type. There are sixteen different people types as shown by the sixteen combinations of the letters. Find the pattern you chose.

ISTJ	ISFJ	INFJ	INTJ
ISTP	ISFP	INFP	INTP
ESTP	ESFP	ENFP	ENTP
ESTJ	ESFJ	ENFJ	ENTJ

Each type of mental processing is different from the others in important ways. As you come to understand the type ideas better, you will see how they affect your life with your friends and family, at school, or in a job.

If you are a teacher, the activity you have just completed is one you may want to use with students. With young students in mind, I wrote it in language as simple as I could. You may photocopy and reproduce the activity for students, giving credit to this publication. Use it only as a *discussion* starter, as a first step in thinking about type. This brief exercise is not an instrument developed through research.

People Types and Tiger Stripes shows how an understanding of the types of mental processing is important for teachers and other professionals concerned with instruction, training, supervision, and guidance. In my own work to understand student motivation and learning styles, I have come to the conclusion that an understanding of the types is fundamental. It is crucial in explaining why certain approaches to instruction or supervision work with some people and not with others. The fact that a person prefers Sensing perception over Intuitive perception, or prefers an active (extraverted) approach to problem solving over a reflective (introverted) one, is not just an interesting curiosity. It is information that many professionals have used to make dramatic improvements in the effectiveness of their work.

> **"As you come to understand the type ideas better, you will see how they affect your life with your friends and family, at school, or in a job."**

The Myers-Briggs Type Indicator® Instrument

The four dimensions of type (E–I, S–N, T–F, and J–P) and the ideas behind the sixteen types represent the lifelong work of Isabel Briggs Myers. In 1962 Educational Testing Service published the Myers-Briggs Type Indicator® instrument, a paper and pencil instrument Isabel developed with her mother Katharine Briggs over a twenty-year period. Regarded as a research instrument, it did not have wide circulation or usage until CPP, Inc. (formerly Consulting Psychologists Press, Inc.) assumed responsibility for publishing it in 1975. The Indicator was developed specifically to carry Carl Jung's theory of psychological types (Jung, 1923/1971) into practical applications.

The rest of this book will be more useful to you if you have taken the Myers-Briggs Type Indicator (MBTI®) instrument and are aware of your own type profile. The Indicator was written to be taken by people who have not yet studied Jung's types. Spontaneous responses probably give a more accurate profile, so the time to take the Indicator is *before* you continue reading this book. If you have not yet taken the MBTI instrument, you may find a person qualified to administer the instrument and interpret the results through a number of organizations. You may also take the MBTI instrument online. Please see the resource section in the back of this book for more information.

The remainder of this chapter and appendix A will help you get started on deciding which of the mental processing types is a best fit for you.

The Sixteen Types

The MBTI assessment was designed to identify a person's preferences on four pairs of opposites, as shown in table 1.5. The MBTI instrument uses a shorthand designation for the eight characteristics: E for Extraversion, I for Introversion, and so on as indicated in figure 1.5. Note that N is used for Intuition because an I has already been used for Introversion. While type is reported and explained in four parts, it is not merely a combination of parts. Nor is it static, as the term "type" often connotes. Type is a dynamic system, and each type is an integrated pattern. The dynamics of the types are the subject of chapter 8.

Table 1.5 Four Preferences Are Scored to Arrive at a Person's Type

Does the person's interest flow mainly to . . .	**E** The Outer World of Actions, Objects, and Persons? — EXTRAVERSION	**I** The Inner World of Concepts and Ideas? — INTROVERSION
Does the person prefer to perceive . . .	**S** The Immediate, Real, Practical Facts of Experience and Life? — SENSING	**N** Possibilities, Relationships and Meanings or Experiences? — INTUITION
Does the person prefer to make judgments or decisions . . .	**T** Objectively, Impersonally, Considering Causes of Events and Where Decisions May Lead? — THINKING	**F** Subjectively, and Personally, Weighing Values of Choices and How They Matter To Others? — FEELING
Does the person prefer mostly to live . . .	**J** In a Decisive, Planned, and Orderly Way, Aiming to Regulate and Control Events? — JUDGING	**P** In a Spontaneous, Flexible Way, Aiming to Understand Life and Adapt to It? — PERCEIVING

So that you have a good idea about all sixteen types, I have included in appendix A the booklet *Descriptions of the Sixteen Types* (Lawrence, 1998). Read all of it. When you have taken the Indicator and know which type it reported for you, the compact descriptions will give you a good way to verify the results and then select a type that seems to you a best fit. The descriptions include the values and priorities associated with each of the types, showing the similarities of kindred types and the contrasts between dissimilar types.

You will also benefit from reading a full description of your best-fit type. Many publications contain full descriptions of the sixteen types. I most often recommend the descriptions in *Looking at Type®: The Fundamentals* by Charles R. Martin (CAPT, 1997). Each description is two pages in length and contains information about the interests and behaviors common to that type.

After reviewing these type descriptions, you should be better able to decide which of the preference types is your best-fit type. Try on your hypothesized type and test its usefulness to you. As you decide on your best-fit type, remember that the activity at the beginning of this chapter is just an exercise to get you started on the concepts. It is not an instrument validated by research.

Don't expect to understand type concepts quickly. Their meanings will present themselves to you at times and in circumstances that will surprise you. As you come to understand type, you'll enjoy watching for type differences in the people close to you.

Jung's Theory of Psychological Types

The great Swiss physician-psychologist C. G. Jung developed one of the most comprehensive theories to explain human personality. Where other observers saw people's behavior as random, Jung saw patterns. What he called "psychological types" are patterns he observed in the way people prefer to perceive and make judgments.

The Mental Processes

In Jung's theory, all conscious mental activity can be classified into four mental processes or functions—two perception processes (Sensing and Intuition) and two judgment processes (Thinking and Feeling). What comes into consciousness, moment by moment, comes either through the senses or through intuition. To remain in consciousness, perceptions must be used. They are used—sorted, weighed, analyzed, evaluated—by the judgment processes, Thinking and Feeling. The following descriptions of these mental processes were adapted from *Applications of the Myers-Briggs Type Indicator to Medicine and Other Health Professions* (McCaulley, 1978).

Perceiving processes: Sensing and Intuition. Sensing (S) is the term used for perception of the observable by way of the senses. Intuition (N) is the term used for perception of meanings, relationships, and possibilities by way of insight.

Sensing (S) types use Sensing and Intuition, but prefer, and therefore develop, Sensing. With good type development, the expertise in Sensing can lead to a differentiated awareness of present experience, acute powers of observation, a memory for facts and detail, and a capacity for realism, for seeing the world as it is. Traits characteristically developed as a consequence of a preference for Sensing include a reliance on experience rather than theory; a trust of the conventional and customary way of doing things; and a preference for beginning with what is known and real, and then moving systematically, step-by-step, tying each new fact to past experience and testing it for its relevance in practical use. To most Sensing types, "real intelligence" is characterized as soundness, accuracy, and common sense. Sensing types are attracted to careers and settings where skillful application of well-learned knowledge is more important than developing new solutions; where working with tangibles is more important than using theory and insight; and where dealing with the immediate situation and using sound, conventional wisdom is more important than making bold breakthroughs.

> **"What comes into consciousness, moment by moment, comes either through the senses or through intuition."**

Intuitive (N) types use Sensing and Intuition, but prefer, and therefore develop, Intuition. With good type development, Intuition provides insight into complexity; an ability to see abstract, symbolic, and theoretical relationships; and a capacity to see future possibilities, often creative ones. Attitudes characteristically developed as a result of a preference for Intuition include reliance on inspiration rather than on past experience, an interest in the new and untried, and a preference for learning new materials through an intuitive grasp of meanings and relationships. To most

Intuitive types, "real intelligence" is shown by insight in grasping complexities, and flashes of imagination or creativity. Intuitive types are attracted to careers and settings where it is more important to find the pattern in complex systems than it is to deal with the practical details; where creating new knowledge is more important than applying existing knowledge; where working with theory and imagination is more important than dealing with tangibles; and where intellectual challenge is more important than the enjoyment of the pleasures of everyday events.

Judgment processes: Thinking and Feeling. Thinking (T) is the term used for a logical decision-making process, aimed at an impersonal finding. Feeling (F) is a term for a process of appreciation, making judgments in terms of a system of subjective, personal values. Both Thinking and Feeling are considered *rational* processes because they use reasoning to arrive at conclusions or decisions.

Thinking (T) types use both Thinking and Feeling, but prefer to use Thinking for making judgments. With good type development, expertise in Thinking leads to powers of analysis and an ability to weigh facts objectively including consequences, unintended as well as intended. Attitudes typically developed from a preference for Thinking include objectivity, impartiality, a sense of fairness and justice, and skill in applying logical analysis. Thinking types are attracted to areas where tough-mindedness and technical skills are needed.

Feeling (F) types use Thinking and Feeling, but prefer to reach judgments through Feeling. With good type development, Feeling leads to development of values and standards, and knowledge of what matters most to themselves and other people. Attitudes typically resulting from a preference for Feeling include an understanding of people and a wish to affiliate with them; a desire for harmony; and a capacity for warmth, empathy, and compassion. Feeling types are attracted to areas where understanding and communication with people are needed, and they find interpersonal skills more interesting than the technical skills.

Preferences Among the Mental Processes

Everyone uses both of the perception processes—Sensing (S) and Intuition (N)—and both of the judgment processes—Thinking (T) and Feeling (F). But everyone prefers one of each pair over the other. That makes four preference pairs:

Sensing plus Feeling (SF), Sensing plus Thinking (ST), Intuition plus Feeling (NF), and Intuition plus Thinking (NT). Myers called the SF combination sympathetic and friendly, the ST practical and matter of fact, the NF enthusiastic and insightful, and the NT logical and ingenious. In chapter 11 of this book is a discussion of the patterns represented in the four combinations.

Jung observed that in each person's preferred pair one of the processes is dominant. It has the leadership in the personality; it serves as the center post, and the other processes are helpers in the person's mental framework. Using my own preference pair as an example, Intuition plus Thinking (NT), you know more about me when you know that Intuition is dominant, and my Thinking process is a helper to the dominant, Intuition. People with Intuition dominant see the world in terms of possibilities. Possibilities come into my mind continually, and I evaluate them mainly with my second preference, Thinking. However, in the NT combination, when Thinking is dominant, logical order is the first concern, and the Intuition process serves the dominant Thinking by supplying possibilities for making an orderly system work well.

> **"Extraversion means looking outward for interests, values, and stimulation. Introversion means looking inward for these."**

The nature of the dominant process and other aspects of the dynamics of the sixteen types are discussed in chapter 8.

The Third Dimension: Extraversion and Introversion

Jung identified a third dimension of personality structure: Extraversion–Introversion. He invented these terms. He created them from the Latin components and assigned to them quite specific meanings. These meanings have been distorted, if not corrupted, in American common usage. Staying close to the Latin, extraverting means *outward-turning* and introverting means *inward-turning*. We all do both regularly, every day. We turn outside of ourselves to act in the world, and we turn into ourselves to reflect. Of course, action without reflection is blind and may be fruitless; and reflection that does not lead to action may be futile. Both extraverting-action and introverting-reflection are essential. However, each person is not equally at home in action and reflection. Those who prefer Extraversion often say "When in doubt, act." Those who prefer Introversion are more likely to say "When in doubt, reflect on the matter more deeply."

To extravert is to think out loud, to reveal half-thought ideas, to process one's experiences outwardly as a means of doing one's best mental work. To introvert is to keep ideas inside, where the best mental work goes on, and polish the ideas until they are ready to be exposed. So people who prefer Extraversion, whom we call Extraverts, are seen as more outgoing, and those who prefer inner processing, whom we call Introverts, are seen as reserved. Extraversion means looking outward for interests, values, and stimulation. Introversion means looking inward for these.

Extraversion and Introversion also refer to how the dominant process—S, N, T, or F—is used. A person whose preference is for Extraversion most often uses the dominant mental process outwardly, where it is visible to others. A person whose preference is for Introversion most often uses the dominant process inwardly, privately. It is no surprise that people who prefer Extraversion are easier to get to know; they show their dominant process most readily. It takes longer to get to know the ones who favor Introversion, who reserve their dominant for the inner life.

The Fourth Dimension: Judging and Perceiving

Briggs and Myers elaborated Jung's ideas of psychological type and showed a fourth dimension that is present, but not highlighted, in the descriptions given by Jung. The fourth dimension is the attitude taken toward the outer world. When a judgment process (Thinking or Feeling) is used in running one's outer life, the natural drive is to have things decided, judged, settled, planned, organized, and managed according to plan. In this personality pattern, the drive is always toward closure, toward having a settled system in place. This is the Judging attitude toward the outer world, represented by the letter J as the fourth letter of the type designation—for example, ENFJ.

When a perception process (Sensing or Intuition) is used to run one's outer life, the natural drive is toward keeping things open to new perceptions. The person wants to stay flexible, so as to adapt to changing circumstances, and to experience life as widely as possible. In this personality pattern, the drive is always toward keeping plans and organization to a necessary minimum so one can respond to new perceptions and adapt flexibly to new circumstances. This is the Perceiving attitude toward the outer world, represented by the letter P as the fourth letter of the type designation—for example, ENFP.

Thus the fourth letter of the type designation is a J or a P. As we get to know a person, the J–P aspect of his or her type is often the first to be noticed. A person's planful or spontaneous nature is quickly apparent.

Directing one's outer life in a planful way, as Js do, seems readily understandable. What is the P way? Being receptive and spontaneous may not appear to be ways of *directing* one's life. They appear reactive and not proactive. Aren't the P types proactive? The analogy of steering a sailboat or skateboarding can help make this concept clearer. These are activities that require many adjustments in a short span of time, actions that appear spontaneous and impulsive rather than based on judgment. Actually, many judgments are happening very quickly. And each adjustment, the steering required, quickly takes into account the changing conditions and how they interact with the intentions of the person controlling the action. There are good reasons to believe that the Perceiving types tend toward occupations that require this kind of steering, adjusting to changing events; occupations such as fine artist, artisan, journalist, craftsman, actor, or psychologist.

To summarize briefly, in Jung's theory of psychological types, all conscious mental activity occurs in two perception processes (Sensing and Intuition) and two judgment processes (Thinking and Feeling). Everyone uses all four processes, but we differ in how much and how well we use each of them. In every person, one of the processes is dominant, and that process indicates the basic way the person addresses life. If a person uses the dominant process mainly in the world of people and things, that person's orientation is called Extraverted. The person who uses the dominant process mainly in the inner, private world of ideas and thoughts has an introverted orientation. Briggs and Myers added the fourth dimension, and a J or P at the end of the set of letters that is the shorthand designation of each type. The J means a Judging, planful way of running one's outer life. The P means a Perceiving, spontaneous outer life.

Questions Often Asked About Type

Following are some questions and answers about type that have been adapted with permission from an unpublished document written by Mary McCaulley, Ph.D., co-founder with Isabel Myers of the Center for Applications of Psychological Type. Dr. McCaulley worked closely with Myers and co-wrote the second edition of the *MBTI® Manual.*

Q: ***How does a person get to be a type?***

Jung believed that we are born with a predisposition for one type. However, environmental factors are very important, since they can foster type development or get in its way. One of the four mental processes (S, N, T, or F) and one attitude (E or I) are your natural bent, according to Jung, and these natural preferences make up the heart of type.

Type may not be clear in young people; that is, the dominant process may not yet be developed enough to organize and integrate the personality. The first task of a young person in type development is to have one of the processes emerge as leader in the personality. A later task is to gain balance by developing the auxiliary process, also known as the second favorite process. The other two processes also have to be developed, at least passably, because all four processes are needed every day of our lives. In middle life, some people begin to focus on their third and fourth processes and can become very skillful in them.

Q: ***How do you develop a mental process?***

By using it purposefully to achieve something you think is important. A good example comes from the use of Sensing. Development of Sensing provides a direct and keen awareness of physical realities and excellent powers of observation. If you are sitting on a train, watching the scenery go by, you are using your Sensing but not particularly developing it. If you are driving yourself around a strange city, you will probably concentrate your Sensing to notice and remember landmarks—this process develops your Sensing. Of course, this kind of focus and effort requires both perception and judgment, the dominant helping the auxiliary to develop, and vice versa.

Q: *Doesn't type fence you in?*

Not if you understand it. An understanding of type frees you in several ways. It gives you confidence in your own direction of development—the areas in which you can become excellent with most ease and pleasure. It can also reduce the guilt many people feel at not being able to do everything in life equally well. As Isabel Myers put it, "For most people, really understanding their own type in particular, and other people's types in general, is a releasing experience rather than a restricting one. It sets one free to recognize one's own natural bent and to trust one's own potential for growth and excellence, with no obligation to copy anyone else, however admirable that person may be in his or her own different way." Finally, acknowledging your own preferences opens the possibility of finding constructive values instead of conflicts in the differences you encounter with someone whose preferences are opposite yours.

Q: *Are types kinds of personalities?*

Many things go into the makeup of a personality—genetics, family life, life circumstances outside the family, society's expectations and requirements, and many learned traits; psychological type is just one aspect of personality. Because people's types express themselves in so many parts of their lives, the types are often called personality types. But type is not synonymous with personality. With people who are likely to be put off by the term *psychological*, I refer to the types as mental processing types.

Q: *Are the types essentially different sets of traits?*

No. Type and trait represent different ways of looking at our psychological natures. The types can be identified by their differences in traits, and they are described by their traits. For example, in the *Descriptions of the Sixteen Types*, the descriptive words and phrases used for each type represent traits. But the type preferences categories are not traits. Rather, they are mind-sets, distinct ways of processing experiences that become visible as traits. For example, Extraversion as a type preference is an either–or category, not a trait that is measured as more or less or in degrees of skillfulness. Because this question is too complex for a good short answer, a portion of chapter 2 covers it more fully.

Q: *Can you change your type?*

Outcomes on the Myers-Briggs Type Indicator instrument can be changed depending on how you answer the questions. Different answers to items can result in a report of a different type, but that does not change one's type. Jung believed that each person has a true type that he or she may not yet have discovered. The true type does not change, although it may seem to, as one focuses on developing different mental processes at different stages of one's life. Behaviors can change, of course, but the roots of them remain the same. However, there are many reasons you might take the MBTI instrument two different times and come out as different types. You might still be discovering your preferences and trying them on for size. Or you might be working especially hard to develop one of the mental processes so that you report it on the MBTI instrument with stronger than usual emphasis. Or, you might take the MBTI instrument one time as your "job self," responding as you see yourself acting on the job, and you might take it another time as your "home self," responding as you see yourself in your home environment. If your type differs in two reports, this fact may lead to interesting information about yourself. As you cast your thoughts back to your frame of mind when you were answering the questions, consider how it may have affected your reporting of yourself, and how it may or may not reflect your true type.

Q: *How do you discover your true type?*

Start with what you are sure about. Read all the type descriptions that include the preferences about which you are sure. At this point, you may find a type that you know is yours. If you are still puzzled, start observing yourself. For example, if you are undecided about Thinking or Feeling, start noticing how you make decisions. Are decisions better if you trust your heart (F) or your head (T)? Notice when activities take a lot of energy and effort. See if you can identify which mental process you were using. It is often true that preferred processes seem effortless, and less preferred processes are more tiring. For example, if watching details closely for a long time makes you feel tired, cross, or nervous, you might investigate whether other Sensing activities are also hard for you. You could then look to see if Intuitive activities come more easily. If they do, you could consider whether Intuition might be your preferred process. To test these ideas, you could ask yourself if your hunches, flashes of inspiration, and other intuitions are generally accurate or trustworthy.

Q: ***What is the best type to be?***

For you, the type you really are. Jung's theory says your best satisfactions in life will be those that come through the strengths of your type.

Q: ***Is everyone of the same type alike?***

No. There are many individual differences within each type, because many things influence personality besides type. Some people are at a higher level of type development than others. Even in people of the same type who are well developed, there are big differences. Take an ESFJ for example. You would expect all the ESFJs to share a wish for people around them to be happy, and to work to achieve harmony. Some ESFJs might be interested in education and be teachers; others might become family doctors and others salespersons; still others might find their way of helping in volunteer work or in being a good parent. All these activities offer effective ways of using Feeling in the outer world, as extraverted Feeling types are predicted to do.

Q: ***Can you guess someone's type, and is that a good thing to do?***

When we are trying to understand, influence, manage, or teach someone else, we often do not know the person's type. As soon as we learn type concepts, we see the value of estimating people's types so as to reach them better. Making a wild guess about someone's type is easy and fun, yet often inaccurate, and sometimes the guess seriously defeats its own purpose. If I make a wrong guess about a person's type and act as if it were a truth about the person, I may be increasing rather than closing the communication gap between us.

Accurately guessing someone's type is a skill that takes a long time to develop. Type concepts have been important in my life for nearly forty years, and I am continually correcting misconceptions I have been carrying and learning new ways to recognize characteristics of type. People who know type concepts well will tell you that the learning never ends.

When you do want to guess someone's type preferences, to improve communication between the two of you, treat your guess as a hypothesis to be checked out, then listen carefully and be ready to change your guess. This book will give you many ideas of behaviors to listen and watch for that are indicators of type preferences.

Talk About Type Concepts

I have explained the type concepts to many people. After getting an explanation of their type and having the opportunity to ask questions, the next best step for most people in learning about type is talking about the concepts with family, colleagues, and friends. You are likely to get the most out of this book if you are part of a small group reading it together. If you have not started talking already, this is a good point to begin your discussions. Convene a meeting. Each person should bring to the meeting his or her MBTI profile and this book. In addition, the group will need several apples, at least one for each person, or a bag of peanuts in the shell. Here are some suggestions for the agenda of the meeting. Keep your own notes for possible further use.

"This book will give you many ideas of behaviors to listen and watch for that are indicators of type preferences."

Share your reactions to your MBTI profiles. If you know each other well, you may want to guess each other's type letters. The object of the meeting is to help each other understand the concepts of "people types." Raise questions you have about the concepts. Your group may want to discuss specific previous parts of this chapter. Discuss opposites and dominants, using the *Descriptions of the Sixteen Types*.

EXERCISE

EAT an APPLE

Now you can stop wondering what the apples are for: They are to help you get a deeper insight into the four mental processes—Sensing, Intuition, Thinking, and Feeling. The idea for this activity was suggested by Alan Bundick, and the instructions follow.

A. This activity is to help you distinguish the mental processes of perception (Sensing and Intuition) and judgment (Thinking and Feeling). Work in pairs, with one partner designated as a recorder. The recorder should mark off four sections on a sheet of note paper. Label one section Sensing, one Intuition, one Thinking, and one Feeling. As both partners talk, the recorder should make notes in each section, as indicated below, starting with Sensing. Each person selects and eats an apple (or peanut), paying attention to each of the four mental processes separately, one at a time. Take three or four minutes for each process.

1) As you eat the apple, list your sense impressions of the apple and its parts: skin, flesh, carpels, seeds—noting colors, shapes, textures, tastes, muscular movements, and tensions. List facts only.

2) List your Intuitions that come to you during the experience. Memories and associations: Who or what do apples make you think of? Can you recall other ways of enjoying apples? Baked? Jellies or ciders? Games? Other memories? Do you recall apples in stories, myths, poems, proverbs, or superstitions? Do you find yourself speculating about this particular apple?

3) List your Thinking judgments. Can you think about apples? Did your sense impressions or your intuitions lead you to make any logical conclusions about this apple? About apples in general? For instance, you might make this logical conclusion based on sensory information, "I'd say this apple has been in cold storage. I say that because . . . ."

4) List your Feeling judgments: How do you feel about trying this experiment? How do you feel about choosing the particular apple you did? How do you feel about eating the apple you chose? How do you feel about apples in general?

B. Each recorder should read to the others in the group what was written in the Sensing section. Get concurrence that all items were sensory data. Then read and process each of the other sections.

C. Then the group should discuss the following questions:

- In what ways is the set of data recorded under Sensing fundamentally different from the kinds of things listed under Intuition?
- Do all members of the group agree?
- Do the two sets of data help to show why people who perceive with their senses more than with their intuition, and who dwell more on sensory data than intuitive data, are fundamentally different from Intuitive types (and vice versa)?
- Can you see why they would be more tuned to concrete facts, in the "here and now," and less tuned in to abstractions, imaginings, possibilities, and speculations?
- Next consider the notes under the Feeling and Thinking mental functions. How are these two kinds of judgment statements basically different? Do they help to show real differences between Feeling types and Thinking types?

Check Your Knowledge of Type Concepts

Before going on to applications of type, you may wish to see how well you grasp the concepts. A Type Concepts test closes this chapter with an answer key included.

Don't be discouraged if you miss items. Learning about the types can be a long, slow process. Fortunately, there are ways to put type concepts to work bit by bit as we learn them. Long before the complexities of all the types emerge in our understanding, we can use the concepts without distorting them or making them trivial. Each or any of the type dimensions—E–I, S–N, T–F, and J–P—can be considered separately. If you have a basic grasp, say, of E and I, you can put it to work. For example, in a brief exchange with someone, guessing E or I may be useful as you decide whether you want to help the person process a thought aloud or allow time for the person to process the thought quietly inside. In considering just E–I in this way, all the sixteen types are sorted into just two categories, Extraversion and Introversion. That is the simplest way of using type ideas. Often, however, it is far more revealing and useful to sort the types into four categories, as I do in chapter 3 in presenting IS, ES, IN, and EN groupings as a practical way of looking at work settings likely to bring out peoples' best work.

After you have completed the Type Concepts test and are reasonably sure you understand the basic type concepts, the next step is talking with others interested in type. Discuss especially the ways that type preferences show up in everyday behavior. Talking type is the best way to hone your ability to use the concepts fluently and appropriately.

TEST YOUR KNOWLEDGE

TYPE CONCEPTS: Part One

(Developed by Anna Nuernberger and adapted by the author)

Record your multiple-choice responses on a separate sheet of paper, and check your answers with the key that immediately follows the test. Some of the items have more than one correct answer.

1. **Type theory is concerned with the valuable differences in personality that result from**
   a. *basic mental health.*
   b. *environmental influences.*
   c. *the way people perceive and judge.*

2. **Extraversion describes someone who**
   a. *is gregarious and talks a lot.*
   b. *is a shallow person.*
   c. *prefers to focus on people and things.*

3. Introversion describes someone who
    a. *prefers to focus on ideas and concepts.*
    b. *is aloof and unsociable.*
    c. *is neurotic.*

4. Sensing describes someone who
    a. *is sensitive and empathic.*
    b. *is sensuous.*
    c. *prefers to perceive through the five senses.*

5. Intuition describes someone who
    a. *has prophetic powers.*
    b. *values imagination, inspirations, and possibilities.*
    c. *has extrasensory perception.*

6. Thinking describes someone who makes decisions
    a. *by means of all the mental processes.*
    b. *logically and impersonally.*
    c. *by taking into account all the data.*

7. Feeling judgment describes who makes decisions
    a. *through immature, emotional judgments.*
    b. *through irrational and illogical judgments.*
    c. *by judging on the basis of human motives and values.*

8. Sensing plus Thinking people are mainly interested in
    a. *facts, which can be collected and verified by senses and analysis.*
    b. *possibilities that reveal themselves in new data and experiences.*
    c. *problems that allow them to use their ingenuity.*

9. Sensing plus Feeling people are mainly interested in
    a. *the impersonal and logical handling of other people.*
    b. *making decisions about facts that take into account how people feel.*
    c. *problems that allow them to use their imagination.*

10. Intuition plus Feeling people are most interested in
   a. *projects that involve them with equipment and tools.*
   b. *possibilities for people.*
   c. *facts about projects.*

11. Intuition plus Thinking people
   a. *enjoy practical problems.*
   b. *are interested in possibilities that they approach with impersonal analysis.*
   c. *choose projects that do not require executive or technical ability.*

12. The "tendencies" of the types
   a. *are the way people are and nothing can be done about it.*
   b. *are the talents you can aspire to realize, and the warnings of what to guard against.*
   c. *are among the most useful learnings you can experience from understanding type theory.*

13. Certain types
   a. *will have trouble with other types.*
   b. *can be of more use to you than other types.*
   c. *will be easier to understand than other types.*

14. In conflicts, you can use your knowledge of type
   a. *by being sensitive to the other person's type.*
   b. *by being certain that the other person is aware of your point of view.*
   c. *to understand what it is that one of you sees and values more highly than the other.*

15. In education, you can use your understanding of type
   a. *to plan more effective learning situations according to type.*
   b. *by expecting a person to focus on processes intrinsically comfortable to him or her.*
   c. *to plan situations that exercise all the processes and give students broad choices in developing their own type preferences.*

(Answers to the Type Concepts Test, Part One)

1. c. The way people perceive and judge. (Sensing and Intuition are the perceiving processes; Thinking and Feeling are the judgment processes.)

   a. Basic mental health is assumed to be associated with good type development, but it is not the basis of the theory.

   b. Environmental influences can indeed affect the way types develop, but they are not the main concern of type theory.

2. c. Prefers to focus on people and things.

   Answers a and b may reveal prejudices you need to look at. Introverts may see Extraverts as overly talkative and shallow because Introverts have little way of knowing how satisfying the company of others can be to Extraverts.

3. a. Prefers to focus on ideas and concepts.

   Choices b and c may indicate either that you do not understand the meaning of the word Introvert or that you have a prejudice that can affect your dealings with Introverts. If you are an Introvert yourself, you may lack the allegiance to your own type that is necessary for an effective and happy personality.

4. c. Prefers to perceive through the five senses.

   Answers a and b are not correct. Being a Sensing type brings with it no assurance that one will be sensitive, empathic, or sensuous.

5. b. Values imagination, inspiration, and possibilities.

   Answers a and c are incorrect. Having a preference for Intuition over Sensing is no assurance that one has, or can attain, prophetic powers or extrasensory perception.

6. b. Logically and impersonally.

   a. In general language, "thinking" is often used to describe all the mental processes. In type theory, Thinking is restricted to judgments made in a logical, impersonal way.

   c. Sensing perception is more associated with seeing all the data (details).

7. c. By judging on the basis of human motives and values. (A Feeling judgment is one that comes to a rational conclusion by weighing the different human values and motives involved.)

Answers a and b are not correct. Emotion in the is defined dictionary as "a strong surge of feeling marked by an impulse to outward expression, often accompanied by complex bodily reactions." When considering type, it is important to distinguish emotion (the visible expression of affect) from Feeling, which is used to indicate a rational process of making decisions. Feeling judgment can be mature or immature. Mature Feeling ensures that transitory pleasures do not outweigh long-term important values. Feeling is rational but not intended to be logical; logic is an aspect of Thinking.

8. a. Facts, which can be verified by senses and analysis.

Choices b and c refer to activities more interesting to persons preferring Intuition rather than Sensing perception.

9. b. Making decisions about facts that take into account how people feel.

a. Impersonal and logical handling of people tends to be more interesting to Thinking types.

c. Problems that allow use of imagination are more interesting to Intuitive types.

10. b. Possibilities for people.

a. The Sensing plus Thinking people are more interested in equipment and tools.

c. Sensing types are more interested than Intuitive types in facts about projects.

11. b. Are interested in possibilities that they approach with impersonal analysis

a. Sensing people are more likely to enjoy fact problems.

c. People with the Intuition, Thinking, and Judging combination are often interested in executive assignments.

12. Both b and c are correct choices.

b. Are the talents you can aspire to realize and the warnings of what to guard against. (The talents stem from the activities of the dominant and the second-favorite processes; the warnings concern the consequences of lack of development of the other processes.)

c. Are among the most useful learnings you can experience from understanding type theory.

a. This answer is partially correct. Type theory assumes that each person has some processes and attitudes that are more comfortable, and that these preferred processes suggest the person's best road to growth. The part of the answer that is wrong is the statement that "nothing can be done about it." The essence of type development is learning to use all one's processes in increasingly skillful and appropriate ways.

13. Answers a, b, and c are all correct.

a. Will have trouble with other types. People who are of very different types may have trouble getting along, especially if they do not understand type differences. They can be of great help to each other if they learn to respect their preferences and their different communication styles.

b. Can be of more use to you than other types. Generally, people who are very much alike have little trouble in agreeing what should be done, but since they have similar abilities and deficits, they will be less help to each other than to people of somewhat different types.

c. Will be easier to understand than other types. Similar types typically, but not always, find it easier to understand each other.

14. Answers a, b, and c are correct. If differences are identified, understood, and respected, they can be discussed rather than fought over.

a. By being sensitive to the other person's type.

b. By being certain that the other person is aware of your point of view.

c. To understand what it is that one of you sees and values more highly than the other.

15. All three choices are correct. Although all of us use all four mental processes, exercise both perception and judgment, and experience both the outer and inner worlds in varying degrees, we learn best when we can learn according to the strengths of our own type.

a. To plan more effective learning situations according to type.

b. By expecting people to focus on processes intrinsically comfortable for them.

c. To plan situations that exercise all the processes and give students broad choices in developing their own type preferences.

2

Type, Motivation, & Learning Style

I BEGAN STUDYING type concepts almost forty years ago. Even though my beginner's understanding was just on the surface of this rich and deep theory, I was able to note many applications for education from the beginning. Through the years since then, my understanding has evolved and deepened in a progression that other people learning about type have also experienced. Your understanding of type may follow a similar pattern.

The Process of Studying Type Theory

Learning about type takes time—and not just the time given to reading about it in this and other books. It takes time to soak in, to show its value, and to get integrated into one's view of human nature. A keen interest in it speeds the process, but it seems to follow a progression that won't be rushed very much.

From my first contact with the Myers-Briggs Type Indicator® instrument and Jung's idea of the psychological types, I saw type theory as an important contribution to my area of work—the improvement of teaching and curriculum work. The outcomes of formal education depend so much on understanding student differences in motivation, interests, learning styles, and aptitudes. I was very grateful to be introduced to a theory that yielded useful insights into these differences in students.

A Progression of Understanding

At the beginning I saw the usefulness of type in terms of the separate dimensions: E–I, S–N, T–F, and J–P. While application to my work was my initial motivation, I soon found my uses of type were superficial until I began to study the meanings of type differences in my own family and among colleagues and close friends. As I explored with them the personal experiences of our own type preferences—how daily life is experienced differently through the eight attitudes and functions—I learned to get beyond the surface in applications to my work. We had to ask of each other uncounted questions, and then try out and agree on language about Introversion and Extraversion that fairly represented these two ways of being in the world, with a minimum of stereotyping. Similarly, we developed our understandings of Sensing and Intuition, Thinking and Feeling, and Judging and Perceiving.

Some questions I asked among my colleagues were about learning styles and interests, as well as problems in classrooms. After hearing the responses of those closest to me, I felt ready to frame questions for people I did not know or know as well. At that point, I was still focused on the four separate dimensions of type. I began to look for evidence of type preferences in action in classrooms, in my own and in other peoples' classrooms where I could be an observer. New understandings about type seemed to come best to me through these kinds of direct experiences at work and at home.

The approach to learning about type I have described so far may be more an Extravert's way than an Introvert's. But I believe that starting in the inner circle of family and friends and gradually working out to wider circles is a general approach for learning about type that will be effective for most people.

In those days, when I started teaching people about type, I concentrated on the four dimensions. If we think of the four dimensions as the first layer of type theory, I stayed in that layer a long time. I knew there was more to type theory, but until I understood the more complex aspects of type by seeing them reflected in my family life, I didn't realize their importance in my work.

Deeper Layers

Next in my progression was recognizing the power of the dominant process, which I described briefly in chapter 1. Soon after, I saw that the *orientation* of the dominant, Extraverted or Introverted, made dramatic differences in peoples' basic motivations and their approach to communication with others. Several years passed before I could call quickly to mind the dynamics of each of the sixteen types. Type dynamics is the topic of chapter 8. So I think it is important to remind the reader again that learning about type requires time, a gestation period. Allow it the time needed.

In my work I have studied many theories concerned with explaining human nature. None has been richer or more rewarding than type theory. The deeper I go into it, the more it reveals. Its value does not fade or become overshadowed by more comprehensive ideas, as have most of the other theories I have encountered. I believe you will find type worth all the effort you give to studying it and using it. I hope this book substantially speeds your process of understanding type. But be aware that you get from one layer of understanding to another only as you make *applications* of the ideas and let the results show you the deeper aspects to study.

Type as a Way of Classifying Behavior

Carl Jung saw his psychological typology as a distinctive way of classifying human behavior. His research showed him that many of our behaviors cluster in patterns that seem to reveal different frames of mind, distinctly different ways of processing our experiences. His theory of psychological types stands apart from other modern theories of psychology. While all psychology is concerned with behavior traits, Jung distinguished types from traits.

Type Preferences Are Not Traits

To understand the difference between type and trait let's use Extraversion as an example. Extraversion can be seen as a type preference *or* as a trait. Jung devised the term to characterize a type preference, one that is the polar opposite of Introversion. It is an either–or category. Like pregnancy—one is either pregnant or not; no one is a lot or little pregnant. The Myers-Briggs Type Indicator instrument *sorts* people into one category or the other. Traits, on the other hand, are not sorting categories; they are characteristics that are *measured*. Treated as a trait, extraversion would be measured; a person would have a lot of it, a little of it, or some quantity in between. You can take a psychological test that includes extraversion and introversion as traits. It is possible for someone to score equally high on both traits, implying that the person may be equally skilled at extraverting and introverting and has both skills readily available when needed; or to score higher on one and lower on the other; or to score low on both, suggesting that these traits are not well developed. That is not what type is about.

> **"We process life experiences with categorically different mental frameworks. We are not all one type, differing just by degree of various traits."**

An analogy here may be helpful. Vehicles come in types as well as traits. When considering buying a new vehicle, we first consider the type: pickup truck, passenger sedan, convertible, sport utility vehicle, minivan. We also consider vehicle traits that are important to us: passenger capacity, hauling capacity, cabin comfort, safety, fuel economy, flexibility in use, reliability record, power of the engine, eye appeal. All of these *traits* are found in all the types of vehicle in some measure. That's the point: traits exist in measurable amounts, types do not. We wouldn't talk about "SUVness": "Mine's more SUV than yours." When someone says "She's too extraverted" or "He's an Extravert off the wall," Extraversion is being treated as a trait and not a type. In line with type theory, it is better to say "She's one Extravert who is too talkative." This way "talkative" is an adjective (trait) that modifies the noun (type) Extravert. That's the equivalent of saying "This SUV has a noisy interior," where the trait, "noisy," modifies the type, SUV. Using the analogy of vehicles, we see the value of considering *both* type and trait.

Essentially, Jung was saying that in the study of human nature we need to look at both traits and types. Mainstream psychology is focused almost exclusively on traits—for instance, assertiveness, sociability, resilience, ambition, sensitivity. More than a 1,000 traits have been identified. Jung's view was that we are more than just bundles of traits; we address life with different types of mind-sets. We process life experiences with categorically different mental frameworks. We are not all one type, differing just by degree of various traits.

Of course, the type preferences have traits that tend to cluster with them; for example, Introverts value privacy more than Extraverts and may have greater capacity for sustained concentration. It is natural for people who prefer Introversion to be more developed in skill traits such as sustained concentration because they cultivate and spend more time using such traits.

When explaining type to people, we use clusters of traits to help define the type preferences. Throughout the book, wherever there are lists associated with the type preferences, the terms listed represent traits. For example, decisiveness and a need for closure and planning are traits that typically go with the Judging type preference; and flexibility, adaptability, and a need for openness are traits that go with the Perceiving type preference. In terms of the vehicle analogy, traits such as cargo hauling capacity go with pickup, and sportiness goes with convertible.

Mistaking Type Preferences as Traits

People often mistakenly treat a type preference as a trait. For example, someone who reports a Judging preference on the MBTI® instrument may say, "I really have to work on my Perceiving skills; I need to be more flexible and spontaneous. Next time I take the MBTI assessment I hope I score as a P." The person sees J and P as traits, something that can be worked on and changed, as one might take some training on assertiveness to become more assertive. The person who reported a Judging preference may indeed work on the traits of spontaneity and flexibility, but doing so does not change one's type. For the person who prefers Judging, working on traits such as spontaneity must be done from a J mind-set. The J has to *plan* when and how to be spontaneous, how to allow time and opportunity for it, or, for instance, have a backup plan in order to be flexible if the original plan is not working. The type preference does not change; the person remains a J who is getting better at traits that do not come naturally to someone who prefers Judging.

In summary, type preferences are not traits, or even clusters of traits. They are preferred ways of being in the world, different mind-sets, different ways of experiencing life's daily events and processing the experiences. The sixteen type designations represent sixteen different patterns of organization of mental energy. It follows, then, that the types also represent different patterns of motivations, interests, learning styles, and aptitudes.

Type and Motivation

Motivation is a key issue in every theory about human nature. Because this is a book for practitioners rather than for theorists, I don't examine this view of motivation in relation to other views. I just address the practical question: What does type theory tell us about people's motivations in their everyday lives? Motivations and learning styles are discussed in this chapter as they appear in schools and colleges. However, readers concerned with people's motivations and learning styles outside formal education, such as parents and trainers who work in organizations, will see that the type differences described here are consistent in all aspects of life, wherever the learning happens, and not just in classrooms.

Schools across the United States, urban and rural, big and small, report that students' lack of motivation for school tasks is one of the most persistent and perplexing problems. Student motivation is, of course, very complex, having its roots in family life, peer relationships, and societal pressures that lie beyond the teacher's range of influence. But teachers do have the power to affect student motivation in some respects; and one key to that power can be seen in the type concepts.

Four Aspects of Motivation

Type theory suggests that we break down motivation into four parts, corresponding to the four dimensions of type:

1. **The Extraversion–Introversion** preference shows the broad areas of a person's ***natural interests.*** Extraverted people are, by nature, continuously alert to events outside themselves, turning outward to pick up cues, ideas, expectations, values, and interests. This inclination to scan the environment gives them a variety of interests. In contrast, Introverted people naturally look inward for resources and cues and pursue fewer interests more deeply. Attending more often to the inner storehouse of perceptions and judgments, Introverts take a reflective approach to life, while Extraverts take an active, trial-and-error approach. Of course, Extraverts often do look inward and Introverts often do turn outward. All four pairs of preferences described in this section refer to habitual, but not constant, tendencies.

2. **The Sensing–Intuition** preference reveals basic **learning style** differences. In learning situations, Sensing people attend most often to the literal meaning they find in concrete experiences. They learn best by moving sequentially through concrete data, with their senses as engaged as possible. Those who prefer Intuition find their attention drawn most often to things that stimulate imagination, to possibilities not found in sensory experience. Their minds work by skips and jumps, looking for patterns wherever the inspiration takes them. The other three dimensions of type also have learning style preferences associated with them, but the S–N differences are the most basic.

3. **The Thinking–Feeling** dimension shows patterns of **commitments and values**. People who prefer Thinking commit to activities that respond to logical analysis and to situations where personal factors don't have to be a primary concern. People who prefer Feeling commit to personal relationships and to situations that call on their harmonizing ability.

4. **The Judging–Perceiving** dimension shows **work habits**. People with a Judging preference are drawn toward closure and want a clear work plan to follow. Disliking unsettled situations, they may sometimes lock into a course of action without looking at enough of the relevant data. People with a Perceiving preference resist closure, wanting to keep all channels open for new data. Disliking fixed plans, they may sometimes postpone decisions, leaving much to be done in a rush as a due date closes in on them.

By taking these four natural motivation patterns into account in planning instruction, by working with them rather than against them, teachers, coaches, and supervisors can better direct people's energies toward learning. The remainder of this chapter and the next two show how type concepts can be used to help focus our own and others' mental energies for effective learning and working.

Type and Learning Style

Motivation and learning style are overlapping categories. When we are focused on how people effectively approach learning tasks, we can see that motivation is a part of learning style. Psychological type and learning style also overlap. However, type and learning style are certainly not synonymous. Type preferences reveal a lot about learning preferences, but some learning strategies are independent of one's type of mental processing.

What is meant by "learning styles"? The term is used variously and loosely in educational literature. I have tried to pin it down with a definition. I use "learning styles" broadly to cover four aspects of psychological makeup:

A. Cognitive style in the sense of preferred or habitual patterns of mental functioning: information processing, formation of ideas, and judgments

B. Patterns of attitudes and interests that influence what a person will attend to in a potential learning situation

C. A disposition to seek out learning environments compatible with one's cognitive style, attitudes, and interests and to avoid environments that are not congenial

D. Similarly, a disposition to use certain learning tools, to use them successfully, and to avoid other tools

"Even in those situations that call on us to produce behaviors quite different from our usual ways of acting, our type preferences don't change."

Researchers report that all of us change some of our learning strategies from situation to situation, from teacher to teacher. Other strategies we want to keep the same in all situations if we can. Type preferences fall in this latter category. There is ample evidence that type preferences remain the same through all situations. Even in those situations that call on us to produce behaviors quite different from our usual ways of acting, our type preferences don't change. So the aspects of learning style that are a reflection of one's type can be expected to persist across situations. That expectation is confirmed by the research on learning styles that involved the MBTI instrument.

Those of us who use type theory as a tool to help us teach and advise students make many assumptions about the ways that students of different types want to learn or ways they do learn most effectively. To see whether these assumptions from type theory were supported by empirical evidence, I examined all the published reports of research that used the MBTI instrument in studies of learning, teaching, and academic aptitudes. I first examined the research reports in 1984 (*Journal of Psychological Type*), and updated the review recently. About one-fourth of the studies gave some indirect evidence of learning style preferences, and another fourth actually tested learning style hypotheses.

More than 80 percent of the studies analyzed learning style differences by examining the four MBTI preference pairs separately rather than using the sixteen preference types. That choice was dictated, in many cases, by sample size; obtaining adequate numbers for the sixteen categories takes a fairly large sample. For that reason, most of the results I have summarized here are given by the four dimensions: E–I, S–N, T–F, and J–P.

With a very few exceptions—where research results were ambiguous or unclear—all of the research outcomes support type theory as presented by Isabel Myers. I have combined and summarized the results in tables 2.1 through 2.4, which report what learning style behaviors or clearly reported preferences were associated with the type preference categories in the research.

Readers who understand type and observe learning styles may feel that some important learning preferences are missing from the tables. For instance, in table 2.3 for ES types there is no mention of a preference for active learning. What you see here is what the *researchers reported*, which is not as encompassing as the anecdotal evidence of teachers who are experienced in using type.

Tables 2.5 through 2.8 provide narrative summaries that are easier to read but are less compact. They incorporate the research conclusions and are somewhat expanded by observations by teachers who know type theory and type behaviors well.

Table 2.1 Learning Preferences Associated with E–I, S–N, T–F, and J–P

Extraversion	Introversion
• talking, discussion • psychomotor activity • working with a group	• reading, verbal reasoning • time for internal processing • working individually
Sensing	**Intuition**
• tasks that call for carefulness, thoroughness, and soundness of understanding • figuring things out sequentially • tasks that call for observing specifics • tasks that call for memory (recall) of facts • practical interests (independent of intelligence)	• tasks that call for quickness of insight and in seeing relationships • finding own way in new material • tasks that call for grasping general concepts • tasks that call for imagination • intellectual interests
Thinking	**Feeling**
• personal connection to content • teacher's logical organization • objective material to study • depth and accuracy of content	• personal rapport with the teacher • learning through personal relationships
Judging	**Perceiving**
• work in steady, orderly way • formalized instruction • prescribed tasks • drive toward closure, completions	• work in flexible way, following impulses • informal problem solving • discovery tasks • managing emerging problems

Table 2.2 Learning Preferences Associated with MBTI® Types by Perception and Attitude Combinations

_ S _ P Types: Structured exploratory observation, hands-on

_ S _ J Types: Structured, didactic, well-organized, sensory-rich instruction

_ N _ P Types: Low structure, inductive instruction

_ N _ J Types: Moderate to high structure, "serious" instruction

Table 2.3 Learning Preferences Associated with MBTI® Types by Quadrants of the Type Table *(See the table on page 7, and the beginning of Chapter 3 for the significance of the quadrants)*

IS _ _ Types	IN _ _ Types
• demonstrations • laboratory work • computer-assisted instruction • films, audiovisual aids	• serious reading • tutorials • independent study • systematically organized courses
ES _ _ Types	**EN _ _ Types**
• television • reports to class on topics selected by students • schedule own time • having a schedule and sticking to it • orderly work on goals set in advance	• reading • self-instruction • courses that put me on my own initiative • working on group projects • meeting a lot of people • opportunities to be creative and original

Table 2.4 Learning Preferences Associated with MBTI® Types by Mental Process Combinations

_ ST _ Types	_ SF _ Types
• demonstrations • laboratory work • television • having a plan and sticking to it • having a study schedule	• student-led demonstrations or presentations • instruction with personal involvement • television • films and audiovisuals
_ NF _ Types	**_ NT _ Types**
• learn through personal relationships • dislike impersonal, didactic instruction • highly value faculty feedback • low-friction student-led discussions • opportunities to be creative and original	• organized teacher lectures • self-instruction • reading, researching • systematically organized discourses

Table 2.5 How the E and I Preferences Affect Learning

EXTRAVERSION	INTROVERSION
Cognitive style that favors	***Cognitive style that favors***
• learning by talking and physically engaging the environment • letting attention flow outward toward events and people • talking to help thoughts to form and become clear • learning through interactions, verbal and nonverbal	• quiet reflection • keeping one's thoughts inside until they are polished • letting attention flow inward • being engrossed in inner events: ideas, impressions, concepts • learning in private, individual ways
Study style that favors	***Study style that favors***
• acting first, reflecting after • plunging into new material • starting interactions needed to stimulate reflection and concentration • having a strong, interesting, external–extraverted reason for studying, beyond studying for its own sake • avoiding distractions that will cut into concentration • studying with a friend • studying to prepare to teach someone	• reflecting first, acting after (if necessary) • looking for new data to fit into an internal dialogue that is always going on • working privately—perhaps checking one's work with someone who is trusted • reading as the main means of studying • listening to others talk about the topic being studied, and privately processing what is taken in • extraverting just when they choose to
Instruction that fits Es: *The extraverting types do their best work with*	***Instruction that fits Is:*** *They like learning situations that let them*
• opportunities to "think out loud;" for example, one-to-one with the teacher, classroom discussions, working with another student, action projects involving people • learning activities that have an effect outside the learner, such as the visible results from a project • assignments that let them see what other people are doing and what they regard as important	• work internally with their own thoughts: listening, observing, laboratory work, reading, writing • processing their experiences at their own pace • present the results of their work in forms that let them keep their privacy • have ample time to polish their work before needing to present it • have time to reflect before answering the teacher's questions • tie their studies to their own personal interests, their internal agenda

Table 2.6 How the S and N Preferences Affect Learning

SENSING	INTUITION
Cognitive style that favors • memory of facts • observing specifics • processing data step-by-step • starting with concrete experience, then moving to abstract concepts • being careful and thorough • aiming toward soundness of understanding • staying connected to practical realities • being attentive to what's in the moment	***Cognitive style that favors*** • being caught up in inspiration • moving quickly in seeing associations and meanings • reading between the lines • relying on insight over careful observation • relying on verbal fluency more than on memory of facts • focusing on general concepts more than details and practical matters
Study style that favors • a sequential approach to new material • beginning with familiar and solid facts • moving gradually toward abstract concepts and principles • approaching abstract principles and concepts by distilling them out of their own personal, concrete experience	***Study style that favors*** • following inspirations • jumping into new material to pursue an intriguing concept • finding their own way through new material, hopping from concept to concept • attending to details only after the big picture is clear • exploring new skills rather than honing present ones • reading
Instruction that fits Ss: *They do their best work with* • instruction that allows them to hear, touch, and see (or read about) the lesson • hands-on laboratory work • relevant films and other audiovisuals • materials that can be handled • computer-assisted instruction • firsthand experience that gives practice in the skills and concepts to be learned • teachers who provide concrete learning experiences first in any learning sequence, before using the textbook • teachers who show them exactly what is expected • teachers who do not move "too quickly" through material, touching just the high spots or jumping from thought to thought • assignments that don't expect them to generate possibilities not based on solid fact • skills and facts useable in the present • being shown what the adult world expects, and not having to discover it for themselves	***Instruction that fits Ns:*** *They do their best work with* • learning assignments that require initiative, individually or with a group • real choices in the ways they work out their assignments and solve their own problems • opportunities to be inventive and original • opportunities for self-instruction, individually or with a group • a system of individual contracts between teacher and students • learning assignments they can feel enthusiastic about, things that spark their imagination (conditions that help carry the work to the finish line) • teachers who keep a lively pace • experiences that are rich with complexities, which may include stimulating lectures • teachers who pose problems, give choices, and challenge students to discover things for themselves

Table 2.7 How the T and F Preferences Affect Learning

THINKING	FEELING
Cognitive style that favors • making impersonal judgments, aiming toward objective truth • keeping mental life ordered by logical principles • analyzing experiences to find logical principles underlying them • staying free from emotional concerns while making decisions • naturally critiquing things, aiming toward clarity and precision	***Cognitive style that favors*** • having settled judgments about human motives and personal values • attending to relationships • personalizing things they care about • staying tuned to the quality of the subjective tone of relationships and seeking harmony • attending to the quality of their own emotional life • naturally appreciating people and their accomplishments
Study style that favors • having objective material to study • compartmentalizing emotional issues to get clear thinking on the task at hand • analyzing problems to bring logical order out of confusion • wanting to get a sense of mastery over the material being studied	***Study style that favors*** • learning through personal relationships rather than impersonal activities • learning by helping, and responding to other people's needs • studying with a friend • wanting to choose topics to study that they care deeply about
Instruction that fits Ts: They do their best work with • teachers who are logically organized • subjects and materials that flow logically and respond to logic • feedback that shows them their specific, objective achievements	***Instruction that fits Fs: They do their best work with*** • teachers who value a personal rapport with students • assignments having a goal of helping people • feedback that shows warm appreciation for the student and his or her effort, and corrective suggestions given in that context • personalized assignments

Table 2.8 How the J and P Preferences Affect Learning

JUDGMENT	PERCEPTION
Cognitive style that favors • having a clear structure in a learning situation from the beginning • aiming toward completions and getting closure • having life organized into an orderly plan	***Cognitive style that favors*** • open exploration without a preplanned structure • staying open to new experience • managing emerging problems with flexible responses • the stimulation of something new and different
Study style that favors • planful and scheduled work; drawing energy from the steady, orderly process of doing the work • wanting to know exactly what they are accountable for and by what standards they will be judged • treating assignments as serious business, and persisting in doing them ***Instruction that fits Js: They do their best work with*** • preplanned structure, and a teacher who carefully provides it • predictability and consistency • formalized instruction that moves in orderly sequences • prescribed tasks • milestones, completion points, with little ceremonies to honor successful completions	***Study style that favors*** • spontaneously following their curiosity • studying when the surges of impulsive energy come to them • finding novel ways to do routine assignments so as to spark enough interest to complete the assignments ***Instruction that fits Ps: They do their best work when*** • they can pursue problems in their own way • they have genuine choices in assignments, as with a system of individual contracts in which the student can negotiate some of the activities • their assignments make sense to them • their work feels like play

3

Using Type Concepts in Planning Instruction

READING ABOUT the learning preferences associated with type differences, as described in chapter 2, brings to mind the obvious questions: How can so many differences be accommodated in one classroom or workplace? How can we honor such diverse learning preferences? This chapter offers some practical answers.

Distribution of the Sixteen Types in Classrooms

The distribution of types among students has major implications for the planning of instruction. The sixteen types are not equally represented in the typical classroom. It is hard to estimate the distributions of types in the general population because different occupations and different educational levels (K–12 and through graduate level) have their own characteristically different type distributions. The estimates in table 3.1 are a composite from several data sets of students, including several thousand school and college students to whom I administered the MBTI® instrument.

Table 3.1 Sample of MBTI® Type Distributions*

Extraversion **66%**	Introversion **33%**
Sensing **70%**	Intuition **30%**
Thinking *(female)* **30%**	Feeling *(female)* **70%**
Thinking *(male)* **60%**	Feeling *(male)* **40%**
Judging **55%**	Perceiving **45%**

*The distributions in this table are consistent with Isabel Myers' estimates, which are based on her three decades of gathering extensive data. The third edition of the *MBTI Manual* (Myers, McCaulley, Quenk, and Hammer 1998) reports a randomized sample of adults done by telephone that showed IS types outnumbering ES types.

This means many more students are ESFJ, for example, than are INFJ, and more are ENFJ than INFJ. The uneven distribution of the first two type dimensions, E–I and S–N, is a crucial fact for teachers, as can be seen in the following figure. A typical classroom of thirty-five students would have a distribution of types corresponding to figure 3.1.

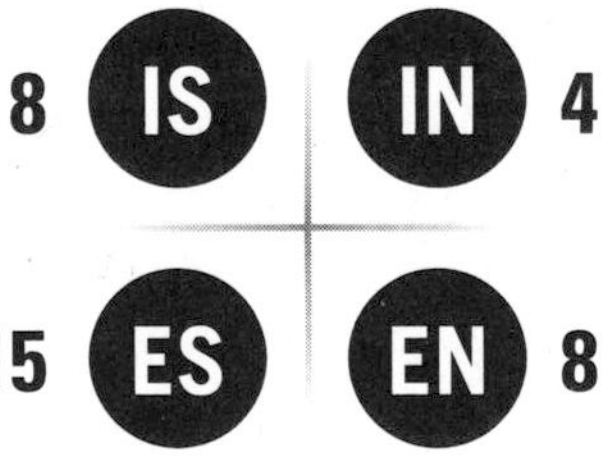

The distribution might be different for elective courses because students' type preferences often influence their choices of electives. The distribution is also different in college samples; in general, college students are more evenly divided between E and I and between S and N.

School Instruction Fits Some Types Better Than Others

If a classroom has four times as many ES types as IN types, what does that mean to the teacher? The question brings us to the second key fact: most school instruction gives an advantage to some types and handicaps others. Consider these three descriptions; do you regard them as typical of school instruction patterns?

- Students work individually on their own tasks with personal sets of materials or books. Quiet is expected so each student can concentrate and think through the work individually.

- When new concepts or rules are introduced, this sequence is typically followed: first the concept is presented verbally, defining it; then examples, illustrations, and/or demonstrations are given; and then (at least sometimes) students are given the opportunity to use the concept or rule.

- The main medium of instruction is words, spoken or written symbols. A student's successful manipulation of words in a dialogue or on tests is the primary way that teachers have of determining a student's achievement. In the case of mathematics and some science knowledge, the symbols of instruction are abstractions representing things other than words.

Are the three descriptions typical? Yes, so much that they seem to be essential. Yet they clearly favor certain types of students. The first one is a natural format for Introverts, who prefer to do most of their work quietly inside their own heads, to keep ideas inside until they are polished and ready to be exposed. Extraverts, *two-thirds* of the students, really do their best thinking with their mouths open. Their thoughts become clearer as they hear them spoken. The most natural setting for Extraverts, the one in which they learn best, is one that allows them to think out loud and to act—that is, to do, make, move, produce—rather than just read and recite words about such actions. The testing of ideas and skills in the outer world tells the Extravert whether the half-formed ideas and skills are worth having. The Introvert, on the other hand, prefers to test ideas against private criteria, in the inner world of the mind—a process that is much easier for schools to manage.

The second classroom practice described above—that of presenting abstractions first and applications after—appeals to the learning style of those who prefer Intuition, not to those who prefer Sensing. Abstractions, such as definitions, theories, lists of procedures and rules, help Intuitive types get into a topic because they want to see the abstract meaning, the relationships to prior knowledge, the "big picture," before they take on new concrete experience.

An Example from a Student

A conversation that I had with a student at a school for learning diesel mechanics illustrates the conventional intuitive bias of instruction—that is, abstractions first and concrete experience after. The student was complaining about paper and pencil tests, saying he did much better with "hands-on" tests in the shop. "I think better with my hands," he said.

When I asked him to give an example, he told of being given a defective alternator he was to take apart, fix, and reassemble. He was given a diagram to guide him in the operation. "I studied the diagram and studied it until I thought I would puke. I couldn't understand it. So I threw down the diagram. I took the alternator apart, carefully laying it down in a pattern. Then I saw the problem, fixed it, and reversed my pattern to put it back together. It worked perfectly."

I asked him if he looked at the diagram afterward. "Yes," he responded. Did he understand it then? "Yes, sure. It made sense then."

To this Sensing type student, the abstract diagram made sense as a map of the complex territory only *after* he first put his senses to work in understanding that territory. It seems likely that similar diagrams he encounters in the future will be more useful to him.

Probably the young man was an ES type. His best learning came when he could use a combination of senses, actively operating on the realities of his tangible environment. Note that he did not follow the prescribed sequence of instruction, beginning with the abstraction, the diagram.

Contrast this student's experience with that of an ENFP, a type with Intuition dominant. He was disgusted with his community college auto mechanics class. It convened for two weeks without books. "All we do is stand around the cars and take parts off and put them back on." He was ready to quit. His mother, knowing about type, urged him to stay until the books arrived. When they came and he then had the words and other symbols he needed to understand the principles, he began to understand the machines and enjoyed the class.

Type and the Skills of Reading

How extensively are standard instruction practices biased toward Introversion and Intuition? No careful analysis has been made, but the bias is widespread. Probably the young child first encounters is in the teaching of reading. Of course, reading is primarily an Introverted activity; it is done quietly by oneself. And it is fundamentally an Intuitive activity, involving abstractions—the printed symbols. But reading need not be taught as if all students were Introverts and preferred Intuition. The skills of reading can be and are mastered by students of all types, and students of all types can leave school with a positive attitude toward reading.

Tragically, many students are alienated by their first encounters with reading instruction. Type theory points to the probability that most of the alienated children are Extraverted and Sensing types. There are data showing that the dropout rate is much higher among Sensing children. Isabel Myers obtained type data from 500 people who did not finish eighth grade; 99 percent of them were Sensing types.

> **"The skills of reading can be and are mastered by students of all types, and students of all types can leave school with a positive attitude toward reading."**

What setting for reading instruction appeals to ES types? They learn best through action, with many chances to talk. Reading aloud with a partner is useful. They can be asked to recall a concrete experience that is worth recording, or the teacher can provide such an experience. If the child wants to report an experience to someone not present, he or she can dictate it and see it transcribed; this process demonstrates writing and recording as activities that are interesting and useful to an Extraverted Sensing type.

To the Sensing types, classroom choral reading of text with unknown words in it is very frustrating; they want to know the words before reading the text rather than guess the meaning of strange words. They need the decoding skills of phonics. Most Sensing children need explicit practice in matching sounds to letters until they have mastered them all and are no longer mystified by the printed symbols. When their first excursions into reading begin with putting sounds to letters and letter combinations, they are more likely to experience reading as enjoyable. I have often discussed this topic with adult Sensing types. Those who now enjoy reading as adults tell me their initial encounters with reading were interesting and fun. And those who don't now enjoy reading, not surprisingly, had frustrating experiences in beginning reading.

Once the basics are mastered, Sensing students can benefit greatly from exercises that focus their attention on the meaning of what they have read; interpretation of meanings requires the use of Intuition, and Sensing children are less likely to do this easily without careful teaching.

While adult reading is mostly a silent, individual activity, type theory suggests that reading can be taught to most children as a social process. Following is an example of how this process might work.

> In a small group with other children at the same level of decoding skills, with the teacher's help, a child sounds out letters and words as other children listen and follow along. The children in the same group then take turns reading aloud from stories containing the mastered words. Sensing types also benefit from writing their own stories, especially reports of events they have experienced, and articles for their own newspaper. ES types in particular benefit from reading aloud to younger children or anyone who will listen. They tend to thrive on any activities that demonstrate reading to be a social transaction. The content of reading, as much as possible, should be words from the students' lives that have a direct connection to their concrete experiences. These techniques, from mastery of the code through writing for the benefit of others, will help eliminate the bias of instruction that disadvantages the ES types.

Type and Testing

Correcting the biases of instruction that harm ES children is perhaps the most crucial unrecognized problem of American education. No doubt the biases are largely unconscious and unintended. In my experience, most textbook writers are Intuitive types, as are the writers of standardized tests. Most are probably unaware that their products reflect their own intuitive way of viewing the world, their way of approaching learning tasks. Writers of pencil-and-paper intelligence tests, usually also Intuitive types, most likely are unaware that their tests have a bias toward the kind of intelligence they value most: intuitive intelligence (manipulating symbols, drawing inferences, and the like).

Considering the biases, it is no surprise that IN students as a group score highest on intelligence tests, followed by ENs, ISs and ESs, in that order. Why do Sensing types, on average, score lower that Intuitive types? First, because the symbols of language have to be translated into meaning. That is done by Intuition types. On paper tests, a double translation is needed, printed symbols into words, and words into meanings. It is a slower and less confident process for Sensing types because they have to use their less-preferred Intuition process to translate the symbols into *concrete* meanings—the kind of meanings that make up the mental storehouse built by Sensing processing of life experiences. The Intuitive types' storehouse, in contrast, is in the form of abstractions. Sensing types are more at home with the facts of a situation. As Isabel Myers has noted, they do not automatically link idea to idea, as Intuitive types tend to do, but want to test ideas against known facts, a process that takes more time. Aiming for this kind of thoroughness, the Sensing types are especially unfairly evaluated by *timed* paper-and-pencil tests.

In my notes of conversations with her, I found an anecdote Myers told that suggests an aspect of Sensing intelligence not reached by such tests. "Speaking of where Sensing people are bright and an Intuitive may stub his toe, at one time somewhere we had a refractory lock which was hard to turn. I was struggling and getting nowhere and Chief [her husband, a Sensing type] said, 'Can't you feel what's going on in there?' And I said I couldn't. That must have meant some sensation there carried a very instructive meaning to which I was absolutely oblivious. I'm sufficiently intelligent, but not on that side." Myers' contrast of her Intuitive intelligence with that of her husband's Sensing intelligence highlights for me the inadequacy of paper-and-pencil tests to measure some aspects of Sensing knowledge.

My experience tells me that the unconscious bias toward intuitive intelligence stretches from kindergarten through graduate school. There is an assumption, certainly from secondary education on, that Intuition is a higher form of mentality than Sensing, that brighter people grow beyond their dependence on sensory processing to the "higher stage" of abstract processing. This view is incorrectly rationalized by citing theories of cognitive development such as those of Jean Piaget and Lawrence Kohlberg. Those theories do not address the mental preferences of Sensing and Intuition as Jung characterized them. Mixing their theories of cognitive development with that of Carl Jung is like combining apples and oranges.

I am reminded of a T-shirt I got from a friend who knows I am left-handed. It reads, "Everyone is born right-handed. Only the greatest overcome it." I hope this book adequately makes the case that the Sensing preference is not something to be outgrown or overcome. I believe the record of American education in the twentieth century is, among other things, a record of neglect of Sensing intelligence—the kind of intelligence possessed by the majority of American students and exemplified by the young diesel mechanics student who bypassed the prescribed instruction process and solved his problem his way.

However, the biases in instruction—the teaching, textbooks, and testing—that handicap the Extraverted Sensing students do not make the instruction ideal for the Introverts or Intuitives. Introverts with a Sensing preference are not benefited by instruction with an Intuition bias. And many Intuition types have told me of the boredom and frustration they have felt when instruction was too cut and dried, too programmed, and too restricted to give them elbow room for their ideas to range through the material in a satisfying way. Many Intuition types said the instruction they experienced was biased against them.

Planning Instruction to Honor the Rights of Every Type

Certainly, all students have a right to educational settings that offer them their best opportunity to develop. That is an ideal everyone subscribes to, and one that everyone knows is still beyond our reach. Type theory provides some new insights into how to improve educational settings to serve all students better.

Trying to improve conventional instruction practices using type theory or any other ideas takes hard work and a lot of time. Having helped many people get started using type in schools and colleges, I know it can be done and is worth the effort. Such a broad and long-term task has to be accomplished one classroom at a time, in small steps. I have included in this chapter ideas for using type that represent many steps, small and large. They can only be undertaken one (or a few) at a time. Start small and confirm for yourself that each step is an improvement. If you begin on a grand scale while you are still new to type concepts, you are likely to undermine your own plan.

You might begin by trying to get more physical activity and constructive dialogue into your instruction plans. Or find more concrete experiences to supplement the abstractions presented in textbooks. Consider starting lessons with concrete experiences before the students open the textbook to read about the subject of the lesson. In this chapter and chapters 9 and 10, you will find a progression of ideas that may take several years to gradually introduce into a classroom or curriculum. Start with one or two ideas where your understanding of type seems most secure.

Following are a number of ways for you to begin using type concepts in planning instruction. The first of these is an exercise called "Four Work Settings." The exercise is made up of four checklists. Use them first to identify *your own* most preferred and least preferred work or learning settings. Follow the instructions for the exercise. You may want to make a photocopy of the two pages so that you also can use the exercise with students.

EXERCISE

FOUR WORK SETTINGS

INSTRUCTIONS:

Step One: *Put a check mark beside those items that are true for you, on all four lists.*

Step Two: *Go back over all four lists. Draw a circle around the check marks for those items that are strongly true of you.*

PATTERN A

I am likely to do my best work in situations that

- ❑ make practical sense to me
- ❑ have a clear organization in them
- ❑ are practical and realistic
- ❑ let me know just what is expected of me
- ❑ let me work at a steady speed, step-by-step
- ❑ require accuracy and careful attention to details
- ❑ require patience

- ❑ don't have many surprises in them
- ❑ let me use my practical experience
- ❑ let me use my memory for facts
- ❑ let me think through a problem by myself before I have to act on it

PATTERN B

I am likely to do my best work in situations that

- ❑ will produce practical results, useful products
- ❑ involve other people or take group effort
- ❑ let me work toward goals step-by-step in an orderly way
- ❑ are real and not just dealing with theory
- ❑ give me a clear picture of what other people are doing and what they regard as important
- ❑ have realistic schedules that don't expect too much too soon
- ❑ let me learn from first-hand experience, on the job
- ❑ let me use the practical skills and facts I possess
- ❑ give me a regular work schedule but give me some variety and time to socialize, too
- ❑ let me work with concrete things, hands-on materials
- ❑ let me "think out loud" with other people

PATTERN C

I am likely to do my best work in situations that

- ❑ let me work in my head with my own ideas
- ❑ let me work toward solutions in my own way
- ❑ give me a chance to be creative
- ❑ let me set my own standards of quality
- ❑ let me work hard when I feel like it and go easy when I need to
- ❑ don't burden me with too many routines
- ❑ have important ideas behind them
- ❑ give me ample time to think out my ideas before I have to act
- ❑ let me use my hunches and inspirations
- ❑ let me follow my curiosity
- ❑ let me work in depth on things of importance to me

PATTERN D

I am likely to do my best work in situations that

- ❑ put me on my own initiative
- ❑ let me plan and carry out new projects
- ❑ involve other people in solving problems, such as group projects
- ❑ let me create new ways of doing things
- ❑ let me try out my ideas to see if they work, to see how other people react to them
- ❑ don't require a detailed accounting of how I use my time
- ❑ pose problems needing more attention to the broad picture than to details
- ❑ provide variety and minimize routine
- ❑ let me figure out how to put theory into practice
- ❑ let me make mistakes without penalties and learn from the mistakes
- ❑ challenge my imagination

What Do Responses to the Exercise Mean?

Look back over your responses and see what patterns you find. As you may have discerned, the A list describes IS preferences for work situations; the B list, ES preferences; the C list, IN preferences, and the D list, EN preferences. You probably put the most check marks on the list that matches your type, and the most circled check marks on that list. Very likely you also put the fewest check marks on the list opposite your type—as ES is opposite IN, and IS is opposite EN.

Now answer the following three questions, to your own satisfaction:

1. Does the list with the most marks reflect work conditions that are usually highly important to you?
2. Would you probably work less productively under the other three sets of conditions?
3. Do the four lists apply as appropriately to schoolwork situations as to other kinds of work situations?

Most people answer yes to all three questions, including young people. Some adults spread check marks across two or three of the lists. Their maturity gives them the flexibility to work well in a variety of situations. Young people may be less adaptable, more polarized toward one pattern. For such students, attention to matching of schoolwork situations to students' types becomes more urgent.

If the sixteen types are distributed in your classroom as they are in the general population, you may find nearly half of your students choosing list B, fewer choosing A and D, and very few choosing C. The four lists were written to apply to any work situation, not just to the classroom. They do not refer to "learning situations" or "learning style" because those terms call to mind the usual features of the classroom (lecture, workbooks, audiovisual materials, et cetera), and those features make it difficult to look more broadly at learning situations. (Later in this chapter, there is a list of classroom features that different types prefer.)

Four Teaching Preferences, Four Teaching Biases

You may find it helpful to go back through the four lists and respond to each item as if it were a question beginning thus: "In my teaching, do I typically provide learning situations that . . . ."

Be critical and mark only the items that describe what you regularly have provided for students. From this analysis you can identify what you *prefer* and what learning structures you are most likely to neglect. A major step in learning to use type in planning is recognizing that our most preferred ways of teaching may be in most cases the least preferred ways of learning for some students.

Through the years, I have often asked students in my classes—every three weeks or so—to give me a brief evaluation of the various aspects of the course, indicating the most valuable and least valuable to them, and giving suggestions for improvement. Early on, from the classes in which we used the MBTI instrument, I learned quickly and dramatically that SJ types had a hard time with my (ENTP) way of structuring the work. They pinpointed blind spots in my planning. It should have been no surprise to me that I was teaching the way I like to be taught. But my image of myself as a good teacher kept me from seeing the areas I was neglecting.

My students' evaluations spurred me to get more serious in understanding what was needed to balance my own inclinations. I still find lots of room for improvement and continue to be surprised at blind spots that turn up. If the "Four Work Settings" exercise turned up a blind spot for you, it may be a good place to begin using type concepts in your planning.

Tips for Using Type in Planning

Here is a procedure for planning instruction that begins with the four lists you have analyzed. When considering instruction plans, keeping sixteen types in mind is difficult if not impossible. It is simpler to start with a model that sorts the types into four sets—IS, ES, IN, and EN—as represented in the four lists you have just used. This approach need not abandon the T–F and J–P dimensions. Rather, they can be used as ways of making adjustments in the four basic models, adjustments to fit the needs of individual students, or of small groups. Making adjustments for T–F and J–P is discussed later in this chapter.

The "four-sets" approach is not the simplest way to start using type concepts in your planning. If you want to start at a more basic level, other options follow these paragraphs.

The Four-Sets Model

I suggest five steps in planning instruction with the help of the IS, ES, IN, and EN lists.

1. Begin with a careful consideration of your own most natural teaching style. Chapter 4, "Type and Teaching Styles," may help you identify relationships between your teaching style and your type. It also offers ways to examine the contrasts between your teaching style and the learning needs of students whose type preferences differ from yours.

   Your basic instruction plan should let you work from your strengths. Your energy for teaching comes in part from the satisfaction of exercising your type preferences. We cannot work well outside the framework of our own types. But we can find teaching styles that accommodate the essential needs of our own types and at the same time provide a good learning environment for students of other types.

The analogy of planning a long trip for a van full of family members may help you think about your instruction plan. The drivers have to look after their own needs and protect their comfort zone, but the trip will be drudgery (and possibly painful) for everyone if the needs and interests of passengers are overlooked.

2. Consider next the needs of ES students because they are the types most often neglected in instruction plans. Check your plan by using the items of the ES list as criteria.

3. Develop alternative activities, variations that will appeal to IS, EN, and IN students. Using the items of those three lists, see what variations you can make in your basic plan and still stay within your comfort zone.

4. If you want to plan adjustments to accommodate T–F and J–P differences, you will find suggestions for that later in the chapter.

5. Double-check your plans by referring to the tables and lists in chapter 2 that show learning preferences associated with the eight type preferences. Ask yourself which of the choices in each dichotomy you prefer.

Plan for the Type Preferences Rather Than for Individual Students

You will notice that my suggestions for planning do not start with giving attention to students as individuals. A teacher just starting to use type concepts should not expect to keep in mind or plan for the types of all the students. I know a few elementary teachers who do it, and some college teachers who can because of small class sizes. Otherwise, a more reasonable expectation is that we plan to teach to type preferences, without regard to which students are which types.

Of course, teachers do encounter students who are enigmatic to them—in areas such as work habits, motivation, or self-management. They are the ones for whom regular teaching plans do not work. In those cases, understanding their types—by administering the MBTI instrument to older students or the Murphy-Meisgeier

Type Indicator for Children® (MMTIC®) assessment to students grades 2 through 8—might be practical as a window into their puzzling behaviors. In most situations, the teacher does not need to first administer the Indicator to students. When a teaching plan takes type into account, the students will respond positively, even when the teacher does not know the types of particular students. Chapter 10 contains suggestions on how to use type in making a plan specific to one student.

Teaching Students About Type

Some teachers find a lot of value in teaching their students about type and using the language of type with them ("We need to do some serious introverting right now, so let's not distract each other" or "Would one of you Sensing types help me explain this more clearly?"). In such cases it would probably be a good idea for the students to take either of the type instruments; be given a full explanation of the type concepts; and be coached in constructive, ethical uses of type. For some students, knowing about type is extremely important to them as they work to make sense of their lives.

> **"Some teachers find a lot of value in teaching their students about type and using the language of type with them . . . ."**

Using the Preferences as a Checklist

When I am planning a unit or lesson, I go through a mental checklist of type preference pairs, starting with S–N. I start there because these perception processes have the most to do with how students encounter new material. I want to use some kind of advance organizer at the beginning to make a bridge to the new material from the concepts and viewpoints they now hold. Intuitive-type students need a "big picture" organizer that shows them the conceptual context of the lesson. Sensing-type students need an organizer that relates to their own concrete prior experience. I want to provide both to help them link old to new. Good teachers have always known how to use examples and analogies that reach both Sensing and Intuitive minds. (The homely but powerful analogies in the parables of Jesus are good illustrations of this technique.)

The E–I preferences are next on my checklist. How can I plan an active, at least dialogue-active, way to get students started in processing the new material? Then, how do I build in a reflection component that appeals to Extraverts as well as

Introverts? This is followed by the T–F dimension, which reminds me that I need two approaches to build their commitment to studying the subject.

The J–P dimension is especially important for me. Being a Perceiving type, unless I plan carefully I tend to neglect the needs of my Judging-type students with a clear structure right from the beginning. In a carefully constructed handout, I tell precisely what is expected of the students. For the Perceiving types, I put into the handout suggested options for reaching the expected outcomes, and I allow students to propose their own options. I have students write individual plans and present them to me for approval or negotiation.

Improving Classroom Routines with Type Concepts

Even the most routine aspects of classroom instruction can be infused with some concrete action to make them more appealing to Extraverts and Sensing types. For example, when drills on reading and writing and other skills are needed, the class can be shifted into two-person teams. Team members can select each other (for example, by writing first, second, and third choices on a piece of paper, from which the teacher selects partners) or can ask to be paired with someone by the teacher. Teachers often find it valuable to keep the same team memberships for several weeks, with the teacher cancelling a team or changing team composition as needed. During team time, members can decide whether to, and when to, work together or separately and how much time to spend in either arrangement. Some teachers give the students the option of handing in joint work or separate products.

The point is that two kinds of accountability must be maintained. First, individual students are responsible for their own work, as well as being responsible to the teacher.

Second, the team members are accountable to each other. If the team members have been taught the concepts of type, and if they know each other's types, they can use their understanding of type to communicate more easily in the process of trying to be accountable.

Of course, students in the K–12 grades can get quite noisy when talking in small groups or pairs. You can deal with that by teaching them quiet voice. Demonstrate quiet voice, speaking just loudly enough for the voice to carry clearly for about two feet. Until your class develops the habit of quiet voice, the volume of the talking will escalate from time to time. When this happens, stop the dialogues and require everyone to work separately without talking. This behavior modification is usually enough to encourage them to work on their self-discipline. They want to talk and will train themselves in quiet voice so that the privilege of talking doesn't get taken away.

Using the Other Preferences

If you have made or revised a basic instruction plan in terms of ES, EN, IS, and IN preferences, you then can consider the T–F and J–P preferences as a means for seeing if the plan has a logical structure and flow to it (T), promotes a warm and respectful interpersonal learning climate (F), is businesslike (J), and has playful elements in it (P). You can use the following list of needs that are usually associated with T–F and J–P differences.

Adjusting Instruction for T–F Differences

T

Thinking types need "order," when order is taken to mean that logic rules the situation. They resent order that is not logical. The teacher can prompt Ts to take leadership in analyzing confusing situations, to use their logic to make situations orderly, and to spell out logical consequences.

T

Thinking types need to achieve, to have a sense of mastery, to know some things deeply and do them well. This need is a natural ally to the school's objectives. Many T children don't know what skills they can develop to the mastery level, and they need specific help in this. Without help, some of them may find mastery in antisocial behavior because the need for mastery is much stronger than the need to please people, including teachers. For the majority of Ts, mastery is most likely to be found in technical areas, many of which are unfortunately unavailable for students to explore until they reach high school.

T

Thinking types need to endure, to persist, and to prevail in [things they are committed to]. They want to have the last word in arguments. They may choose the wrong things to persist in, and they often need help in identifying the values that really are most worthy of their stick-to-it determination. Teachers can avoid useless confrontation with T students by recognizing early signs of persistent resistance and redirecting the students' reasoning power into careful analysis of the situation, looking for cause-and-effect relationships (for example, "We seem to disagree. Tell me how you see the problem . . . . Have you thought about it from this angle?")

F

Feeling types need approval and personal support more than they need to achieve, to prevail, or to be "right." In some F students this need is very strong. Teachers who emphasize independent, individualized activities for students should be especially careful that they have not cut off F students from one of their main sources of motivation: the sense that their work is valued and appreciated. They want warm, rather than cool or impersonal, acknowledgment of their work.

F

Feeling types need to be needed, to know they are helpful to peers and adults. They are turned off by assignments that seem to have no particular value to anyone except themselves in some impersonal, remote sense (as with memorization of many facts and skills that are found in textbooks). Receiving the teacher's personal support and approval does not adequately substitute for the student's need to be helpful. So Feeling types are most likely to profit from work in a harmonious group—when the task involves group members helping each other, with a division of labor and shared responsibility. Examples would be group projects, tutoring, team learning, and drilling with a partner. Projects that have a goal of being helpful to people outside the classroom are especially motivating to F students. They may even warm up to more remote materials if the human side is presented first. Fs want content they can personally relate to, such as stories about people or ethical issues.

F

Feeling types strongly need friendship. They value harmony and will give in on disagreements because they want to preserve satisfying personal relationships. When given the opportunity to call attention to disharmony in the classroom, F students can be very helpful in leading the class toward an improved classroom climate. Many F students value the opportunity to work with a friend. Friends who work together generally will stay on task if they know they will be separated when they abuse the opportunity. Peer affiliation is probably the most powerful force inside middle schools and high schools. The wise teacher will harness it rather than try to fight it.

Adjusting Instruction for J–P Differences

J

Judging types need structure and predictability much more often than do Perceiving types. ISTJ and ISFJ students need these most. If J students have not worked out their own structure for schoolwork, the teacher must provide it. They value an orderly sequence of studies. Js can be comfortable with some variety and spontaneity if they know that an underlying structure is intact or that the structure actually calls for flexibility and spontaneity.

EI SN TF JP

J

Judging types need milestones, completion dates, and a sense of closure. Progress charts and tangible records are useful. Ceremonies, even little ones, to mark successful completions are valued, as are traditions. Persistence is a related J trait, and ceremonies that honor successful persistence will be especially appreciated. (In contrast, persistence does not come easily to Ps, but they need to develop it, so ceremonies are likely to benefit them, too.)

J

Judging types need a system of accountability that is clear and made known in advance. They want to know what they are accountable for and when, how, and by what standards they will be judged. Js will learn out of a sense of duty, for a while at least; but that is not a good substitute for clear expectations made known in advance.

P

Perceiving types need variety, novelty, and change. As McCaulley and Natter (1974) note, the typically structured classroom "can make the perceptive types feel imprisoned, with the result that they spend energy needed for study trying to get freedom. More flexible classrooms are naturally more suited to these students."

P

Perceiving types need autonomy and choice. The need is especially strong in Intuitive Perceiving types. They work much better at tasks they have chosen. They will accept structure and a system of accountability if they have choices within the structure, and especially if they have had a hand in deciding and protecting the structure. For example, a system of individual contracts, in which a student can negotiate some activities, is a structure Ps would enjoy planning and supporting.

P

Perceiving types need opportunities to be spontaneous and freewheeling, to follow their curiosity. The teacher alert to this need will find tasks for Ps that let them explore and find new facts or possibilities for the class to use.

Plan a Unit of Instruction Using Type Concepts

Here are steps you can take to try out the ideas of type in your classroom.

1. Select one classroom group of students with which to try using type concepts. As needed, coordinate your choice of students and your instruction plans with other people. Even if you believe it is not appropriate for your students to answer the MBTI or the MMTIC instrument, you can still use type concepts in many ways to reach students of different types. If you are not going to administer one of these instruments, you can nevertheless use the exercises mentioned in steps 2 and 3.

2. If your students are twelve years or older, decide which to administer: the Myers-Briggs Type Indicator® instrument or the Murphy-Meisgeier Type Indicator for Children (MMTIC) instrument. In most situations, teachers need to coordinate MBTI or MMTIC administration with the school counselor and find out if parental consent is required. If you do use one of the instruments, precede the administering of it with an introduction to the idea, such as the "People Types and Tiger Stripes" activity in chapter 1. The introduction should serve to spark students' interest in

the instrument so they will respond to it seriously. Some students may have difficulty with MBTI or MMTIC instruments because of low reading vocabulary level. Reading the items aloud to them is an option. If you do read the questions to them, each student should have a copy of the MBTI questions booklet to look at as you read. Tell the students they may skip some items. Do not interpret questions for the students. If you read questions aloud, take care to make sure your own type preferences don't show up in your inflections. Make each choice sound equally desirable. After they take the instrument, be sure they have their profile interpreted and their questions answered. Nearly all the students will be keenly interested in their profiles.

3. Decide whether to have the students respond to the four lists entitled "I Am Likely to Do My Best Work . . . ." Steps 2 and 3 are intended to give you some evidence of the types of your students. Having information on that is not essential to this planning sequence, but it is helpful. If you have students who cannot read the Indicator or the other materials, it is possible to recognize characteristics of type in their behavior. Chapter 10 includes a set of observation checklists you can use to estimate students' types by observing the patterns in their behavior. The process is time-consuming, but it may fit your needs. Once again, knowing each student's type is not essential to planning instruction with type concepts.

4. Prepare a plan of instruction—either a new plan you have not implemented before or a revision of a plan you have used. The objective is to incorporate type concepts into the plan. You may want to start with a single dimension of type, such as EI, or you may want to follow the IS, ES, IN, EN process described earlier in this chapter. Prepare it in sufficient detail so that you can have a colleague read it and follow its intent without having to ask you for clarification on major points. You may want to consider preparing a joint plan with one or more partners. In either case, your plan should have a clear rationale based on type concepts.

5. If you need a formal evaluation plan, decide what data you can gather, as progress reports or a final report at the end of the unit, to show tangibly how well your plan worked. If you do succeed in making a better match

between students and the learning setting, what would you expect to improve? Student time-on-task can be estimated by simple observation. Student interest can be sampled by a few questionnaire items. Student achievement can be documented by student products and by teacher-made tests. Organize these ideas into an evaluation plan.

6. Before you implement your plan, have a colleague review it, critique its applications of type concepts, and make suggestions.

Examples of Class Projects Successful with All Types of Students

Following are four examples of instruction plans that have a strong measure of concrete activity in them and have been (predictably) successful with ES students as well as the others. Note that the teachers who planned and conducted these activities did not consciously follow the four-step plan, but in retrospect all the features of the planning process can be seen. All these projects require time, planning, and logistical support. Considering the crowded agendas of schools today, the help of parent volunteers for such activities is highly valuable.

The Greenhouse Project

Sixth-grade students in Jacksonville, Florida, became interested in the processes of plant growth and decided to build a greenhouse so they could house the number of plants they wanted to grow and could continue growing them throughout the winter. Concrete activities were at the center of the plan: presenting the idea to the principal; a field trip to a local greenhouse; letter writing to obtain information about greenhouse construction; dialogues with a nurseryman, a businessman, and a construction foreman (a parent); and maintaining a bulletin board related to the progress of the project.

Science and math became concrete and active for this project as well. Students made charts and graphs for the plant experiments; plotted the sun's movement in relation to the school to choose the best location for the greenhouse; made careful measurements and worked up plans concerning the size, shape, materials, and cost of the greenhouse; and developed the plant experiments. All the students wanted to be involved in some way in the actual construction work: using the posthole diggers, sawing, hammering, and stapling on the plastic covering.

In analyzing the events as they evolved, we could see that most students were drawn to the physically active aspects of the projects. Virtually all parts of the project were performed by teams, with more quiet and reflective activities coordinated with the active work. The teacher who planned the project expected the library research on greenhouses, the sun's path, and design work to appeal especially to INs, as would the plant experiments themselves. He expected that IS types would be attracted to the planning of details, learning from experienced adults, keeping accounts for the fund raising, and calculating materials needed and the cost of them. He later noted that the IS students were also the most reliable in caring for the plants and recording the outcomes.

Adopted Grandparent Program

The adopted grandparent program at P. K. Yonge Laboratory School in Gainesville, Florida, began more than forty years ago and has been successfully adapted at many other schools. It was originated by a second-grade teacher who worked with the administrator of a nearby retirement home to arrange visits for the children to the residents of the home. Her class "adopted" some of the residents and gradually built a strong relationship with them that was beneficial to the adults as well as the children. The residents had all volunteered to be involved and had lively minds. Many of them became frequent visitors and helpers at the school.

The children who chose to go regularly to the retirement home learned about companionship with very old people, the problems of living with infirmities, and death of loved ones. They arranged birthday parties for their adopted grandparents, made craft gifts for them, wrote poems, read to them, helped them eat, and engaged in many other activities with them as they would with their own grandparents. The adopted grandparents in turn gave the children individual attention and help they may not have received otherwise. Many former P. K. Yonge students consider the time with their adopted grandparents as a highlight of elementary school. Needless to say, the diverse activities meant that all the type preferences could be engaged.

The Inner-City Housing Project

Some Nashville, Tennessee, junior high school social studies teachers planned a successful unit for students of their inner-city school. Many of the students had the ability to do well in school, but most were expected to drop out because of what was termed their "defeatist" attitude. Most of the students lived in apartment complexes that were poorly maintained. No one knew the landlord, rent checks went to a real estate company, and requests about repairs mostly went unheeded.

When the teachers learned about the housing conditions, they proposed a project for the students to find out more about the situation and to try to do something about it. Students agreed, without much enthusiasm at first. Investigative teams were formed. After preliminary planning, some teams took a questionnaire, a note pad, and a camera to an apartment building to interview tenants and document the need for repairs. These teams kept records of how much rent was paid, what requests for repairs were made and when and which were honored, and what repairs were still needed. Another team went to city hall to find deeds and other documents that would show who the absentee landlords were.

After a file of facts, figures, and photographs was prepared for one housing complex, a team made an appointment with the landlord and presented him with the file. In several buildings, the students' project resulted in repairs and had other positive results. The teachers learned later that some students and their families became active in tenant cooperatives and earned wages or rent rebates for helping to care for their buildings.

Besides learning something about economics and local politics, the students more importantly gained a sense of their own ability to influence "the system" they had thought to be mysterious and inaccessible.

As with the greenhouse project and adopted grandparents program, the central events of this unit were *active* and *concrete* and were sufficiently varied that all of the sixteen types would find activities of interest.

The Aluminum Can Project

Three middle school teachers had planned a year's theme of human ecology. One activity, suggested by the students, proved to be especially rewarding—collecting aluminum cans to be recycled. It not only led them into the issues of finite resources and recycling, but the income from the sale of the cans paid for the cost of busing them on several field trips: to a plant making aluminum extrusions, to a power plant to see how electricity is generated, to a small company that built solar heating units, to a sewage treatment facility, and to a bird sanctuary.

Among other things, students figured out techniques for saving energy at home and monitored their family's consumption of energy by charting the relative effect of various conservation measures. As they became aware of ecological problems in their community, the students also wrote letters to the editor of the newspaper, and a group of them presented a proposal to the city council. These activities were the more dramatic highlights of a year of study, and they were strong motivating elements for the more typical activities: use of textbooks, films, resource persons, library report work, and some laboratory experiments.

The thread common to the four examples of instructional planning is the emphasis on making active (Extraverting) and concrete (Sensing) experiences the center of attention of students. Other activities, more conventional to classrooms, are sparked in that way and take on new importance for students who are not natural academicians.

Using Type in Classroom-Bound Instruction

Of course, instruction cannot always be planned to incorporate the action, variety, and concrete experiences described in these examples. Type concepts can also help you plan better instruction when you are limited largely to the classroom and media center. Table 3.2 was developed by Margaret K. Morgan of the University of Florida. It briefly shows what has been learned about the classroom learning styles of each of the sixteen types. Note that in the table Sensing types are described as linear learners and Intuitive types as global learners. Linear refers to the sequential approach to learning tasks. The global approach involves intuition leaps, seeking to see the whole of the task first. Also note the preferences of different types for various media of instruction. These preferences are confirmed by research reported by McCaulley and Natter (1974).

Table 3.2 Relating Type to Instructional Strategies

ISTJ • Linear learner with strong need for order (SJ) • Likes direct experience (S) • Likes audiovisuals (S), lectures (I) • Enjoys working alone (I) • Likes well-defined goals (S) • Prefers practical tests (S)	**ISFJ** • Linear learner with strong need for order (SJ) • Likes direct experience (S) • Likes listening to lectures (I) • Likes audiovisuals (S) • Enjoys working alone (I) • Likes practical tests (S)
ISTP • Linear learner; needs help in organizing (SP) • Likes direct experience (S) • Likes lectures, audiovisuals (S) • Enjoys working alone (I) • Wants logically structured efficient materials (IT)	**ISFP** • Linear learner; needs help in organizing (SP) • Likes direct experience (S) • Needs well-defined goals (S) • Needs harmony in group projects (F) • Likes audiovisuals, practical tests (S) • Enjoys working alone (I) • Needs sensitive instructor (IF)
ESTP • Linear learner; needs help in organizing (SP) • Needs to know why before doing something (S) • Likes group projects, class reports, team competition (E) • Likes direct experience (S) • Likes audiovisuals (S) • May like lecture (T)	**ESFP** • Linear learner; needs help in organizing (SP) • Likes direct experience (S) • Likes audiovisuals; practical tests (S) • Needs to know why before doing something (S) • Likes group projects, team competition, class reports (E) • Needs orderly, well-defined goals (S)
ESTJ • Linear learner with strong need for structure (SJ) • Needs to know why before doing something (S) • Likes direct experience (S) • Likes group projects, class reports, team competition (E) • Likes audiovisuals, practical tests (S) • May like lecture (T)	**ESFJ** • Linear learner with strong need for structure (SJ) • Needs to know why before doing something (S) • Needs well-defined goals (S) • Values harmonious group projects, team competition, class reports (EF) • Likes audiovisuals, practical tests (S) • Likes direct experience (S)

Table 3.2 Relating Type to Instructional Strategies (cont'd.)

INFJ • Can be global or linear (NJ) • Wants to consider theory first, then applications (N) • Enjoys working alone (I) • Prefers open-ended instruction (N) • Needs harmony in group work (F)	**INTJ** • Can be global or linear (NJ) • Wants to consider theory first, then applications (N) • Enjoys working alone (I) • Prefers open-ended instruction (N) • Good at paper-and-pencil tests (NT)
INFP • Global learner; may need help in organizing (NP) • Likes reading, listening (N) • Wants to consider theory first, then applications (N) • Needs harmony in group work (F) • Prefers open-ended instruction (N) • Enjoys working alone (I) • Likes autonomy (NP)	**INTP** • Global learner; needs help in coming to closure (NP) • Likes reading, listening (N) • Wants to consider theory first, then applications (N) • Good at paper-and-pencil tests (NT) • Prefers open-ended instruction (N) • Enjoys working alone (I) • Likes autonomy (NP)
ENFP • Global learner; needs choices and deadlines (NP) • Likes seminars (EN) • Likes reading if can settle down long enough (EN) • Likes harmonious group projects, team competition, class reports (EF) • Likes autonomy (NP) • Needs help with organizing (NP)	**ENTP** • Global learner; needs choices and deadlines (NP) • Likes autonomy (NP) • Likes seminars (EN) • Likes reading, listening (N) • Wants to consider theory, then applications (N) • Good at paper-and-pencil tests (NT) • Prefers open-ended instruction (N)
ENFJ • Can be global or linear learner (NJ) • Likes seminars (EN) • Likes reading if can settle down long enough (ENF) • Likes harmonious group projects, class reports (EF) • Likes listening (N) • Likes pencil-and-paper tests (N) • Prefers open-ended instruction (N) • Wants to consider theory, then applications (N)	**ENTJ** • Can be global or linear learner (NJ) • Likes seminars (EN) • Likes reading if can settle down long enough (EN) • Likes group projects, class reports, team competition (E) • Likes listening (N) • Likes pencil-and-paper tests (N) • Prefers open-ended instruction (N) • Wants to consider theory, then applications (N)

4

Type & Teaching Styles

When considering type and teaching preferences, we find two main topics: how our types exert influence on our behavior as teachers and how we may use knowledge of type to adjust our teaching styles to better fit the needs of students. This chapter is mainly about the former. Chapters 2 and 3 are mainly about the latter. While the whole book is about understanding the role of psychological type in people's behavior, this chapter focuses specifically on teaching behavior.

What Research Reveals About Type and Teaching Preferences

Teachers and researchers who understand type concepts see ample evidence that teachers' types affect how they teach and what they prefer to teach. Much more needs to be learned about type differences in teaching styles, but research is already supplementing observation to provide some interesting facts about the ways teachers of different types behave in their classrooms.

The following come from four sources: Hoffman and Betkouski (1981), DeNovellis and Lawrence (1983), the data bank at the Center for Applications of Psychological Type, and my review of the research reported since the Hoffman and Betkouski review.

Teachers' Choices of Levels and Subjects

While all types are found in all occupations, people are attracted to and stay in jobs that are in harmony with their types of mental processing. For example, among physicians, Es are more prevalent in family practice and Is make up the majority of anesthesiologists and radiologists. Among teachers, the types are distributed differently in subgroups according to teaching level and subject areas.

Levels

As shown in table 4.1, all types are represented in all levels of education but in quite different proportions. More Ss than Ns teach in elementary and middle school grades; Ss and Ns are about equal in high school; more Ns than Ss are found in college and university teaching, with about two-thirds of university teachers reporting a preference for N. This pattern is consistent with type theory: the proportion of Intuition types increases as the subject matter becomes more abstract.

More Feeling types than Thinking types choose the lower grades, while more Ts than Fs are found in postsecondary education. This distribution is also consistent with type theory: the more impersonal curriculums of higher education attract more Thinking types.

Of special interest in the table is the representation of the sixteen individual types at the various levels of education. While the four NF types—INFJ, INFP, ENFP, and ENFJ—are about equally represented at all levels, the four SF types—ISFJ, ISFP, ESFP, and ESFJ—are three times as likely to be in pre-school and elementary grades as in higher education. The four ST types—ISTJ, ISTP, ESTP, and ESTJ—are fairly evenly distributed across the levels, but the NT types—INTJ,

Table 4.1 Percentages of Teachers at Different Levels of Education, by MBTI® Types

	ISTJ	ISFJ	INFJ	INTJ
A Pre-School	3.0	20.0	7.0	4.0
B Elementary	10.7	17.9	5.1	2.1
C Middle & Jr.	11.7	12.2	5.0	4.5
D High School	11.9	10.6	7.7	5.4
E Adult	10.1	11.4	3.1	2.6
F Jr College	12.1	8.2	5.0	7.0
G University	12.8	6.1	7.5	10.9
	ISTP	**ISFP**	**INFP**	**INTP**
A Pre-School	0.0	4.0	8.0	2.0
B Elementary	1.7	4.9	4.6	1.5
C Middle & Jr.	2.3	3.2	5.9	2.4
D High School	1.5	2.5	6.3	2.9
E Adult	4.4	4.8	6.1	1.8
F Jr College	0.7	2.1	8.0	4.6
G University	1.7	1.7	8.1	5.4
	ESTP	**ESFP**	**ENFP**	**ENTP**
A Pre-School	0.0	8.0	12.0	1.0
B Elementary	0.9	5.7	10.2	1.5
C Middle & Jr.	1.8	3.8	10.1	3.9
D High School	1.1	2.3	11.4	3.5
E Adult	4.0	5.3	8.3	3.5
F Jr College	1.4	2.8	13.6	5.0
G University	1.2	1.7	9.1	5.3
	ESTJ	**ESFJ**	**ENFJ**	**ENTJ**
A Pre-School	6.0	12.0	8.0	5.0
B Elementary	8.5	12.4	7.2	5.2
C Middle & Jr.	9.1	11.5	7.8	4.3
D High School	11.3	8.5	8.8	4.3
E Adult	10.1	11.4	13.6	5.3
F Jr College	6.8	8.2	7.8	6.6
G University	6.5	4.4	8.0	9.6

Note: Numbers preceding bar graphs represent the percentage of the sample falling in that type.
Source: CAPT *Atlas of Type Tables*, 1986. Used with permission.

INTP, ENTP, and ENTJ—clearly tilt toward higher education. This distribution is also consistent with type theory: the SFs are more oriented to the concrete and personal teaching roles, while the NTs are drawn to the abstract subjects and academic roles.

A comparison of the table with estimates of the sixteen types in the general population shows several striking contrasts. The IN types, who make up about 10 percent of the population, are very much overrepresented among teachers at all levels. ISFJs are overrepresented among teachers at all levels except the university, as are ISTJs at all levels except pre-school.

The four SP types are dramatically underrepresented among teachers. While together SPs make up about 30 percent of the general population, in the field of teaching they only represent about 10 percent. This can be a real problem for SP students because teachers who share a similar mind-set and who emulate the SP kind of good type development will be scarce. The explanation for the scarcity is not difficult to find. Formal education is conducted mainly with an NJ bent.

I have administered the MBTI® to many school and college faculties, and I have seen the type distribution patterns of many more. It is very unusual for one or more types to be entirely missing from the faculty type table. But the distribution of the faculty among the sixteen types is often mismatched with that of the students. In general, student tables show more Extraverts, more Sensing types, and more Perceiving types than are represented in the faculty. Most striking of all in the faculty type tables is the relative absence of the SP types. The research can't show us a cause-and-effect relationship, but we can speculate that the generally lower grade point averages of the SP group, and the higher representation of these types among school dropouts, are affected by the mismatch of types between students and faculty. My own opinion is that the way the SP types see the world does not easily fit into the usual classroom practices of our schools and colleges. Some behaviors and viewpoints that are natural expressions of their types are often misunderstood and misinterpreted by their teachers. The SP learning style and instruction plans to accommodate it are discussed in chapters 2 and 3.

Subjects

Teachers' choices of subjects to teach are also predictable from type theory. The sample list that follows, drawn from the CAPT data bank, shows that Ss are attracted to teaching of practical courses, and Ns to courses emphasizing theories and ideas. Ts are attracted to teaching of mathematics, science, and technical skills, and Fs to language arts and fine arts.

Art, Drama, Music	50% are NF types
Coaching	50% are SJ types
English	66% Ns, 66% Fs
Foreign Language	70% Fs
Health	Evenly distributed
Mathematics, 7–12	66% Ss
Science, 7–12	66% Ts
Special Education	Evenly distributed
Industrial, Technical	45% in two types: ISTJ, ESTJ

The Teacher in the Classroom

In this section about teaching styles and in the next three sections, I summarize what research has shown about the tendencies of teachers when they are sorted by types. The differences reported are statistically significant, but the differences may not be large.

Type Preferences and Teaching Styles

A teacher's actual behavior in the classroom is influenced by many things besides his or her psychological type. Some of the statements describing your type will fit you, and others may not. A sign of a good teacher is the ability to flex one's teaching style to better fit the needs of those being taught. The style that results from the flex may not be the same as the natural inclinations of one's type.

Extraversion–Introversion differences. Extraverted teachers are more likely than their Introverted counterparts to engage students in classroom or school projects and to give them choices about what to study and how to go about learning tasks. Introverted teachers are more likely to structure learning activities through the materials they select for students. Extraverted teachers are more likely to be constantly attuned to the changes in student attention and activities. Introverted teachers are more attuned to the ideas they are trying to teach and tend to center the control in themselves.

Sensing–Intuition differences. Sensing types tend to emphasize facts, practical information, and concrete skills. Intuition types tend to emphasize concepts and relationships and the implications of facts for understanding larger matters. Sensing-type teachers tend to keep things centralized and focus activities on a narrow range of choices. Intuition-type teachers are more likely to give a wide range of choices to students, allow them to make small groups more often, and expect independent and creative behavior from them. At the elementary and middle school levels, Intuition-type teachers are more likely to move freely around the room than their Sensing counterparts.

Thinking–Feeling differences. Thinking-type teachers make relatively few comments about student performance, and these are likely to be objective statements. Feeling types are more likely to praise and criticize, support and correct, in words and by body language. Thinking types have students spend more of their time focused on what the teacher is doing or saying.

In elementary and secondary classrooms, Feeling-type teachers have students spend more time in their individual work and are more likely than Thinking-type teachers to move from student to student, attending to each student's needs, and usually seeking some dialogue. Feeling type teachers seem better able to attend to more than one student at a time, in contrast to Thinking types who typically deal with the class as a whole.

Judging–Perceiving differences. The classrooms of Judging-type teachers are more likely to be orderly, with adherence to structure and schedules. Perceiving-type teachers encourage more movement around the classroom, more independence, more open-ended discussions, and more socializing in study groups.

Student Reactions to Teachers' Management Styles

The classrooms of I, S, and J teachers are likely to be quiet and orderly. When students in these classrooms get off task, they are apt to daydream, doodle, and do other passive, withdrawn activities. In contrast, the classrooms of E, N, and P teachers typically have more movement and more noise. In these classrooms, students have a greater voice in decisions about activities. When students get off task, they are likely to do so actively and noisily. The E, N, and P teachers spend more time trying to get students settled down to work.

Structure and Flexibility in the Classroom

IJ teachers seem to need the most structure in the classroom; EJs need somewhat less; IPs need even less; and EPs need the least structure of all. In fact, EP teachers often do things that will *bring* unpredictability into the classroom—e.g., encourage open-ended discussions, ask students to create projects, permit socializing in study groups.

Clearly, the amount of structure a teacher needs for personal equilibrium will suit the needs for external structure of some of the students in the classroom and will not fit others at all. What are the implications of these differences for instruction? It is unrealistic to ask teachers to change their needs for structure. There are two alternatives to the mismatch between student and teacher needs. First, students can be placed with teachers so as to obtain a better match between teacher style and student need for classroom structure. This is not a solution for use on a broad scale; grouping by types is *not a good idea* for reasons discussed elsewhere in this book. But in individual cases, especially in the early grades, students who need special support can be placed with a teacher whose structure style is most helpful to their growth.

> **"Clearly, the amount of structure a teacher needs for personal equilibrium will suit the needs for external structure of some of the students in the classroom and will not fit others at all."**

The second way to deal with various structure needs is for teachers to learn the techniques to meet a diversity of student needs without pushing them beyond their own equilibrium.

As an example of the latter solution, one Judging-type mathematics teacher in a middle school was able to keep his natural style, but to redirect it more appropriately. He realized that his own need for order and control was resulting in overbearing supervision of his students. He redirected his need for order to an inanimate object: a chart he kept for himself, on his desk, showing all the students' names and the objectives of the lessons. He exercised his Judging by marking on the chart as the students completed their tasks.

In another example, a Perceiving-type fifth-grade teacher realized he was too unstructured for many students and found a solution in individual student contracts. Students who needed more structure got more tightly drawn contracts. He also arranged for election of class officers. Students debated and decided on a set of class rules, and the officers were charged with the responsibility for reminding everyone of those rules.

Type and Questioning Styles

The kinds of questions teachers ask students, and the ways they ask them, can reflect the teachers' own preferences for Sensing or Intuition. Sensing teachers are likely to start a sequence of questions with a request for facts and details; the responses they are seeking are predictable. Intuitive teachers are likely to start with questions that call for synthesis and evaluation: "What's the main theme (issue, problem) here?" or "What is the author trying to say in this paragraph?"

Because Intuitive teachers personally like questions that stimulate imagining and hypothesizing ("If you were . . . ?" "What might have happened if . . . ?"), they may assume that all students like, or should like, such questions to answer. Sensing students are put at a disadvantage with these questions, unless other questions that engage Sensing come before them. For example, the following questions will engage Sensing types: "What did you see happening?" "Which facts are most important? Why?" "Which facts give you clues why so-and-so did such-and-such?" This sequence of questions carries the student from the known to the unknown, from the givens to the speculative. It helps Sensing students connect with the teacher's intention and also models a good mental discipline for Intuitive students.

Sensing teachers may neglect to ask students to synthesize, to hypothesize, and to attend to the "big picture." Intuitive teachers may allow students to be too casual about the facts, as long as they have the concepts right.

While teachers instinctively lean toward questioning styles that reflect their type preferences, they can readily train themselves in strategies that are fair and appealing to all types of students (see chapter 3 for more details).

Teachers Report Their Teaching Styles

In another study, teachers described in detail the ways they view and conduct teaching. The following are representative descriptions of the teaching process provided by teachers in a study by L. L. Thompson (1984). The extensive interview data were sorted by teachers' type and summarized by the four mental process combinations.

The role of the teacher is to . . .

ST: Set an example for students, be a role model, and share knowledge and experience.

SF: Instruct, discipline, encourage, support, role model, and serve others.

NF: Encourage, inspire, provide variety and creativity, and motivate students to develop.

NT: Encourage, inspire, help students develop as citizens and persons.

Ideas for teaching come from . . .

ST: State and local curriculum guides, textbooks, and experience.

SF: Curriculum guides, manuals, textbooks, workshops, other teachers, and experience.

NF: Concepts from content of subject taught; courses, reading, knowledge of student development; and "ideas from everywhere."

NT: Concepts from subject area, knowledge of students' needs and development, synthesis of ideas from many sources.

Teaching is planned by . . .

ST: Making complete, detailed plans in advance for year and term with specific objectives.

SF: Establishing complete objectives and detailed teaching plans using yearly school calendar; taking students' abilities into consideration.

NF: Structuring plans around general goals, themes, and students' needs; then adapting plans to students' needs week to week.

NT: Making a plan according to an overall yearly structure; organizing by concepts or themes; determining details by student levels.

Typical method of teaching is described as . . .

ST: Following daily routine, directing activities.

SF: Following ordered daily pattern adjusted for person-centered interactions.

NF: Using a flexible daily pattern depending on topic and student need.

NT: Having a flexible daily routine that depends on topics and student needs, with interaction based on expectations for order and learning.

Students' work is evaluated by . . .

ST: Using points and percentages in a systematic way.

SF: Using points and percentages, plus extra credit options.

NF: Using a number of factors, only one of which is grades.

NT: Using a number of factors.

The teacher feels successful if . . .

ST: Student grades and behavior improve.

SF: Student behavior and grades improve, and there is the feeling of having contributed to students' education.

NF: Student learning and participation increase, and there is the feeling of having made a personal contribution to students' education.

NT: Students have increased involvement with learning.

I have used the Thompson results as the basis for an exercise to demonstrate to teachers the reality of type differences and how they influence teaching style. My approach is to sort teachers into four groups by the process combinations—ST, SF, NF, NT—and have each group first provide responses to the topical questions that mirror the Thompson study categories (see figure 4.2.) Then I ask them to read the summaries from the Thompson study. And finally I invite them to discuss the implications for flexing their teaching styles to accommodate type differences in students.

Figure 4.2 Topical Questions to Understand Type Differences in Teaching

The role of the teacher is to ______________________________

Ideas for teaching come from ______________________________

I plan my teaching by ______________________________

In regard to daily teaching routine, I ______________________________

I evaluate students' work by ______________________________

I feel successful in my teaching if ______________________________

EXAMINING and ADJUSTING TEACHING STYLES

We all can benefit from help, practice, and constructive feedback in tuning-up our teaching techniques to do a better job with students whose types are most different from ours. Following is a discussion activity for teachers or prospective teachers. I have used it successfully with middle, high school, and college faculties to exemplify the improvement needs of the teachers and the assistance process. The objective is to plan some teaching practices that will fit the needs of one's most opposite types and obtain feedback on the planned ideas. The activity organizes participants into groups by the type preference combinations that teachers say are most difficult to bridge from teacher to student. Allow a minimum of one hour for the exercise.

1. Form four type-alike groups: SJs, NPs, NJs, and SPs.
2. Ask each group to do the following:
   a. Read the list of teaching preferences reported by researchers (see figure 4.3).
   b. Discuss and confirm and/or clarify the statements referring to the two type preferences the small group members have in common: Sensing and Judging, Intuition and Perceiving, Intuition and Judging, and Sensing and Perceiving.
   c. Turn to chapter 2 and read "Summaries of the Learning Preferences Associated with E, I, S, N, T, F, J, and P." Read only the descriptions of your *opposites* (i.e., NP is opposite SJ, and NJ is opposite SP).
   d. Discuss and write on newsprint the changes you would be willing and able to make in your teaching practices to better engage and evaluate the students whose learning preferences are most opposite your own.
3. Combine opposite small groups (the SJs will join the NPs, and the NJs will join the SPs).
   a. In each combined group, each subgroup should use its notes to report what was produced in step 2 and invite clarifying questions from the other subgroup.

Figure 4.3 Teaching Practices Summary

_S_J Teachers' Tendencies

- emphasize facts, practical information, concrete skills
- centralized instruction, focus activity on a narrow range of student choices
- expect quiet and order
- need clear classroom structure and schedules
- questioning style starts with requests for facts and specifics, expecting predictable responses
- may neglect Intuitive students' need to see the big picture first

_N_J Teachers' Tendencies

- emphasize concepts, relation-ships, implications of facts
- give students choices
- use small group work
- expect independent, creative work from students
- expect order, with adherence to structure and schedules
- allow noise if work is orderly
- questioning style starts with request for synthesis, evaluation, big-picture questions
- May neglect Sensing students' need to start with observable specifics

_N_P Teachers' Tendencies

- emphasize concepts, relation-ships, implications of facts
- give students choices
- use small group work
- expect independent, creative work
- expect student movement during study time, and some noise
- encourage open-ended discussions
- questioning style starts with request for synthesis, evaluation, big-picture responses
- may neglect Sensing students, need to start with observable specifics
- may be too casual about the facts if students get the concepts

_S_P Teachers' Tendencies

- emphasize facts, practical information, concrete skills
- focus activity specifically on what students should accomplish
- expect students to be free to express themselves
- expect diverse learning styles
- expect movement and some noise during study time
- questioning style starts with a request for observed facts and details, expecting predictable responses
- may neglect Intuitive students' need to see the big picture first

4. Reconvene as one group. Have a reporter for each work group tell the whole group what was accomplished in the work group. Clarify and discuss the results and insights from this exercise.

This exercise is especially effective when it is repeated with the following variation: Ask participants to prepare lesson plans designed to reach students of their opposite type preferences. Then repeat steps 2d, 3, and 4 to critique the lesson plans. Participants usually begin to see that type-different colleagues can be an important resource to them for improving lessons plans that will be effective for all the students in their classrooms.

Type and the Teaching Team

Teachers involved in team teaching find that type differences and similarities may play a part in how well their teams function. The combination of types on a teaching team often makes a difference in the team's productivity, compatibility, and flexibility. A good mix of types is a strong asset to a team.

Readers who are in teams may be helped by reviewing the table in appendix B. Does your team have a balanced mix of types, with three or four of the columns (ST, SF, NF, NT) represented? Are three or four quadrants also represented (IS, ES, IN, EN)? An ideal team has all eight preferences represented. If your team lacks any of them, someone on the team must usually take on the responsibility for the point of view and disposition that would come naturally to a person with that preference.

Consider your own strengths as a team member. Read back through the information about teaching styles on the previous pages and think about their relevance to you.

Following is an activity I designed for members of teaching teams. It is useful for considering the mix and balance of types on any kind of team; with a little alteration I have used it in many different organizational settings besides schools. Your team may find it helpful as a way to start a dialogue about type-related issues affecting the team.

EXERCISE

THE GREEN-WHITE CONFLICT

Here is a description of a conflict between two teachers. Through the use of type concepts, analyze the conflict and consider what might be done to improve the relationship.

Understanding the Green-White Conflict. Two members of a teaching team frequently seem to have misunderstandings. Mr. Green is often the "idea man" of the team, suggesting with enthusiasm that the team try this or that. Generally his ideas seem sound to the team, but in need of some refinement and attention to practical details. Ms. White, another team member, is usually the first one to question Mr. Green's ideas, on grounds of practicality, and she states her position in such a blunt way that she sometimes causes hard feelings. At that point, Mr. Green "clams up," and his idea fades away without the team dealing with it further. Outside of team planning meetings, Green and White seem to get along quite well. Analyze the Green-White relationship by answering these questions:

1. What types are Green and White? Make a guess.
2. How can you explain the conflict in terms of type theory?
3. Assuming you are a member of their team and feel a need to help them, what would you say to Green? to White? Would you say it privately or during a team meeting? Write your remarks just as you would say them; put them in quotation marks.
4. Do you identify more with either Green or White? Would you be comfortable in the role of peacemaker between these two? Do your responses to these questions relate to your own type?

The Green-White exercise will yield many more insights if you can discuss it with a colleague or two. After you have discussed it, you can compare your analysis and action plan with the following one.

Possible Actions for the Green-White Conflict. Chances are that Ms. White doesn't even know her blunt reaction (T) caused hard feelings. Quick to make a judgment (J) based on awareness of missing details (S), she is probably an STJ. Choosing to speak to her in the meeting or in private would depend on your comfort in the two settings. There are advantages to talking directly about the conflict in the meeting, at the time it happens. When the problem is talked out in the meeting, there is less chance that members will wonder who talks to whom outside the meeting and who is seen as wrong or right. In the meeting you might say "We need fresh ideas, and we also need to look at them carefully for practicality and detailed planning. Let's look at Mr. Green's proposal as a beginning concept, and when we're clear about what he has in mind, let's analyze it for practicality."

If you choose to speak to Ms. White privately, you might say, calmly and straight to the point, "I think you came across too strongly with Mr. Green. I'd say his feelings are a reality we have to recognize next time. Your knack for spotting quickly what is missing in a proposed plan is a real asset to the team, but I'll bet Mr. Green feels you never heard what he did say." Then you might counsel Ms. White in more sensitive approaches to sharing her point of view.

Mr. Green, full of interesting possibilities (N) that were not thought out completely (P) was hurt by the critical analysis (F) and retreated too quickly to withdrawn silence. The retreat suggests Introversion; where an E most likely would have argued and defended the plan, an I might believe that the worth of the plan did not depend on anyone accepting it. Mr. Green might respond favorably if you say something in the meeting such as suggested in the earlier paragraph. If you choose to speak to him privately, you could say, "I expect Mrs. White has no idea that she caused hard feelings. She's blunt, but I think her bluntness comes from her logic, not from her feelings. She certainly isn't alert to other people's feelings the way that you are."

The Green-White episode illustrates the value of having type concepts as one of the tools of teamwork. When team members know about type, the differences can be talked about directly in the meeting, as they arise. For example, using the Green-White exercise, other members might have spoken up and said, "I think we have some type differences getting in our way. I hear some Intuitive possibilities getting discarded because the Sensing specifics haven't been worked out. Can we put the type differences to work for us to get a good action plan out of this?" In this way, type can be used to address the conflict directly while steering the meeting away from behaviors that might be interpreted as a personal attack, and counterattack. Using type concepts allows us to talk about sensitive areas of personality differences in a more objective way. When Ms. White's behavior is seen as a natural expression of her type preferences, her team members can more easily assume that her intentions were only constructive and can then move the team's work along with fewer emotional snags.

The following essay by Isabel Myers (1962) seems especially useful for understanding situations such as the Green-White conflict. Myers wrote about using type for understanding and improving relationships in any areas of life, and her ideas certainly apply to teacher-student and teacher-teacher relationships. As you read it, you will recognize the roots of the Green-White exercise.

Type and Human Relations

by ISABEL BRIGGS MYERS

The effects of type in this field do not lend themselves easily to statistical verification but can be explored by personal observation and experience. The conclusions reached from the writer's observation and experience are therefore offered as a frame of reference for the reader's own explorations. Recognition of the type differences, when carried over into the field of person-to-person relationships, may afford a useful system for understanding others whose attitudes or actions seem unreasonable. Type theory would hold that type differences yield differences in interests, values, and problem-solving techniques which may facilitate or handicap a working relationship between two or more people. Where two individuals interacting with one another are of similar type, there is a better chance of communication of ideas. Sensing types like facts; Intuitives like possibilities; Thinkers like logical principles; Feeling types like a human angle. A good sound idea can be presented in any or all of these forms, but difficulties may be expected to occur if, say, the Thinker attempts to force logical reasons upon a Feeling type or possibilities upon the Sensing people.

It has seemed to the writer that most people get around this difficulty by picking friends mainly from their own type column, a fact generally apparent if one enters his friends upon a Type Table. In marriage there is a significant tendency to prefer likeness to difference, especially on SN. But parents and children have no option. They are stuck with each other's types, for better or worse.

The type differences, and the resulting family conflicts, can appear very early. A six-year-old girl with Feeling said in dismay after a week's visit from a five-year-old Thinker, "He doesn't care about pleasing, does he?" Basically, he never will. He has to have reasons. The small Feeling type will do things for the sake of "pleasing" but is quite unmoved by logic. If one expects to influence either, he must give him a motivation that means something to his type.

As individuals grow up, each type can profit by learning how to get along with the other. The Thinker is by nature impersonal and critical. He likes effects to follow logically from causes, and he forgets to reckon illogical human motives and reactions among the causes. In any disagreement, therefore, he tends to state his position bluntly, without concern for the feelings of the other people involved. The effect is to stir up antagonism which makes agreement needlessly hard.

Feeling types, on the other hand, set great value upon harmony and good feelings and are very aware of the likes and dislikes of the people around them. They assume that the Thinker is equally aware and resent his tactlessness toward others as well as toward themselves. What the Feeling types need to remember is that most of the time the Thinker does not even know how people feel about things. He needs to be told, calmly and plainly, before trouble starts, so that he can count people's feelings among the causes to be reckoned with and act accordingly.

What the Thinker needs to remember is that the Feeling types prize harmony and really prefer to agree with him if given a chance. He should start every discussion by mentioning the points on which he agrees with them. If they can feel that he is basically in the same camp with them, they are ready to make concessions to preserve that harmony and stay in the same camp. The points of difference can then be discussed rather than fought over. And the Thinker's logic and the Feeling type's understanding of people can both be brought to bear upon the problem.

Clashes between the types arise out of the very fact that makes opposite types mutually useful to each other: the fact that each sees the side of the problem which the other naturally overlooks. For instance, the Intuitive by nature likes to think things up; the Sensing type likes to get things done. The Sensing type puts his faith in the actual, the Intuitive in the possible. When an Intuitive comes up with a blazing new idea, his natural course is to present it in rough and sketchy form, trusting his listener to concentrate on the main point and ignore the details that have not been worked out. The Sensing type's natural reaction is to concentrate on what is missing, decide the idea won't work (which it won't in that form), and flatly turn it down. Result: one wasted idea and much hard feeling. Either type could avoid the collision by a little respect for his opposite. The Intuitive should be realistic enough to foresee the Sensing type's reaction and prepare for it, work out the details of his project, and get together the necessary facts in inescapable form. The Sensing type on his part should concede the Intuitive type's idea a fighting chance. He can say, "It might work if" and then bring up all the objections that experience suggests and ask, "What would you do about this and this and this?' The Intuitive then spends his energies happily against the obstacles, changing his ideas as necessary, and often ends with a solution valuable to them both. When compromise between opposite types is necessary, the best compromise is that which preserves to each party the advantage he considers most important. The Sensing type wants the solution to be workable, the Thinker wants it systematic, the Feeling type wants it humanly agreeable, and the Intuitive wants a door left open for growth and improvement. People often go to the mat for a scheme as a whole, when what they really care about is one particular merit that could as well be incorporated into another plan.

Whenever people differ, a knowledge of type helps to cut out irrelevant friction. More than that, it points up the advantages of the differences. No one man has to be good at everything. He only has to be good at his own stuff and decently appreciative of the other fellow's. Together, thanks to their differences, they can do a better job than if they were just alike.

5

Type Is a Four-Letter Word

Uses and Abuses of the MBTI® Instrument

THERE IS NO DOUBT about the effectiveness of the MBTI® instrument, and the underlying concepts, when it is used well. My experience tells me that competent and ethical uses of it are more common than the misuses. In this chapter, however, I concentrate on the misuses to help new users avoid them. Sound and ethical uses are described in chapter 12.

In his article "Second Thoughts" about the MBTI instrument, Ron Zemke (1992) reported views of critics and supporters of the Myers-Briggs Type Indicator® assessment. I can confirm, from more than thirty years of experience using the instrument, that attitudes about it range from giddy zealousness to passionate criticism.

Why such emotional reactions to a psychological instrument? It is, after all, just an instrument. I have observed several hundred people in the helping professions use and misuse the Indicator and its underlying concepts, and I have listened to many critics and supporters. In my experience, the responses at the extremes—praising it as panacea and criticizing it as trivial or hurtful pop psychology—come from misuses of it, from misunderstandings and mistakes that can be avoided. This chapter is about avoiding the pitfalls and staying on an ethical path to get the most out of using the Myers-Briggs® instrument and concepts.

The Indicator has two special features of its construction not found in most other psychological instruments. These can be sources of abuse by those who use it without understanding. The first is its appearance of being simple, and the second is the unusual nature of its scales and scores.

Misuse Arising from the Indicator's Appearance

Although the Indicator is the result of very sophisticated development, it appears simple for several reasons: (1) it is self-administering; (2) the questions are concerned with everyday events; (3) in the self-scoring and template scoring versions of it, it is a straightforward tabulating of votes for each pole of four scales; and (4) the descriptions of the types by Isabel Myers, which portray each type at its best, can seem to some like horoscopes, even though they actually represent the essence of a complex theory plus the results of extensive research and exquisitely careful writing.

> **"The nontechnical language of the instrument's items and the type descriptions was chosen so that respondents would feel at ease in exploring the ideas of type."**

Plain Language

The nontechnical language of the instrument's items and the type descriptions was chosen so that respondents would feel at ease in exploring the ideas of type. The descriptions emphasize the positive aspects of each type for the same reason. Unfortunately, the nontechnical appearance also seems to invite misuses of the Indicator by those who haven't studied the *MBTI® Manual.*

The apparent simplicity of the MBTI assessment leads some people into using it without adequate preparation. Often people are attracted to using it in their work after taking it themselves and being impressed by the accuracy and usefulness of the type description that goes with their MBTI results. If a trainer involves them in some exercises that show practical implications of type theory in work settings (or family relationships, learning styles, careers, et cetera), they are more impressed. They know they themselves can conduct exercises like that, and they feel they could easily manage an instrument that seems so nonthreatening—if they can get good-quality training materials. They somehow obtain the MBTI materials and begin administering them. Unfortunately, they didn't order or read the essential document, the *MBTI® Manual*, which explains what the authors intended, explains the complexities and subtleties, provides appropriate language for giving interpretations, summarizes the research behind the instrument, provides cautions, and gives guidelines for dealing with ethical issues—as do all good manuals for psychological instruments. An even worse practice is skipping the MBTI assessment altogether and using a short-version based on MBTI concepts assessment from the Internet—because it costs nothing. There is no short-version. To my knowledge, MBTI-like instruments that appear on the internet have not been validated by research. Those who compose their own MBTI-like questionnaire, even paraphrasing Myers' items, are ignorantly and unethically ignoring the mountain of work that went into constructing the Indicator's items—thousands of variations in wording tested on thousands of respondents to produce the phrases that work.

Who Is Qualified?

Professionals such as psychologists, counselors, and some educators, who are qualified by virtue of their formal education to purchase most psychological instruments from the tests' publishers, may be able to purchase the MBTI assessment materials even if they have not taken training in the Indicator's appropriate uses or read the manual. It is assumed that these professionals will act according to the ethics of their profession, but they do not always do so. In addition some practitioners, who have had no formal education in using psychological instruments but have access to the Indicator through others in their organizations, begin using it without coaching or adequate self-study.

Some professionals are qualified to purchase the MBTI materials by virtue of their education. Training programs for becoming certified to use the MBTI instrument are available for others. For information about qualifications and training programs contact CPP, Inc. (www.cpp.com) or the Center for Applications of Psychological Type (www.capt.org).

The children's counterpart of the MBTI instrument is the Murphy-Meisgeier Type Indicator for Children® (MMTIC®) instrument. In its new version published by CAPT, the MMTIC instrument and its support materials are available to teachers and parents online. The cautions in this chapter about misuses of the MBTI instrument generally apply to the MMTIC instrument as well because the two are grounded in the same theory, have similar construction features, and are subject to the same misunderstandings when their special features are not understood.

Consequences of Not Being Prepared

The poorly prepared user may set off unfortunate consequences: clients who aren't helped to distinguish between type and stereotype; who settle for and spread around quick, easy, shallow interpretations; who see type as a way to excuse their own faults; who see it as a means to try to manipulate others, to classify people for job assignments, to cater to the boss, or to use it as a pastime such as speculating about the types of celebrities. Their misuses of the Indicator also create critics who are so put off by the consequences of misuse that they dismiss the MBTI instrument and the theory behind it, sometimes with disgust.

Any instrument in the hands of someone not skilled in using it is a blunt instrument. And, in the exhilaration of getting acquainted with a new tool, we all run the risk of overusing it—like the proverbial child with a new hammer who suddenly realizes everything looks like a nail. With the MBTI assessment, new users are tempted to see possibilities of its use that stretch beyond its range; they want type theory to explain too many things. Psychological makeup is far too complex to be reduced to one set of explanations. Type is just one template to place on the human experience.

Misuse Arising from Confusion About Scales and Scores

The four dimensions or indices in the MBTI assessment, each represented as a dichotomy, are

- **E–I: Extraversion–Introversion**, one's orientation of energy;
- **S–N: Sensing–Intuition**, one's perception preference;
- **T–F: Thinking–Feeling**, one's judgment preference; and
- **J–P: Judging–Perceiving**, one's orientation to the outer world.

The instrument is constructed so that the response to each item is a vote for one side of the dichotomy or the other, on one of the four dimensions. In type theory, everyone uses all eight aspects of mental processing but has a constitutional preference for one side on each dimension: one is used most naturally, is most trusted, and is given priority. When the MBTI responses are scored, two outcomes are reported: a four-letter type designation, such as ESFP, and a preference clarity category (pcc) on each of the four dimensions—a pcc of slight, moderate, clear, or very clear—indicating the confidence one can have that the Indicator sorted the person into the best-fit preference category, based on the votes the respondent gave to each side of the dichotomy.

Scales

Misuse of the MBTI instrument also arises from the unusual nature of the scales and what the scale scores mean. Unlike nearly all other psychological measurements, the MBTI assessment *does not* measure traits or strength of traits. True to Jung's theory, the MBTI results indicate type preferences, not trait strengths. An MBTI score that reports a person's preference for Introversion over Extraversion, for example, says nothing about the person's skillfulness in introverting or extraverting. The score only reports that the person's responses placed him or her in the Extraversion or Introversion category and shows by the ppc how clearly the person prefers one mode over the other.

Scores

Scoring of the instrument, of course, produces scores. But since the Indicator does not measure strength of traits, the numerical outcome can easily be misinterpreted. The confusion comes when respondents assume or are incorrectly told that the numbers or a pcc of "slight," "moderate," "clear," or "very clear" reflect on their maturity or personality balance. Such misconceptions may be stated in many ways, such as "This extreme score means you overuse . . . or you neglect . . . " or "A low score is good because it means balance between the opposites . . . " or "You need to develop some balancing Extraversion . . . " or "Your Introversion score means you have good powers of concentration and are good at reflecting and considering things deeply." Another gross misunderstanding shows up in such statements as "I need to get my Extraversion score up; a lot of extraverting is expected of me in this new job." No such interpretations of MBTI scores are warranted.

There are, of course, skills of extraverting and introverting, but they are not measured by the MBTI assessment. Someone with a report that shows a clear preference for Introversion would be expected to be more skillful at introverting than extraverting. But the MBTI scores say nothing about that person's introverting skills relative to another person. Someone whose MBTI report shows a very clear preference for Extraversion may, by virtue of training, experience, and maturity, have better introverting skills than a less mature person whose report shows a very clear preference for Introversion.

If they do not represent skillfulness or strength of character, what do the MBTI scores mean? They indicate simply the confidence one can have that the instrument sorted the respondent into the best-fit category. They do not even mean the extent to which one mode is preferred over the other. For example, I score a slight preference for Extraversion, but I have no doubt at all about my type preference being ENTP. Here is the essential point. The MBTI assessment was designed specifically to designate a four-letter type, and the only function of scores is producing the four-letter hypothesis type. Isabel Myers called her instrument an *indicator* because its main function is to be a pointer; for each respondent it points to one of sixteen type descriptions and says, in effect, "Try this on. This is my best estimate of the psychological type represented by your responses to the MBTI items."

What the Numbers Mean

Myers' intentions on the topic of reporting scores to respondents are most clearly stated in the *MBTI® Manual,* (2nd edition): "Quantitative interpretation of the MBTI scores is not recommended. Scores were designed to show the direction of a preference, not its intensity" (Myers and McCaulley, 1985, page 58). If the respondent feels that the reported type is a good fit, there usually is no need for discussion about the numbers, or even for reporting the pcc to the respondent. When a respondent is not confident of the fit, or is uncertain about a preference, the preferences clarity categories can be used in the discussion to help find the type that rings most true.

For example, if the Indicator scored a client as an ISTJ but the person felt that the description of that type was not a close fit, the practitioner would look in that person's results for a score in the "slight" range and use that as a clue to suggest an alternate type description for the client to consider. With a slight pcc for Introversion, for example, the practitioner would suggest ESTJ as an alternate type to consider for a better fit.

The numerical part of the scores is also useful in answering the client's question, "If I responded to the MBTI questions another time, perhaps in a different frame of mind, what are the chances I would come out the same type?" High pcc scores indicate a high chance of coming out the same, while a pcc of "slight" means more chance of another type being reported.

> "In effect, psychological type is taken into account in job placement by using it to sharpen the job description and the interview process."

Wrong Uses of the MBTI® Instrument

Because the MBTI assessment does not measure competence, its use as a screening device is fruitless and often harmful. Consider, for example, a situation in which the management team decided that finding an SJ type to fill a vacancy in an administrative assistant position was desirable. They had candidates take the MBTI assessment to screen for that type. An internal candidate whose record of competence put her at the top of the list did not come out SJ on the Indicator, and the job was given to an external candidate who did. There are at least two big mistakes here. Coming out one type or another on the MBTI instrument is no assurance of skillfulness, and type should never be considered a barrier to the development of any particular skills. Second, because the Indicator is a self-report instrument, people taking it in a hiring situation can fake their responses in the direction of what they perceive will best fit the job description and not report their natural tendencies.

A good use of psychological type in hiring situations would begin in a similar way, analyzing the job's tasks in light of type preferences: Which types are likely to find the tasks easy or difficult? The next step is not administering the MBTI assessment to applicants, but planning out criteria and questions for the interviewing process that will encourage candidates to report their experience in performing such tasks. In effect, psychological type is taken into account in job placement by using it to sharpen the job description and the interview process. This way you are more assured of getting someone with the skills and experience that you need regardless of his or her type preferences.

Putting together work teams based on MBTI results is another area where misuses occur. They occur mainly because of the assumption that the Indicator measures skillfulness (for example, "Let's put an F on that team to deal with the other members' abrasiveness"). Misuses also happen because of clumsiness of the consultants or facilitators who are assisting the team building process. Using poor entry techniques, they inadvertently cause people to be secretive or defensive about their MBTI results or to feel manipulated. (Good entry techniques are described in chapter 12.)

Here is a good example of using type concepts in selecting a team member in a middle school. After being introduced to psychological type, teachers on one team recognized they had no Judging type on the team and saw a relationship between that fact and their frequent problem of getting closure on team tasks. A team member was retiring, and they asked the principal if a Judging type could take her place. The principal wisely said the MBTI instrument wasn't used for screening, but he asked the team to help interview candidates for the job. He suggested they write some questions to put to the candidates, questions about work style that might reflect the Judging-related traits they were seeking. They did, and they were pleased with the way their questions worked in the interviews. The new hire brought to the team's work the traits they were seeking. Later, when the new teacher took the Indicator, she scored a preference for Judging. Of course, many people with a Perceiving preference have well-developed skills of organizing and scheduling for closure. The new teacher's skills would not depend on scoring as a J on the Indicator.

Case-by-case evidence of the value of the MBTI concepts in team development is easy to find, as it is in family relationships, personal development, teaching and learning, and other areas. In addition there is mounting evidence of its value from carefully constructed research studies.

Reliability, Validity, and Practical Effectiveness

MBTI practitioners are cautioned not to use the "T" word, *test*, when describing the MBTI assessment to clients—so as not to raise anxieties clients may carry about the kinds of tests that have right and wrong answers. Nevertheless, it is certainly a psychological test, validated by all the standards that psychometricians set for such tests. Those who critique such instruments generally regard the MBTI assessment as meeting or exceeding expectations for reliability and validity—that is, for getting consistent results and for accomplishing what it was designed to do. When researchers have commented on the *MBTI® Manual*, they praise it as setting a new standard by which manuals for psychological instruments can be judged.

The most-consulted reference guide for psychological instruments, the Buros Mental Measurements Yearbook (Buros 1989), a source devoted to critical reviews, gave the MBTI assessment a favorable report. "The MBTI is an excellent example of a construct-oriented test that is inextricably linked to Jung's (1923) theory of psychological types . . . . [It] is not surprising that it is held in high regard by many who subscribe to this aspect of Jungian theory. It is also not surprising that those who do not accept the tenets of the theory reject, or more typically ignore, the considerable body of evidence regarding the validity of the MBTI that now exists."

The User Affects Reliability and Validity

The practitioner's essential concern is very specific: Will the MBTI results be valid and reliable for my clients? The answer depends on three conditions, all of them under the practitioner's control: the fit of the MBTI assessment to the application planned for it, the skill used in introducing the indicator into the situation, and the expectations held for outcomes from its use.

Appropriate Uses

I have seen some really bad applications of the MBTI assessment. The Indicator cannot provide valid data when it is used inappropriately—for example, when used before and after some research intervention to try to show how peoples' behaviors, attitudes, or personalities were changed for the better by the intervention. I have read research studies in which students were being taught a set of human relations skills, and the researcher administered the Indicator before and after to see if students came out more E and F after the training. There is no basis for supposing someone's type would change even if some skills were improved or attitudes changed. And there is no basis in MBTI outcomes for deciding that someone has better or worse human relations skills because he or she is an I or an E or a T or an F.

There are good applications where type is a variable being used to predict behavior or performance, but such applications require the skills of a researcher: careful attention to research design issues—sample size, control of other variables, comparison groups, et cetera. This kind of use is beyond the scope of practitioners not trained in research methods.

> **"The validity and reliability of the MBTI assessment for individual clients depends on the skill of the practitioner."**

The rule of thumb for getting a good fit is to avoid using the MBTI assessment to do something *for* or *to* employees or students and to confine its use to helping them use type concepts as a tool in their work, as part of their language for problem solving.

Practitioner's Skill

The validity and reliability of the MBTI assessment *for individual clients* depend on the skill of the practitioner. If the clients get a positive introduction to the Indicator, they will give straight answers to the MBTI questions, attend carefully to the explanation of results, remain open to type ideas, and accept help in testing out the ideas and using them well. The MBTI results and underlying ideas will be valid and reliable for them.

When a practitioner is not skilled, there are risks. For example, many people have a tendency to treat others as stereotypes, to categorize them and treat them according to those categories rather than as individuals. When introduced to type, they are likely to see it as a new way to sort, label, or manipulate others. The practitioner who is not skillful in using type concepts is likely to present them in ways that reinforce such tendencies to stereotype.

Practitioner's Expectations

Unrealistic expectations for outcomes on the MBTI instrument can cloud its usefulness and make its results invalid and unreliable—for example, expecting a one-hour or one-time orientation to type to be an adequate introduction; expecting employees to embrace it when the boss does not; expecting type, by itself, to be highly predictive of performance; and expecting the MBTI assessment to serve as a candidate screening device, as previously mentioned.

Following is an example of an appropriate expectation for using the Indicator: a large accounting firm had a good introduction to type, with the boss making clear his support for type and encouraging its inclusion in the way the company did business. One of the accountants, on learning that his type, ENFP, was uncommon among accountants, and doing some self analysis, began to see type as a clue to some sources of frustration in his work life. He went to the boss to discuss the problem. The boss recognized the problem and saw an opportunity to shift the employee to a new, emerging role within the organization that would call on the natural inclinations of his type: developing new clients. The results were good in all respects.

The Ethics of Using the MBTI Instrument

Ethical guidelines for using the MBTI assessment are essentially the same as for any psychological instrument. However, there are some special guidelines. Because of the practical insights type concepts provide into individual and group functioning, and because the Indicator's language and concepts are understandable to non-psychologists, the MBTI instrument has attracted users who have not before had to consider the ethics of gathering and using psychological data. Their previous professional training or experience may not have taught them the essentials, such as taking the instrument must be voluntary; results must be given only to that person; and the person must receive an individualized explanation of the results, including what is indicated and not indicated by the results. These and other ethical guidelines are included in chapter 12.

The ethical problems are compounded because clients themselves can be naive about what constitutes a breach of ethics. They often get excited about using type concepts, and they talk about and apply them freely without considering the ethical fallout. Practitioners must not only model ethical behavior for them but also must teach them explicitly how to use type concepts and how to take precautions so that their good intentions don't backfire.

This chapter has highlighted misuses of the MBTI assessment and the negative consequences that follow the misuses. I took this approach to dramatize for new MBTI and MMTIC users the responsibilities that go with effective use of the instruments and their underlying concepts. All of us want to be ethical, but sometimes in our drive to be effective and get results, we run the risk of overlooking or obscuring the ethics of a situation. When we do that, we jeopardize our own credibility and the long-term effectiveness of our work.

6

Type & Stereotype

Why Do We Stereotype?

STEREOTYPING IS a part of human nature. We tend to stereotype those who are most different from us because we understand them less well—a rule that holds true for type differences as well as for cultural, racial, religious, and political issues. For example, Extraverts may stereotypically project onto Introverts the awkwardness they themselves would feel when stuck without having something to say or some action to be involved in. The comfort the Introvert feels in reflection and silences may not occur to the Extravert. The opposite projection, of course, is a risk for Introverts. MBTI® practitioners have a special responsibility to examine their own stereotypes and to teach about type in ways that minimize clients' stereotypical use of type concepts.

No one wants to be guilty of stereotyping, but we all are. Why? A dictionary definition of stereotype gives clues. When used in describing ideas, stereotype is defined as "A standard mental picture held in common by members of a group and representing an oversimplified opinion . . . or uncritical judgment . . . an over–simplified generalization making it easy to dismiss divergent groups." Why do we stereotype when all we mean to do is have helpful labels for experience?

Cognitive psychologists remind us that it is human nature to categorize. We can't deal with the daily bombardment of perceptual stimuli in raw form; the stimuli are too overwhelming in number and variety for each to be acknowledged in its uniqueness. So we sort them into categories and deal with them in these sets. Doing our mental processing in categories simplifies the perceptual field enough for our minds to work comfortably. The dark side of this process is that our drive for order and mental comfort leads us to form and use poorly constructed categories that are too simple, uninformed, and often biased. Those categories become stereotypes, categories that tend to close our thought processes rather than keep them sensitive to possible bias.

Type and Stereotype

We who use type concepts certainly want to avoid stereotyping the sixteen psychological types. No doubt most of us who use type theory were drawn to it because it gives us constructive categories to think with—categories that are vast improvements over the familiar ones people use to sort each other. Our common goal is to give people more helpful categories to put in place of less helpful ones. Carl Jung, Katharine Briggs, and Isabel Myers worked hard to select terms for psychological type that would avoid bias and minimize stereotyping. Those of us who use type strive to continue that process. It surely is not a finished job.

Regardless of our efforts, we are all caught at some time or another with our biases showing. Being an Intuitive type, my dominant Intuition colors and steers my perceptions in such a way that I cannot be sure that my views of the Sensing process or of Sensing types aren't stereotypes, at least in some respects. Time and again my Sensing friends have helped me see the stereotypes I might be using. Type theory tells me that Sensing is my least developed mental process or function and the most unconscious of my four mental processes. I believe it. Sensing just doesn't get much respect in the flow of my thought processes, so how can I expect it to assert itself and show up my stereotypes for what they are? How wonderful to have some Sensing friends who help me break my stereotypes about Sensing. If I, who have been studying type for nearly forty years unwittingly use language that stereotypes people when I talk about the types, what happens in the minds of those I teach, who first learn about type from me? Perhaps the stereotypes get embellished and hardened as they are passed on.

Just as I am guilty of unfavorable stereotyping of people with types and type preferences different from my own, so I am guilty of favorable biases creeping into my language and thoughts about my own type preferences.

It Happens to All of Us

None of us is immune from stereotyping. One person, very knowledgeable about type, and whose name we know well, wrote these descriptive phrases about Thinking types: "Thinking types . . . are relatively unemotional people and uninterested in people's feelings . . . . [They] tend to relate well only to other Thinking types . . . . [They] may seem hard-hearted . . . . " We all know some Thinking types who may be accurately described by these phrases, but do you detect stereotyping here? These are Isabel Myers' words, from the 1962 *MBTI® Manual* and reprinted on page 14 of the first edition of *Introduction to Type®*. They are part of the section called "Effects of Each Preference in Work Situations."

Isabel Myers was a very careful writer, to say the least. It is impossible to overstate the exquisite care she took in finding the right words for describing type—clear words that would not stereotype or have misleading connotations. Her perfectionism in writing is typified in the fact that she spent thirty years writing the manuscript of *Gifts Differing*, her only book besides the *MBTI® Manual*. I understand she would take it off the shelf every week or so to change a word or two. Isabel Myers was a dominant Feeling type, an INFP. If stereotyping were to appear in her descriptions, where would it most likely be?—her description of the mental process opposite her dominant, her least conscious process: Thinking.

Several of us with a preference for the Thinking process objected to the phrases, called them to her attention, and she changed them to read "Thinking types . . . do not show emotion readily and are often uncomfortable dealing with people's feelings." She eliminated the second phrase, "[They] tend to relate well only to other Thinking types", and she changed "hard-hearted" to "firm-minded." Allen Hammer, editing *Introduction to Type* for its fourth edition, chose to eliminate the first phrase. Its closest counterpart in the new list of phrases describing Thinking types was "respond more to people's ideas than to their feelings."*

Are these wording changes nit-picking? Not to me. When we introduce someone to type, the credibility of type theory *for that person* is on the line. Our task is to find and use language that reduces the risk of type being distorted into stereotype.

Watching Our Language

What are some signs of stereotyping, some red flags that we can watch for in our language? Phrases containing absolutes, such as *always* and *never*, are suspect. For example, "You can always count on Sensing types to . . . stuff envelopes . . . take minutes of the meeting" might be a stereotype used by an Intuitive to relegate mundane tasks no one likes. A statement such as "Never trust an NF with balancing a checkbook" is another example. Another sign is excusing one's behavior on the grounds of type: "I'm allowed to be spacey, I'm an Intuitive" or "That's my J compulsiveness."

In dividing up jobs, some people who know about type are quick to assume that the decisions about who gets what jobs can be based on a superficial look at type preferences, without other considerations such as familiarity, desire, or skillfulness.

The Risk of Stereotypes in Humor

Watch for stereotypes in anecdotes and humor. Humor often relies on exaggeration to get its punch, and exaggerations of type characteristics may result in unwanted negative stereotypes. Some humor is grounded in stereotype, of course—for example, ethnic humor such as Polish jokes or blonde jokes. This is humor at the expense of the group that is stereotyped. Jack Benny made a career out of the stereotype of himself that he created as the basis for most of his jokes. This is a benign stereotype, of course, because he invented the image and it hurt no one. A more recent comedian, Bill Cosby, writes humor with much of the same non-stereotyping tone.

---

*For readers interested in examining ways that type bias persists among those of us who use and teach about type, particularly the stereotyping of Sensing types, see Allen Hammer's insightful article, "Typing or Stereotyping: Unconscious Bias in Applications of Psychological Type Theory" in the *Journal of Psychological Type*, Volume 10 (1985).

Through the years, I have found cartoons helpful in introducing type concepts. I thought I had screened them for stereotypes, but my wife Carolyn, a Feeling type, spotted some I missed in the cartoons dealing with the Thinking and Feeling preferences.

One is a Trudy cartoon by Jerry Marcus, a single panel, showing her confronting her husband with an exasperated look on her face. He is seated in his easy chair, his hands folded, with a smug look on his face. She is saying, "Your argument is logical, sensible, fair, perceptive and factual and I hate you."

I had been using it to show that Thinking types believe an issue should be settled when they produce an objective, impersonal, and logical argument, while Feeling types don't want it settled until the reasoning gives adequate weight to the human, personal consequences of the decision. Carolyn showed me the stereotypes. The Feeling type (Trudy) seems to be giving in to the Thinking type's argument, acknowledging logical reasoning as superior, though distasteful. Feeling gets the last word but loses the argument. Thinking wins. In the way I was using the cartoon, not calling attention to the stereotyping, I let pass not only the implication that Feeling judgment is subordinate to Thinking judgment but also that Thinking is for men and Feeling is for women. I still use the cartoon at times, but now I add a discussion about stereotyping.

A Frank and Ernest cartoon by Thaves is another I have used. In its single panel, the two characters are looking up at a very dark and starry night. One says, "Do you realize all the rest of our galaxy is moving away from us at one-third the speed of light?" The response is "Do you suppose it was something we *said?*"

In using the cartoon, I thought I was making the point that Thinking types give more attention to impersonal phenomena in looking for life's meanings, while Feeling types are more likely to look to personal events as the source of understanding. Until Carolyn showed me, I had missed the stereotype: it is silly for Feeling types to apply Feeling criteria where they don't belong. I have since found a companion cartoon that shows a Thinking type looking silly applying impersonal analysis where it doesn't fit, and I use the two cartoons together.

Persona, Shadow, and Stereotype

Carl Jung's concepts of persona and shadow help us understand why we are more likely to stereotype some groups and not others and why we are not likely to recognize our own stereotyping when we do it. The persona is the part of me that I show the world, the part I am comfortable enough with to allow it to represent me to other people. The shadow is the back side of the persona, the dark side away from the light of public exposure, where I might hold aspects of myself that I tend to deny in consciousness.

How does this relate to stereotypes? First we need to look at the relationship of type to persona and shadow. The persona is expressed most easily through our favorite and second most favorite mental processes, while the third and fourth processes most often carry the contents of the unconscious shadow. In my own case, my Feeling and Sensing processes are mainly in the shadow; they are less mature, less conscious, less controllable and predictable when in my conscious life, and more worrisome. So when people and situations call on my Feeling and Sensing processes, my shadowy and immature versions of these processes color my perceptions and give me an unconscious bias that results in stereotypes. I am likely to see immaturity or threatening motives in those others who are so different from my persona, who remind me of my shadow side, the part of me I want to keep hidden. So when I project onto their behavior the dark meanings that come out of my shadow, I have produced a stereotype.

An Activity for Identifying Stereotypes

No doubt stereotyping is related to the attitudes of Extraversion, Introversion, Judging, and Perceiving as well as to the four mental processes. To demonstrate the extent to which we all carry with us stereotypes of type preferences that are opposite ours, try this activity with some friends or colleagues who know type concepts. Choose one dimension of type, E–I, S–N, T–F, or J–P. I will illustrate with E–I. With your group, complete three tasks:

1. Each person chooses a partner whose E–I preference is the same. The partners in each Extraversion pair will individually think of specific

people he or she knows are Introverts and write down four or five words or phrases that accurately describe the Introverted characteristics of those people, taking care to use unbiased descriptors. Using the same care, the partners in each Introversion pair will individually use the same process to identify the Extraversion characteristics of their sample of Extraverts. Allow three or four minutes for this step.

2. Partners discuss the words they wrote individually and edit them as needed to replace the words that might be seen as stereotyping. Schedule five minutes for this step.

3. Each pair of Es then gets with a pair of Is to present both sets of descriptors, to discuss any stereotyping suggested in the two lists, and to find unbiased replacement words.

> **"Carl Jung's concepts of persona and shadow help us understand why we are more likely to stereotype some groups and not others and why we are not likely to recognize our own stereotyping when we do it."**

During your discussion, you will find more stereotyping than you suppose. This discussion time is also a good opportunity for exploring the meanings of appearances—that is, for asking the group members of the opposite preference questions about their Introversion or Extraversion. For example, in a recent discussion an Introvert asked the Extraverts, "Why do you seem to need to fill every silence in a conversation?" And an Extravert said, "Help me understand why Introverts often seem to be aloof." You can give this discussion all the time you have available; in my experience, we always have to end it before the people feel finished with it. After the discussion, I believe you'll agree that stereotyping is natural and inevitable.

Sometimes when I use this activity, we take lists prepared by E and I pairs and combine them into composite lists. Some words appear on several people's lists. On one recent occasion, we worked as a combined group to first screen the lists for words that seemed to have a bias. (Remember that the foursomes had already screened their descriptors for stereotypes.) As a whole group we applied the first of three criteria: *Does the word suggest bias for or against?* We quickly spotted and scratched off several words—for example, *entertaining* and *superficial* on the Extravert list prepared by Introverts, and *loner* and *quiet assurance* on the Introvert list prepared by Extraverts. We all knew people for whom the words were accurate, but we all agreed the terms applied to special cases and not the general categories of Extraversion and Introversion. With such words gone, the lists looked like the following:

Extraversion	Introversion
active	thoughtful
open	quiet
talkative	reserved
sociable	shy
outgoing	serious
friendly	deep
lively	careful
enthusiastic	brief
expansive	discreet

The second stereotype-detecting criteria we applied to each term was: *Could the term be misleading by implying a negative opposite trait for people of the other preference?* We decided this criterion eliminated most of the eighteen words listed above. For example, using *active* for Extraverts could imply *passive* or *inactive* as traits of Introverts; *open* could imply *closed;* using *thoughtful* for Introverts could imply *thoughtless* or *unthinking* as a trait of Extraverts; and *quiet* could imply *loud* or *noisy* for its opposite.

Each time I use this activity, participants come to a clear conclusion that explicitly stating the opposite you *intend* to convey is important to avoid misunderstanding. So we decide to use words only in pairs. For example, *active* and *reflective* make a good pair, as do *outgoing* and *reserved*, or *expressive* and *quiet*. By finding good pairs, we returned most of the eighteen words to the list. But good pairs were hard to agree on, and such "good" lists never get very long. So we agreed that when we introduced Extraversion and Introversion to people we would give the descriptors only in balanced pairs.

We then used a third criterion for screening out stereotypes: *Does the word distinguish between the preferences, or could it be applied also to the opposite or other preferences?* We decided that *friendly* didn't distinguish between Extravert and Introvert. And some Extraverts regarded themselves as *shy*, so those words were eliminated. Also eliminated were *open* and *thoughtful* because they were not distinctive to Extravert or Introvert. Seven other words on the composite were also eliminated because they did not meet this criterion—*lively, people-oriented, enthusiastic, expansive, careful, brief,* and *discreet*. They were dropped because they could apply to more than one of the eight preferences that make up the types.

This activity always has the effect of making participants alert to the need for care in choosing descriptors for the type preferences. Participants uniformly speak of it as a powerful learning experience.

What We Can Do

Having stereotypes in our conceptions and language about type is natural and inevitable, but we can guard against them and head them off. And we must do so if we are to grow.

- We can be alert to the spots where we are most vulnerable to stereotyping, which will differ for each of us.
- We can be aware, those of us who use and teach others about type concepts, that we have a common challenge. In our enthusiasm and in our desire to convince people of the value of type, we may overstate and overgeneralize—a sure source of stereotyping.
- We can ask our opposites to help us spot possible biases as we talk about type and to suggest alternate, unbiased language.
- We can realize that improving our language about type requires an improvement in understanding of opposites and therefore a deeper knowledge of type.
- And, finally, we can accept the fact that the quest to drive out our stereotypes about type never ends.

We can help each other. One of my fondest memories of Isabel Myers is the effective way she helped people improve their understanding of type by gently offering them an appropriate word to replace a biased one they had used. She'd say, "I believe they'll understand better if you say . . . " or "I used to say it that way until my ISTJ husband showed me a better wording." In the same spirit, we can help each other.

7

Psychological Type & Education

THIS CHAPTER is comprised of an essay by Isabel Briggs Myers that was written in October 1971, and not published elsewhere to my knowledge. She wrote it to describe how type theory can be used to understand the learning of children from their early years in school. Its relevance for today's educational settings will be evident to you as you read it. Isabel Myers was always concerned that many children are taught, very early, in ways that make them lose confidence in themselves and cause them to come to hate school. She graciously gave permission to include her thoughts here.

Taking Type into Account in Education

by ISABEL BRIGGS MYERS

Schools are being told that they are accountable for educating every child. They are required to teach the basic skills, so that every child grows up able to read, write and balance a checkbook. And they are required to plant various sorts of knowledge, deeply enough so that it will germinate, take root and bear fruit.

Both demands are better met if the schools take into account the type differences among children. These are not quantitative differences that can be expressed simply as a higher or lower degree of mental ability. They are qualitative differences, differences as to the kind of perception and the kind of judgment that the child prefers to use. It is his preferences that make his type. Children of different types have a different "mix" of abilities, different needs, interests and motivations, and different degrees of success in school.

The preference that has the most conspicuous consequences in education is the choice between the two kinds of perception, the choice between Sensing and Intuition. Sensing focuses interest and attention upon the concrete reality that is apparent to the five senses. Sensing children are more interested in doing something, almost anything, with almost any tangible object, than in listening to what anyone is saying unless it has to do with action or adds something definite to their picture of the physical world. In contrast, Intuition focuses interest and attention upon the end results of one's own unconscious processes, which include the translation of symbols-words into meaning, and meaning into words. Intuitive children thus tend to take a positive interest in language, spoken or written, and acquire a facility that is convenient in class and in verbal ability tests and also enables them to state clearly and usefully to themselves the relationships and possibilities suggested by their Intuition.

> **"If we are to have a system of universal education that does justice to all the types, I think we must draw a sharp distinction between skills and knowledge."**

It is therefore understandable that, as most schools are now run, Sensing children have less use for school than Intuitive children do (often no use at all), that on the average they make lower grades and score lower on intelligence tests (though not enough lower to account for their grades), and that they far more frequently drop out.

If we are to have a system of universal education that does justice to all the types, I think we must draw a sharp distinction between skills and knowledge. Knowledge spreads over a tremendous variety of subjects, each of which may be interesting and useful to certain types and a waste of time to others. But the basic skills are essential for all the types, and should be taught in such a way as to give every child what he needs.

The usual first grade has a substantial majority of Sensing children and a smaller number of Intuitives. The Sensing children do not want to have to cope with anything unexplainable. The Intuitives do not want to be bored by anything tedious and dull. Except for an occasional child who may have been let into the secret by an Intuitive parent or have found it out for himself, none of the children, Sensing or Intuitive, know that letters stand for sounds.

In most first grades, nobody (for a long time) tells them this one crucial fact that makes sense of the process of learning to read. Reading thus consists of memorizing "sight words," recognizable only by their general shape. A new word is an insoluble mystery until teacher tells you what it is. Content is necessarily restricted to repetition of the few words thus far memorized. "Dick. See Dick. See Dick run." This method of teaching manages to frustrate both the Sensing children and the Intuitives. Reading, which ought to be a magical extension of one's own experience, is both unexplainable and dull.

To meet the needs of the Sensing children who want things to be explicit and the Intuitive children who want unlimited possibilities, first grades should introduce intensive phonics at the very beginning, so that every child in the class knows that there is a perfectly good way to tell what new words are. He is going to be able to read, very soon, up to the limits of his speaking vocabulary. And removal of the artificial limits on vocabulary means that he can read vastly more interesting things. He can, in fact, attempt anything he cares to tackle.

From the standpoint of the child's success in school and his development as a person, with ambition, initiative, and confidence in himself, the start of first grade marks a crucial fork in the road. That is the point at which he decides either that school makes sense or that it does not, that it is interesting or boring, that he can or cannot do these new things. If he cannot do the new things, his only defense against the humiliation of being "dumb" is to decide that such things are not worth doing.

The pitfall in the teaching of arithmetic skills is basically the same as the pitfall in teaching reading. The children who try to cope with the symbols without recognizing the realities these stand for are doomed to frustration. They never win through to the beautiful certainties in the realm of numbers. They just memorize incantations; "7 and 5 is 12." "11 minus 4 is

7." "5 times 7 is 35." When the teacher gives you the first two numbers of an incantation, you have to remember the third. If you forget that third number, there is nothing you can do about it. And if you are given a problem and can't see what kind of incantation to use, there is nothing you can do about that.

The solution is to establish the reality of numbers first. The symbols then can be understood as a way of talking about reality. There should be no operations with disembodied numerals, no incantations, no memorizing, no flash cards for "addition facts" and "subtraction facts," no verbal drill, until the children are thoroughly familiar with manual operations with quantities. For many Sensing children, things you can touch and move are real but words are not.

The form in which a question is put can change the whole spirit of the proceedings. "How much is 7 and 5?" implies that the child ought to know by this time and the teacher wants to find out whether he does or not. This is wrong side to. The child is the one who should be doing the finding out. "Find out how much is 7 and 5!" is an invitation to action. Using number blocks, for instance, the child can take a block that is seven squares high and stand it against the number tower. Naturally it reaches to seven. Then he can take a block that is five squares high and stack it on top of the seven. Together they reach to twelve. Every time he does it they reach to twelve. In fact, he can see that they have to reach to twelve; the seven block is always three squares short of ten; the first three squares of the five block always get you to ten; the other two squares always stick up beyond ten and reach to twelve. A similar certainty has to exist in the case 17 and 5, 27 and 5, and so on up.

Consistent use of this approach gives the child a picture of the number system as a whole, the place of any given number in that system, and its relation to other numbers. When he starts doing operations with numerals instead of blocks, he knows the quantities they stand for and what he is doing with those quantities. And when he is given a problem, he has a decent chance of seeing what he must do to solve it.

Reading, writing and arithmetic are well-defined skills that every child needs to acquire. But knowledge, as distinguished from skills, is another matter. It has no limits. Schools must decide what tiny fraction they will try to teach. If we take it as axiomatic that a child should be taught things that are of lasting benefit to him, either by making him more effective or by otherwise enhancing his life, one brutal conclusion follows. There is no use in teaching a child things he intends to forget.

Nothing will stick in a child's mind long enough to do him any good unless it interests him, and here type plays a major role. The combination of a child's preferred kind of perception and his preferred kind of judgment tends to concentrate his interest in fields where these find scope, as shown in the comparison on page three of *Introduction to Type*. His remaining preferences influence the kind of work he will like to do in those fields. Hence knowledge that is relevant, even illuminating, for a person with a given set of preferences can be acutely boring to a person with the opposite set. Aside from routine warnings against common dangers, like carbon monoxide and the signing of documents unread, there is probably no body of knowledge that can profitably be "taught" to every child regardless.

Time and effort spent in trying to teach a child something against his own will are worse than wasted. Real harm is done. If a child is not interested in what he is supposed to be learning, he is bored. And the habit of being bored is disastrous for children, because it destroys their native curiosity. Babies and preschoolers have a great urge to make sense of the world. They devote their energies happily to finding out one thing after another, whatever fixes their curiosity at the moment. They learn at a tremendous rate, and they remember what they learn, because it becomes a part of their world as they know it. Learning is high adventure, not a chore.

"Children in all the grades should be given maximum opportunity to learn the things that have meaning and interest for them in terms of their own kind of perception and their own kind of judgment."

School should be a continuation of the adventure. Children in all the grades should be given maximum opportunity to learn the things that have meaning and interest for them in terms of their own kind of perception and their own kind of judgment. To the extent that they are given this opportunity, they gain not only in interest but in application and intelligence as well. People of any age, from six to sixty, apply themselves with greater vigor to the task in hand when they are interested. People of any age are more intelligent when they are interested than when they are bored.

A child permitted to study what interests him learns more and remembers it. The most valuable outcome, however, is the effect upon the development of his perception and judgment. A purposeful finding out about almost anything develops his perception. And a self-imposed doing of whatever is necessary to that end develops his judgment far more than would mere obedience to a teacher's authority. The lifelong importance of adequate development of perception and judgment is shown in past and current studies with the Type Indicator. Good perception and judgment are associated with achievement, which is reasonable because they make a person more effective in whatever he sets out to do. They are also associated with mental and physical health, which again is reasonable because they enable a person to cope more competently with his problems and thus lessen or eliminate strain.

Ways of making room for individual interests and study can be worked out in any school where authority will accept the idea. In fact, they can be worked out independently by any teacher. A seminar approach can be taken, in which the class is given a bird's-eye view of the different aspects of the subject and then allowed to sign up to work on whichever aspect each finds most interesting. Or a list of individual projects can be designed to appeal to widely different types. Flexibility can be achieved by framing some exam questions for Sensing types, others for Intuitives, everyone being permitted to leave out the two he likes least. Or it may be announced in advance that everyone may formulate and answer one question of his own, substituting it for one not in his field.

Where students are old enough to take the Type Indicator, as in seventh to twelfth grades, their types can be ascertained, subject to confirmation by the students themselves. Teachers can then learn by direct observation how their subjects need to be presented in order to catch the interest of ST, SF, NF, and NT types respectively, and can share their findings with other teachers. Feedback to the students about their types can add to their understanding of themselves and others, can reassure them that it is all right to be the kind of person they are, and can relieve the strain of personal conflicts at home or elsewhere by showing how these arise from differences in type. It can even help them to develop their perception and judgment. *Introduction to Type* has instructions how to do it, exercising each kind of perception and each kind of judgment, separately, in turn, to find out what each can contribute to the solution of a problem.

Children in lower grades can also practice using the different kinds of perception and judgment one at a time in appropriate ways. Exact observation will exercise Sensing. Figuring out possible ways to solve a difficulty will exercise Intuition. Thinking out all the unintended consequences that may result from an action will exercise thinking. Weighing how other people will feel about things will exercise Feeling.

An early clue to a child's type may be obtainable from his response to these activities. The Sensing child should find the Sensing exercise easier and more fun than the Intuitive exercise. The little Thinker will prefer Thinking about [logical] consequences to guessing about other people's feelings. And so on. An observant teacher may be able to draw useful inferences as to the way each child's mind works and what will help him most. Whether she does or not, the children will benefit directly from practice in these four different, important ways of using their minds.

2

Part Two: Advanced Applications

8

The Dynamics of Type

More Than Four Preferences

MARK AND SAVANNAH are a couple who responded to the Myers-Briggs Type Indicator® (MBTI®) instrument as part of a couples study group at their church. They reported ENTJ and INTP and confirmed that the descriptions of those types fit them very well. They also learned that one of the processes—S, N, T, or F—is dominant in each person's mental makeup. That made sense to them. But what startled the couple and got them confused was learning the ENTJ and INTP both have Thinking as dominant. They saw their mental processing and habits of thought as being very different. They agreed that they both favored Thinking over Feeling, but they were puzzled about the differences they saw in their uses of Thinking. To get an idea of their puzzlement, I suggest you reread the descriptions of the two types, as they appear in figure 8.1 on page 126.

Even though they both had Thinking as dominant, ENTJ and INTP read as two distinctly different kinds of mind. Savannah and Mark quickly saw that Thinking is not just one concept, one component in a combination of four preferences, such as E+N+T+J, or any other combination that includes T. They had come to the door of a new level of understanding about people types: that the processes operate in attitudes; specifically, that an introverted T is different from an extraverted T.

Figure 8.1

ENTJ	INTP
Intuitive, innovative ORGANIZERS; analytical, systematic, confident; push to get action on new ideas and challenges. Having extraverted THINKING as their strongest mental process, ENTJs are at their best when they can take charge and set things in logical order. They value: • Analyzing abstract problems, complex situations • Foresight; pursuing a vision • Changing, organizing things to fit their vision • Putting theory into practice, ideas into action • Working to a plan and schedule • Initiating, then delegating • Efficiency; removing obstacles and confusion • Probing new possibilities • Holding self and others to high standards • Having things settled and closed • Tough-mindedness, directness, task focus • Objective principles; fairness, justice • Assertive, direct action • Intellectual resourcefulness • Driving toward broad goals along a logical path • Designing structures and strategies • Seeking out logical flaws to improve things	Inquisitive ANALYZERS; reflective, independent, curious; more interested in organizing ideas than situations or people. Having introverted THINKING as their strongest mental process, they are at their best when following their intellectual curiosity, analyzing complexities to find the underlying logical principles. They value: • A reserved outer life; an inner life of inquiry • Pursuing interests in depth, with concentration • Work and play that is intriguing, not routine • Being free of emotional issues while working • Working on problems that respond to detached intuitive analysis and theorizing • Approaching problems by reframing the obvious • Complex intellectual mysteries • Being absorbed in abstract, mental work • Freedom from organizational constraints • Independence and nonconformance • Intellectual quickness, ingenuity, invention • Competence in the world of ideas • Spontaneous learning by following curiosity and inspirations • Using critical analysis to improve things

Looking again at the two type descriptions, they began to figure out that the outward use of T and the inward use of T represent quite different behaviors, priorities, and motivations in one's mental processing. Exploring these differences took them into what is referred to as type dynamics, the subject of this chapter.

The Myers-Briggs Type Indicator assessment provides scores on four separate dichotomies—E–I, S–N, T–F, and J–P—and reports a preference on each one—such as E, S, F, and J. On the surface the four preferences are apparently independent of each other. When respondents are told that the four letters taken together—for example, ESFJ, represent one of the sixteen types, it is natural for them to conclude that a type is a composite or addition of four separate qualities—E plus S plus F plus J. This natural conclusion about the four type letters is wrong. Each type is a distinctive, dynamic organization of mental energy, greater than the sum of four preferences. The name we use for the energy systems of the sixteen types is type dynamics.

Many, perhaps most, people who learn about the psychological types through the MBTI instrument do not learn about the theory of types as dynamic wholes, as Jung and Myers wrote about it. It is not surprising that they consider the types to be sets of four separate preferences. The confusion comes about, in part, because a self-report instrument with four separate scales is used to identify the types.

When Jung developed his theory of psychological types he foresaw it being used by professionals trained to treat psychological problems; they would learn the theory of type dynamics and apply it in their work. He did not anticipate the need to identify the types with an instrument such as the MBTI. Myers and Briggs saw the need for the ideas of type to be available to people in everyday life, not just in psychotherapy. When they decided to develop an instrument for identifying type preferences, they faced the problem of how to have people self-report their tendencies and interests in a way that would show one of the sixteen types as the best fit. In an instrument, they could not teach people Jung's complex theory and have them pick a type that seemed best to them. They decided the most sound way to proceed was to have people vote on the four preference pairs separately. They devised four scales and wrote items for each scale.

The person who has scored E, S, F, and J, for example, is shown the Myers-Briggs® description of the type Jung called extraverted feeling with sensing, the type to which Myers and Briggs gave the shorthand label ESFJ. If the person reads the type description and it seems to be a good fit, the person has selected a type, not just four preferences.

If a type is more than the four preferences, what should readers of this book know about the whole patterns of the types and the dynamics of them? Some of your clients will be ready to learn about the dynamics of the types, and if you have the knowledge and the opportunity, you can teach them how to apply this more in-depth information about type. This chapter is about the theory of the dynamics and includes some ideas you can use with your clients. The central feature of type dynamics is the belief that each type has one of the mental processes that is dominant and favored and a second mental process that is auxiliary, a helper to the dominant. How they function in the personality and work together is the main subject of what follows.

“Our troubles come from faulty perceptions and poor judgments, and our progress certainly comes from clear perceptions and sound judgments.”

Type Theory Is About Perception and Judgment

Jung's theory of psychological types is about patterns of conscious mental activity. At the most basic level, it is about perception and judgment. In Jung's view, all conscious mental activity is either perception activity—awareness, taking in data—or judgment activity—making decisions about what has come into awareness.

Perception and judgment are basic in the human condition. Our troubles come from faulty perceptions and poor judgments, and our progress certainly comes from clear perceptions and sound judgments. We may not think about it often, but the quality of any human activity—caring for a child, building a house, fighting a fire, running a business, playing tennis, preparing a meal—depends on the quality of perception and judgment that goes into them. Jung saw that the ways we go about perceiving and judging differ, and the differences come in patterns.

One of the points of confusion for people learning about type is the use of the terms *perception* and *judgment.* We who talk and write about type use the terms at three different levels of meaning. To avoid confusion, I will discuss the definitions of the three here. The first is the broad meaning given in the two previous paragraphs: the processes of awareness and data collecting, and acts of making judgments, decisions. The second and third meanings are specific meanings in the theory of types, one provided by Jung and the other devised by Myers and Briggs.

Perception, in Jung's *specific* meaning, refers to the two mental processes of Sensing (or Jung's word, sensation) and Intuition; in his view, all perceptions come by way of those two processes. His *specific* meaning for *judgment* is the exercise of the two ways of deciding: Thinking and Feeling.

The third meaning, given by Myers and Briggs, is also specific: the Judging–Perceiving dimension of type that is represented in the J–P index of the Indicator and the last letter of the four-letter type designations. Specifically, the last letter indicates which mental process shows in a person's *outer life*, the preferred judgment process (T or F) or the preferred perception process (S or N). Throughout this book I try to make clear which of the three meanings I am using in any situation. Here, discussing the dynamics of type, it is essential that meanings aren't confused.

Three Meanings of Perception and Judgment

1) Broad meanings:
   perception = awareness, taking in data
   judgment = making decisions
2) The mental processes:
   The *perception* processes = Sensing and Intuition
   The *judgment* processes = Thinking and Feeling
3) The fourth dimension of a type designation: the **Judging (J)** or **Perceiving (P)** preference, as in ENFP or ENFJ.

Also, please note that in Jung's work, none of the preferences are capitalized, and Jung called Sensing *sensation*. For ease of reading and because this work is about applying the MBTI instrument, I will use the preferences with initial capitalization and use Myers' Sensing term.

Dynamic Relationships of the Mental Processes

While Carl Jung gave much of his attention to the unconscious mind and how it influences our behavior, he developed his system of psychological types in contrast to show how we process our conscious experiences. In effect, he showed us sixteen different dynamic patterns of normal, conscious mental processing. And the dynamics of each type is governed by one mental process that steers the others: the dominant process. Following are some questions and answers to help you study the dynamic patterns of type.

Q: ***What is the dominant process?***

Jung said that *all* conscious mental activity can be sorted into four categories: the two ways of perceiving—Sensing and Intuition—and the two ways of judging—Thinking and Feeling. Everyone regularly uses all four, but not at the same time, for equal amounts of time, or equally well. From childhood, each of us has come to rely on one process more than the others. It seems more trustworthy, and so we trust it and use it more. And the more we use it, the more mature and reliable it becomes. Its use seems most natural and interesting, and it draws our attention more than the others. That one mental process becomes dominant, the center post, the core of the personality.

Q: ***Why do people need a dominant mental process?***

If one of the mental processes were not dominant, in charge of a person's conscious mental life, the person would not have a central theme to organize consciousness. In people with the Feeling process dominant, for example, conscious mental activity is organized around keeping their lives in harmony with the values they prize most highly. They personalize their experiences, including objective events, so they can deal with them with their best skills. This approach is the polar opposite of people with Thinking as the dominant process, who objectify personal events so they can use their best skills, logic, and objective analysis.

There needs to be one dominant function because mental processing cannot be organized both ways: Feeling and Thinking. The contrasts between Feeling and Sensing, or Feeling and Intuition, are not so dramatic, but the mental process that is dominant shows its distinctive kind of organization of mental activity. The dominant serves to unify people's lives.

Dominant Process

- Favorite among S, N, T, or F
- Governing force
- Unifies one's life
- Best-developed and most-used process
- "The general"

Q: How do the four kinds of dominant process differ?

Those who have Sensing perception as the center post, the dominant mental process, are above all else practical people. Their close attention to data provided by the senses makes them well attuned to immediate experiences, the literal facts at hand, the concrete realities. People who have Intuitive perception as the dominant process have their consciousness mainly focused on associations, abstractions, theories, and possibilities that do not depend directly on the senses. Above all else, they believe in insights and imagination to set life's directions.

People in whom Thinking judgment is the strongest mental process are above all else logical and have orderly, analytical minds. All experience must fit into logical mental systems, or the systems must be reworked to accommodate perceptions that don't fit. Children of this pattern may not seem logical by adult standards, but internally the drive is to test and organize all experience by logical criteria, even if the logic is still undeveloped. They naturally treat people and things (and themselves) impersonally.

Finally, people with Feeling judgment as the dominant mental process direct their lives toward human values and harmony, above all else. They weigh all experience as being harmonious or dissonant with the values and priorities of their own lives and the others they care about. They are naturally more attuned to the subjective world of emotions and values, and more alert to the human issues in any situation.

Q: *What keeps the dominant from making a person one-sided?*

If people trust and develop only one of the four mental processes, their lives tend to be essentially one-dimensional. Unfortunately, we all know such people. There are some whose perceptions are not focused or tempered by good judgment. What they perceive from moment to moment, day to day, stirs their interest, and they flit from one interest to another without adequately weighing the value of what they are doing or the logical consequences. They may be unstable like a sailboat with too much sail and not enough keel. And we know others whose judgments are locked so tightly that they remain unmoved by fresh perceptions. They are like the sailboat with a keel too heavy for its small sail, keeping a steady course but not making much progress. To avoid such one-sidedness, people must develop another of the mental processes to be a major, reliable helper to the dominant. Jung called the second process the auxiliary. It is needed to balance the dominant process, just as balance is needed between sail and keel.

Auxiliary Process

- Second favorite among S, N, T, or F
- A perception process (S or N) if the dominant is a judgment process (T or F)
- A judgment process (T or F) if the dominant is a perception process (S or N)
- Used in the outer world if the dominant is Introverted
- Used in the inner world if the dominant is Extraverted
- "The general's aide"

Q: *Can any of the other three processes be the auxiliary?*

In Jung's theory, the two kinds of perception—Sensing and Intuition—are polar opposites of each other. Similarly, Thinking judgment and Feeling judgment are polar opposites. In a person with Intuition dominant, it follows that Sensing is necessarily the least developed and least trusted (and trustworthy) of the four mental processes; it could not be the auxiliary. That is not an arbitrary feature of the theory, but rather a logical condition in human experience. In the instant that conscious attention is focused on intuitions, it cannot simultaneously be focused on sensations, and vice versa. I may shift quickly from one to the other, but not attend to both at once. Thus, I attend to my Intuitive perception and develop my Intuitive capacities at the expense of my Sensing perception. The concentration of energy in Intuition means a withholding of energy from its opposite, Sensing.

Because of the polarity concepts just described, a person with Intuition dominant cannot have Sensing as the auxiliary because Sensing, being the polar opposite of Intuition, will be the process that is least accessible in consciousness and least developed. The reverse is true for people with Sensing dominant, and the same principle applies to the other dominant-auxiliary combinations. *So the auxiliary is always formed in the dimension that the dominant is not in.* That is, a person having Sensing or Intuition as the dominant process will develop either Thinking or Feeling as the auxiliary process. Similarly, a person with Thinking or Feeling judgment as the dominant process will have Sensing or Intuitive perception as the auxiliary process.

Most important is the balance provided by this arrangement. A dominant in the perception dimension is balanced by having the auxiliary in the judgment dimension, and vice versa. Good perception is only effective when sound judgment gives it direction and purpose. And judgments are sound only when they are informed by adequate, clear perceptions. One balances the other as it completes and complements the other with a totally different kind of mental processing.

Q: *How does the auxiliary balance the dominant?*

Perception and judgment are not expected to be evenly balanced—whichever is dominant will always be in charge; but the auxiliary must be developed so that one-sidedness is avoided. Balance does not mean equal development or equal influence in the personality. Rather, the auxiliary complements and supplements the dominant. If we continue the sailboat analogy, we understand that the sail and keel need to be balanced. If the boat is for racing, sail is dominant and some stability is given up for the potential of speed and maneuverability. But there still must be adequate keel for stability. If the boat is for cruising, stability is the dominant concern, but the sail capacity still must be enough to make the trip interesting.

In the personality, a person who has a perception process (Sensing or Intuition) as dominant is most interested in being open to and taking in experiences. But this person needs a well-developed judgment process (Thinking or Feeling) as auxiliary to test the value and logical soundness of the perceptions. The person with T or F dominant needs a well-developed perception process (S or N) as auxiliary to give the judgments enough data to be sound.

Q: ***What are the main differences between the dominant and auxiliary combinations?***

When we combine dominant and auxiliary processes, eight sets are formed.

Dominant Auxiliary	**Dominant Auxiliary**
SENSING with Thinking	INTUITION with Thinking
SENSING with Feeling	INTUITION with Feeling
THINKING with Sensing	FEELING with Sensing
THINKING with Intuition	FEELING with Intuition

The meaning of the eight sets can be illustrated by the varied emphases in the left-hand column of the table above. People who prefer Sensing with Thinking focus their practical outlook on the aspects of the world that are readily subject to logical analysis—the objects, machinery, and more impersonal transactions of life. In contrast, those who prefer Sensing with Feeling attend primarily to the practical side of human needs. Still different in emphasis, the people who prefer Thinking with Sensing wish to put their system of logical order on the practical matters of the world. And those people who prefer Thinking with Intuition wish to put their system of logical order on the abstract and intangible matters of the world.

The differences suggested here are subtle but not superficial. Those who prefer Intuition with Thinking, for example, may test their Intuitive inspirations with logical analysis, and the analysis may shoot down the inspiration. However, if the inspiration is compelling enough, no amount of illogic discovered in the idea will be enough to kill it. In a showdown, Intuition will win because it is the dominant process in Intuition with Thinking people. In contrast, a person who prefers Thinking with Intuition would likely sacrifice the Intuition in such a showdown.

The Attitudes: Extraversion and Introversion

You'll recall that Sensing, Intuition, Thinking, and Feeling are called the mental functions or processes. In Jung's theory all mental processing can be sorted into these four categories. The other elements of type—Extraversion, Introversion, Judging, and Perceiving—are not mental functions but are the *attitudes* or *orientations* in which the functions are used. First we'll consider Extraversion and Introversion.

> "**Extraversion and Introversion are called the attitudes or orientations to life, referring to the *orientation* of the person's *dominant* process.**"

Q: ***How do Extraversion and Introversion affect the dominant?***

Extraversion and Introversion are called the attitudes or orientations to life, referring to the *orientation* of the person's *dominant* process. People who use their dominant process primarily to run their actions *in the world outside themselves* are extraverting the dominant and are referred to as Extraverts. To balance their extraverted dominant, they mainly introvert their auxiliary function to run their inner lives. In contrast, people who *reserve* the dominant process primarily for the *personal world* of inner thoughts and reflections are introverting the dominant and are referred to as Introverts. They mainly extravert their auxiliary function to run their outer lives.

Extraversion and Introversion provide the second way that the auxiliary provides balance to the dominant: if the dominant is Extraverted, the auxiliary brings balance by being mainly Introverted, and if the dominant is Introverted, the auxiliary brings balance by staying in touch with extraverted aspects of one's experience.

The dominant process tells the most about a person. Extraverts, by definition, reveal their best, their dominant, first. Introverts, reserving their best for their inner, their favored world, reveal mainly their auxiliary process to others. Only close associates will be allowed to see the most valued process in operation. Thus we come to know Introverts more slowly. It is through a well-developed extraverted auxiliary that Introverts function effectively in their outer world. In contrast, it is through a well-developed introverted auxiliary that Extraverts obtain reflection and depth in their inner world.

Q: *How do the eight patterns change into sixteen?*

When Extraversion and Introversion are added to the eight dominant-auxiliary combinations, represented in the table on page 134, the MBTI preferences become sixteen: eight Extraverted sets and eight Introverted sets.

Consider, for example, how the Extraversion–Introversion dimension expands the Thinking with Intuition pattern. This was illustrated at the beginning of the chapter by the case of Mark and Savannah (the ENTJ/INTP couple). The Extraverted version describes people such as Mark, who direct the energy of the dominant Thinking into the world of people and things, to manage as much of it as they can. They want to extend their personal logical systems into the world around them, their favored arena for personal expression.

In contrast, Introverted Thinking with Intuition types, such as Savannah, want to exercise their dominant Thinking process mainly in the inner realm of ideas, of private mental activity, and they strive above all else to have orderly, logical minds. They direct the energy of their auxiliary process (Intuition) mainly outward to run their outer (Extraverted) lives, and this gives them the *appearance* of having Intuition as the dominant process. When we meet an Introvert, we first see the auxiliary.

Q: *When do we see the general, and when do we see the aide?*

In *Gifts Differing*, Myers used the analogy of the general (the dominant process) and the aide (the auxiliary) to show the relationship of the process that is Introverted and the one that is Extraverted. The general who is Extraverted leaves the tent to take care of outside business directly, leaving the aide in the tent to continue working there. The general who is Introverted sends the aide to deal with the outside business while remaining in the tent working there and awaiting a report from the aide. Anyone who deals with the aide of the Introvert will benefit from knowing that the one in command is in the tent and can be only somewhat represented by the aide. Of course, our mental processes do not wear the insignia of rank, and it is not so easy for someone to know if the mental process they are meeting is the one in charge.

Simple symbols can show these ideas. Capital letters are used to represent the dominant process, and small letters are used to represent the auxiliary process. Using Myers' general–aide–tent analogy, a triangle is used to represent the tent walls, the dividing line between the inner and outer worlds that people live in. Here are two examples to illustrate the relative roles of the dominant and auxiliary in the extraverted and introverted attitudes. The first is for ESFJ and the second for ISFP. Both are Feeling-with-Sensing types but differ as to which process is extraverted and introverted.

ESFJ

Feeling judgment is dominant *and* extraverted.
Sensing perception is auxiliary *and* introverted.

ISFP

Feeling judgment is dominant *and* introverted.
Sensing perception is auxiliary *and* extraverted.

The people represented by the first symbol make their Feeling judgments public, naturally and frequently. Their antennae are out to pick up Feeling signals, and they are the practical harmonizers and weavers of compromises. The general is there to do the public business.

The people represented by the second symbol have no less wealth of Feeling, but it is reserved as a private process, revealed only to family and close friends, and it is more often seen in deeds than in words. The aide does the public business, and the aide's work is the practical usefulness of the Sensing process. Of course, the general knows what the aide is doing and will come out to do business with us if the general sees it as important enough. Loyal and devoted, ISFPs harmonize matters through a receptive, quiet helper role, in contrast to the activist and often warmly assertive stance of those who have Feeling dominant and extraverted.

Q: *Why are Extraversion and Introversion called attitudes or orientations rather than mental processes?*

Jung asserted that all conscious mental activity can be sorted into the four functions or processes: Sensing, Intuition, Thinking, and Feeling. In that view, where do Extraversion and Introversion fit? Aren't they conscious mental processes? Extraversion and Introversion are *attitudes* or *orientations*, not processes—that is, they tell the direction of a process, outward or inward. "Attitude" as used in this context is a synonym for direction: outward facing or inward facing. Each process is oriented, and mostly used, inwardly or outwardly.

Thus for people who have the INTUITION with Thinking pattern, the Intuition may be Extraverted or Introverted, and the auxiliary Thinking needs to be in the opposite attitude to provide balance. So the complete name for the Extraverted INTUITION with Thinking type is Extraverted Intuition dominant with Introverted Thinking auxiliary. If the person, however, preferred Introversion, the name would be Introverted Intuition dominant with Extraverted Thinking auxiliary.

Keeping Type Language Clear

Functions
Four basic mental processes:
Sensing, Intuition, Thinking, and Feeling

Perception
The two functions or processes for perceiving:
Sensing and Intuition

Judgment
The two functions or processes for decision making:
Thinking and Feeling

Attitudes
Two directions for the flow of energy:
Extraversion (outward) and Introversion (inward)

In subsequent paragraphs, we will see how to recognize ENTP as the shorthand for the former and INTJ as the shorthand for the latter—and all of the other type designations as well. If you want to skip to those paragraphs and learn the rule for recognizing the dominant and auxiliary in any type, please come back to this section for further review.

Q: *How do E and I provide balance?*

For each of the sixteen types, Jung's dynamics show the dominant and auxiliary in different attitudes—if one is extraverted the other is introverted. Why didn't Jung let the general and the aide (in Myers' terms) both be outside the tent? Or both be inside the tent?

The answer is not difficult to find. Jung and other professionals who use his theory of types have observed and written about people who seem to be so dominated by events outside themselves that they do not see their personal role in a situation, or they seem unable to reflect on the consequences and learn from them. In type terms, they extravert not only their dominant but their auxiliary as well. They do not have a good means for introverting the role their auxiliary should play. Conversely, there are people who introvert both dominant and auxiliary and have no good way of functioning in the world *outside themselves*. Engrossed deeply in their inner lives, they pay insufficient attention to what is going on around them and do not take effective action. In Myers' view, personal effectiveness requires that the Introvert have a well-developed auxiliary process for extraverting and the Extravert a well-developed auxiliary process for introverting. In her words, "The Extraverts' auxiliary gives them access to their own inner life and to the world of ideas; the Introverts' auxiliary gives them a means to adapt to the world of action and to deal with it effectively."

In summary, the auxiliary process provides balance to the dominant in two essential ways: (1) a dominant from the perception dimension, Sensing or Intuition, is balanced by an auxiliary from the judgment dimension, and vice versa, and (2) when the dominant is mainly extraverted, the auxiliary is mainly introverted, and vice versa.

The Dominant and Auxiliary Provide Balance

- Between perception (S or N) and judgment (T or F)
- Between attention to the outer world (E) and the inner world (I)

Judging and Perceiving Reveal the Dynamics

The *patterns* in type theory are complete when Extraversion and Introversion are added into the eight sets of dominant–auxiliary combinations. Using just the letters of the preferences and lowercase letters for the auxiliary, we can see the sixteen types. Notice that the J (Judging) and P (Perceiving) letters do not appear in these shorthand descriptors.

ST Combinations	SF Combinations	NF Combinations	NT Combinations
IS+t	IS+f	IN+f	IN+t
IT+s	IF+s	IF+n	IT+n
ES+t	ES+f	EN+f	EN+t
ET+s	EF+s	EF+n	ET+n

Q: ***How does the Judging–Perceiving dimension fit into the sixteen patterns?***

If the sixteen types can be designated this way, why are J and P needed? As explained in chapter 1, the J–P dimension refers to the preferred way of conducting one's outer life, in a planful or spontaneous way. Briggs and Myers devised this fourth dimension for two reasons: to provide a pair of descriptive categories for the planful (J) or spontaneous (P) behaviors people *show in their outer lives* and to provide *a way of identifying the dominant process* in each type. The first purpose is obvious, and the J–P descriptions are very useful. The second purpose, to be a pointer to the dominant, needs explanation.

Consider the problem of a self-report MBTI instrument that has no J–P dimension. Suppose a person scores E, S, and F on the Indicator. How can anyone know from the results whether Sensing or Feeling is dominant? One possibility is to regard the one with the higher preference score as the dominant, with the lower score being the auxiliary. In this instance, ES+f could be used as a shorthand designation to show that Sensing had the higher score, and EF+s to show Feeling having the higher score.

That solution was not acceptable to Myers and Briggs. They wanted an instrument fully consistent with Jung's theory. Following the theory, an Extravert with Sensing dominant will be Sensing dominant *no matter how high the score* for Sensing or whether the score for the auxiliary, in this instance Feeling, is *higher*. In my own case, if the ENTP type description is the best fit for me, which it is, it should not matter whether my N score was higher than my T score. If one's type were reported by designating the dominant according to the higher score between N and T, and if my T score were higher, I would be directed to the ENT profile with Thinking dominant, which is ENTJ. But when I read the ENTJ description, I know it is not describing me.

> **"The patterns in type theory are complete when Extraversion and Introversion are added into the eight sets of dominant–auxiliary combinations."**

Q: *How does the J–P preference indicate the extraverted mental process?*

Myers and Briggs found that they could identify the dominant by means of the J–P preference. Here is the basic rule: the J–P designation indicates the mental process that is *extraverted;* for Extraverts, that is the dominant; for Introverts, that is the auxiliary.

Let's see some examples. It helps to keep in mind the order of the four preferences reported by the MBTI instrument, such as ENTP; the two mental processes are in the middle—N and T—and the attitudes (orientations) are on either end—E and P.

On the MBTI assessment, my type is reported as ENTP. The four letters direct me to the type description for ENTP, which is short for Extraverted Intuition dominant with Thinking auxiliary. Just by seeing the four letters, you can tell that Intuition is the dominant—by using the J–P rule. My last letter, P, says that my *perceiving* process (the letter in position two is *extraverted,* showing in my outer life. Because Extraverts show their dominant outwardly, the P points to my *dominant.*

Position 1	Position 2 *Perception* process	Position 3 *Judgment* process	Position 4
EI	SN	TF	JP
E	N	T	P

Contrast this with the other ENT type, ENTJ. The last letter, J, says that the judgment process (the letter in position three) is *extraverted*, used in the outer life. Because Extraverts show their dominant outwardly, the J points to the *dominant*. So the dominant is Thinking, and ENTJ stands for Extraverted Thinking dominant with Intuition auxiliary.

Let's contrast these with the introverted NT types, INTP and INTJ. In INTP the P says that the *perception* preference (N), in position 2, is extraverted, used outwardly. For Introverts, we know that the process that is extraverted is the auxiliary, so Intuition is the auxiliary and Thinking is the dominant. INTP thus stands for Introverted Thinking dominant with Intuition auxiliary.

In the case of INTJ, we know the J means that the *judgment* preference is extraverted. We also know that Introverts use their auxiliary for their extraverting. So Thinking is the auxiliary, leaving Intuition as the dominant. INTJ thus stands for Introverted Intuition dominant with Thinking auxiliary.

Here is a formula to use for finding the dominant in any of the four-letter type designations:

Step 1: J–P points to the letter of the mental process that is Extraverted; J points to position 3, T or F; P points to position 2, S or N. Mark that letter with an E, as the Extraverted process.

Step 2: If the first letter is E, then the marked letter is the dominant. If the first letter is I, then the marked letter is the auxiliary.

Use the formula to identify the dominant on several types and check your results by using the following table. It is just like the table presented earlier, but with the Myers-Briggs terms added.

ST Combinations	SF Combinations	NF Combinations	NT Combinations
IS+t ISTJ	IS+f ISFJ	IN+f INFJ	IN+t INTJ
IT+s ISTP	IF+s ISFP	IF+n INFP	IT+n INTP
ES+t ESTP	ES+f ESFP	EN+f ENFP	EN+t ENTP
ET+s ESTJ	EF+s ESFJ	EF+n ENFJ	ET+n ENTJ

Another Way to Check Your Results

- For E _ _ Js, the third letter is the dominant
- For I _ _ Js, the second letter is the dominant
- For E _ _ Ps, the second letter is the dominant
- For I _ _ Ps, the third letter is the dominant

Knowing the dominant of each type, without having to stop and apply the rule, does not come quickly. I used the type concepts in my work for several years before I could quickly bring to mind the dynamics of each of the types. The knowledge of this deeper layer dramatically extended my effective uses of type, as it will for you. But it does take time. You can see in appendix A that each of the type descriptions is headed by the four-letter type designation. Note that the dominant function in each case is given in a larger font. That should help you remember more quickly the dominant for each type.

The Third and Fourth Mental Processes

Jung saw that a person's conscious mental life consists mainly of the activity of the dominant process. The auxiliary is also often in consciousness, but it plays a secondary, helping role. What about the less preferred mental processes: the third and fourth ones?

Q: ***What are the third and fourth mental processes called, and how do they work in the dynamics?***

Using again the example of my own type, ENTP, N is dominant and T is auxiliary. The mental processes that do not appear in my type letters are S and F, my third and fourth preferences. How do S and F work in the dynamics of my type? In each type, the mental processes that are not represented in the four letters are what Jung called the third, or *tertiary*, and the fourth, or *inferior*, processes. They can serve the dominant process also, but they are much less available than the auxiliary. The tertiary process is more accessible than the inferior but less than the auxiliary.

> "Jung called the opposite of the dominant process the *inferior* process because it is at the bottom of the hierarchy of the four processes for that type."

Jung called the opposite of the dominant process the *inferior* process because it is at the bottom of the hierarchy of the four processes for that type. Some others refer to it as the shadow. Jung used the term *shadow* to cover more than the inferior process, so I do not use it in relation to the type preferences. The inferior process is the least developed of the four for each person and is the most childish of the processes when it does appear in conscious life. It is the process we have the least control of and is the one that has taken over when we say "I wasn't being myself just then." *Was That Really Me? How Everyday Stress Brings Out Our Hidden Personality* by Naomi Quenk (2002) is an excellent book on the dynamics of the inferior process.

Being in one's dominant process just happens. It is automatic. A well-developed auxiliary is easily accessible. But it takes *conscious effort* to stay in one's third process, and even more effort to access and use the fourth process. We are mostly unaware of the functioning of the third and fourth processes, except when we deliberately call on them to help out. For example, when I am writing I try to lock into my Sensing while I am proofreading. Also in my writing I work to call on my Feeling process when trying to personalize my NT abstract reasoning that tends to get too heavy.

In chapter 10 you will find what we call a zigzag method for problem solving. This method shows you how to engage the four mental processes when working through a problem.

Through conscious effort, over the course of a lifetime, some people do become quite aware of the functioning of the third and fourth processes, and as this awareness increases control also increases. To the extent that they remain out of our awareness and control, they represent blind spots that may get us into trouble.

Tertiary Process

Third favorite among S, N, T, and F

The opposite of the auxiliary (as S is opposite N, and T is opposite F)

Less developed and less accessible than the auxiliary

Later in developing than the auxiliary

Inferior Process

The opposite of the dominant (as S is opposite N, and T is opposite F)

The least developed process

Our relatively childish and primitive perception or judgment processes

An escape from the conscious personality

Is in charge when "You don't act yourself"

A source of much undiscovered personal energy

Q: ***In what ways are the third and fourth processes our blind spots?***

For each type, it is important to remember which mental process is the least used and least trusted. Recall that the inferior process is always the polar opposite of the dominant process, as Sensing is the opposite of Intuition, and as Thinking is the opposite of Feeling. The third and fourth processes are your blind spots; they represent areas that are most neglected. Whenever I am working with someone to solve a problem, I try to keep in mind not only the person's dominant but also the inferior—seeing the dominant as the best avenue to good communication and the inferior as a probable roadblock. To explore for yourself the nature of the blind spots, now that you know about the dominant and inferior, I suggest you turn back to the descriptions of the sixteen types in appendix A. The material there takes on a deeper meaning when the concepts of the dominant and inferior are applied. The descriptions of the types are placed so that opposite types are across from each other. Examine, for example, the ENTJ and ISFP opposites. To understand the ENTJ's blind spots, read the ISFP description and consider it being played out in a childish, immature way. And vice versa: consider what an immature version of ENTJ might look like to get an idea of the blind spots of the ISFP type.

Although it might seem that the tertiary and inferior processes might cause most troubles in a personality, it is actually neglect of the auxiliary that causes the most serious problems. A dominant not supported by an adequate auxiliary means one-sidedness not only in the perception–judgment balance but also neglect of either the inner life or outer life. (The problems of an unsupported dominant were described earlier in the chapter.)

Q: ***How can we help the third and fourth mental processes to develop?***

In *Gifts Differing,* Isabel Myers argues for helping the inferior process to develop by letting it play but not by pressing it into service. For example, when working with a Sensing-dominant student, a teacher is not helping, and is probably harming, the student by requiring learning activities that depend mainly on Intuition for a sustained time. And with Intuition-dominant students, the surest way to bring out their worst behavior is to keep them on tasks that require them to follow uninspiring routines, step-by-step, with careful attention to details.

The inferior process can be developed in two ways, according to Myers. First, the inferior process can be developed through enjoyable and recreational activities. For example, someone with Intuition dominant may enjoy activities that are sensory in nature such as gardening or woodworking. Someone with Sensing dominant may express their Intuitive function through recreational reading. A Feeling-dominant person I know gets genuine pleasure in keeping a ledger, and another who is Thinking dominant finds recreational enjoyment in caring for animals.

Second, the inferior process can be developed by letting it serve the dominant process in some way that is important to the dominant. An illustration of this second method can be found in the work of Isabel Myers herself. She was an INFP—an Introvert with dominant Feeling—and her heart's desire was the perfecting of the Indicator. To accomplish this goal, prompted by her dominant Feeling, she mastered statistics and research design—fields that are totally grounded in the

Thinking process, and she would spend weeks doing mathematical work to discover one fact that might improve the Indicator.

Here are other examples of the inferior being developed as it serves the dominant. An excellent ESTJ elementary school teacher uses her inferior Feeling process every day to gauge the effect of her lessons on the inner-city children whom she teaches. She works hard to remain sensitive to them individually because she knows her carefully crafted instruction plans will not succeed with these at-risk students without the fine-tuning that comes by taking their emotions into account. An ISTJ department manager, who supervises more than thirty people, mostly Intuitives, deliberately starts her day using her inferior Intuition process to keep the big picture in mind, to check her map of long-term plans, and to stay in tune with her people. The staff is grateful for her dominant Sensing process that keeps everyone focused on the immediate targets and the means to reach them.

Finally, I can use myself as an example of dominant Intuition, inferior Sensing. Knowing that many of this book's readers are Sensing types, I regularly edit with my Sensing eye as I go along, asking myself, is what I am writing practical and explicit enough? Does it provide enough concrete examples, moving from specific experience toward abstract generalization? How well I have succeeded in making it readable for Sensing types is difficult for me to know, but what you are reading did get a Sensing critique as best as I could provide it (with the help also of some Sensing people who read all or parts of the manuscript).

The approach to developing one's third mental process is the same as has just been described for the inferior process. As with the inferior, it is best treated with invitations and not demands and certainly not with the same standard of quality performance as we apply to our dominant. My own third mental process is Feeling, which is dominant for my wife. As an ENFJ, her Feeling process is Extraverted, very present, very articulate—a dramatic contrast to my largely unconscious and inarticulate introverted Feeling. I'm certain my Feeling judgment and awareness of emotions have grown and matured under her influence, especially when she invites me into Feeling playfulness—but not when she puts me under pressure or moves into a mode of instructing my Feeling!

The Practical Benefits of Knowing Type Dynamics

The main benefit of studying type dynamics is a better understanding of our own tendencies—our basic mind-set and our blind spots. My dominant process tunes me in automatically to some viewpoints and life experiences and tunes out others. Knowing that, I can be more alert to the perspectives I naturally neglect and work to attend to them with more careful discipline. When we experience the most uncertainty, confusion, and distress, when we feel off-balance and out of control, we can be fairly sure that our inferior is active. Because the inferior stays almost hidden from consciousness, it is difficult to understand. But the off balance experiences can alert us to the fact that the inferior is afoot. We then can look for its effects and better see how to compensate for our blind spots.

> "Being aware of the dominant and inferior mental process is especially important when working with students or employees whose types are most different from our own."

By knowing the dominant and inferior processes of people close to us—family and friends—we may be able to notice the subtle differences in their type dynamics. Staying tuned in to them becomes easier, and cooperative problem solving works better, when we can anticipate how their dominant or inferior will react in given situations. When a family member or close friend is also a confidant who knows and can talk about type dynamics in everyday relationships, you will both find that your type skills are sharpened and that you will begin to have insights that can be useful in other parts of your lives.

Being aware of the dominant and inferior mental process is especially important when working with students or employees whose types are most different from our own. The teacher who effectively engages students' attention and interest does so by finding some common mental ground. In type theory, the common ground includes shared perceptual data and/or shared judgments. These usually are easy to anticipate in students who are like us in type, but they are hard to find in students whose types are unlike our own. Fortunately, the study of type gives us ways to understand and work with the mental patterns of different types, even when we cannot "be there" and know existentially what they are experiencing.

Now that you are aware of the dynamics of the types, you can read Myers' type descriptions more deeply. If you turn again to the sixteen type descriptions in appendix A or in publications such as Charles Martin's *Looking at Type®: The Fundamentals*

(CAPT, 1997), you'll see that the opening paragraphs are about the dominant process being used in its favored attitude—Extraverted or Introverted and the interests and skills associated with it. The text of each description then tells of the balancing, supplementary role of the auxiliary process, and the difficulties each type may experience if the auxiliary process is not well developed. And some of the descriptions include statements about the least developed process, the blind spots it represents, and ways to keep it from being disruptive.

To close this chapter, I have included a type concepts test similar to that in chapter 1. Before proceeding in this second section of the book, you may want to use this quiz to check your grasp of the main concepts of the dynamics of the types.

TEST YOUR KNOWLEDGE

TYPE CONCEPTS, Part Two

Record your multiple choice answers on a separate sheet and check your responses with the key that follows this test. Some of the items have more than one correct answer.

1. The term *dominant process* in type theory means
    - *a. either Extraversion or Introversion.*
    - *b. either a Judging or Perceiving attitude.*
    - *c. the favorite process, the one used most.*

2. The auxiliary process is
    - *a. the opposite of the dominant.*
    - *b. the least used process.*
    - *c. the second favorite.*

3. If the favorite process is a judgment one, the second favorite is
    - *a. also a judgment one.*
    - *b. a perception one.*
    - *c. any of the other processes.*

4. If the second favorite process is a judgment one, the favorite will be
   a. *a perception one.*
   b. *also a judgment one.*
   c. *any of the other processes.*

5. One's attitude to life is either
   a. *Judging or Perceiving.*
   b. *Extraversion or Introversion.*
   c. *the dominant or the auxiliary process.*

6. One's attitude or orientation toward the outer world is
   a. *either Judging or Perceiving.*
   b. *governed by the favorite process.*
   c. *governed by the second favorite process.*

7. The effects of the combinations of perception and judgment
   a. *are arbitrary and unpredictable.*
   b. *produce the different types of personalities.*
   c. *produce different sets of interests, values, needs, habits of mind, and surface traits.*

8. The last letter in the four-letter type designation indicates the mental process you use in the outer world
   a. *if you are an Extravert.*
   b. *if you are an Introvert.*
   c. *for both Extraverts and Introverts.*

9. The Introverts rely on their auxiliary process
   a. *for dealing with the outer world.*
   b. *for dealing with the inner world of ideas.*
   c. *in the same way as the Extraverts.*

10. The Introverted Judging types (with IJ in their type designation) have as their favorite process
   a. *a judgment process: either Thinking or Feeling.*
   b. *a perception process: either Intuition or Sensing.*
   c. *any of the four mental processes named in a and b.*

11. The Extraverted Judging types (with EJ in their type designation) have as their favorite process

  a. *a judgment process: either Thinking or Feeling.*

  b. *a perception process: either Sensing or Intuition.*

  c. *any of the four mental processes named in a and b.*

12. A well-developed auxiliary process is necessary

  a. *to prevent superficiality in Introverts.*

  b. *to help Extraverts put their best foot forward.*

  c. *to help both Extravert and Introvert achieve balance and to keep them from ignoring either world.*

13. In types whose favorite process is a judgment one, the perception auxiliary provides

  a. *help in making quick decisions.*

  b. *the raw material needed as a basis for judgment.*

  c. *a second line of attack when the favorite process does not work.*

14. In types whose favorite process is a perception one, the judgment auxiliary provides

  a. *a steadiness of purpose.*

  b. *a means of evaluating the worth of their perceptions and the uses to be made of them.*

  c. *help in suspending judgment when data are insufficient.*

15. The remaining processes, after taking into account the dominant and auxiliary

  a. *should be suppressed.*

  b. *are not necessary and can be ignored.*

  c. *can make contributions toward greater effectiveness.*

(Answers to the Type Concepts Test, Part Two)

1. c. The favorite process, the one used most. Sensing, Intuition, Thinking, and Feeling are mental processes, one of which will be the favorite or dominant.

   a. Extraversion and Introversion are defined as attitudes, not mental processes.

   b. A Judging or Perceiving attitude refers to how one runs one's outer life, and the dominant may or may not show itself in one's outer life.

2. c. The second favorite.

   a. The opposite of the dominant conflicts with it and therefore is the least developed of the four processes. The auxiliary, to be helpful, must serve the dominant process, not compete with it.

   b. The opposite of the dominant is the least used, least trusted process.

3. b. A perception one. Its responsibility is to supply facts and understanding as a basis for judgment.

   a. If both dominant and auxiliary were judgment processes, there would be no balance. Also, the auxiliary would be opposite the dominant.

   c. The opposite of the dominant is excluded as a candidate for the auxiliary. The opposite is the least developed process and the slowest to develop because the energy that flows to the dominant is denied to its polar opposite.

4. a. A perception one. When the second favorite process or auxiliary is a judgment process, it is because the favorite or dominant process is perception and needs a judgment assistant for balance.

   b. If both dominant and auxiliary were judgment processes, there would be no balancing perception.

   c. One of the other processes would be the inferior process, which cannot be the favorite.

5. b. Extraversion or Introversion. This is the "attitude to life" because Extraversion means "to be focused outwardly" and Introversion means "to be focused inwardly." Orientation signifies the attitude (direction) of the dominant process; in Extraverts, the attitude of the dominant is outward, and in Introverts the attitude of the dominant is inward.

   a. The J–P preference indicates whether a person shows a judgment or perception process to the outer world. Stated another way, it shows which function preference is Extraverted. And still another way, J–P show whether the person takes a Judging or Perceiving attitude toward the outer world. While E–I shows one's attitude to life, J–P shows the orientation or attitude toward one's outer life.

   c. The dominant and auxiliary are mental processes that are used in the Extraverted or Introverted attitude.

6. a. Judging or Perceiving.

   b. Only the Extravert's attitude toward the outer world is governed by the favorite process.

   c. Only the Introvert's attitude toward the outer world is governed by the second favorite process.

7. c. Produce different sets of interests, values, needs, habits of mind, and surface traits.

   a. The combinations of perception and judgment, when understood in type theory, give us a way to increase our ability to predict people's behavior.

   b. The types are produced by more than the combination of preferences of perception and judgment. Types result from the combinations of the E–I preference, the dominant and auxiliary mental processes, and the J–P preference.

8. c. For both Extraverts and Introverts.

   a. and b. It is important to keep in mind that, by definition in the theory, J–P points to the process used in the outer world by all types.

9. a. For dealing with the outer world.

   b. Introverts use their favorite or dominant process for dealing with the inner world of ideas. Consequently, the "best side" of Introverts is not seen by the casual observer, who mainly witnesses the less-developed auxiliary (second favorite) process.

   c. Extraverts, on the other hand, use their favorite process in the outer world, and the observer sees the best of them at once.

10. b. A perception process, either Sensing or Intuition. (The J in the four type letters indicates that the outer process will be Thinking or Feeling. For an Introvert, the outer process is the auxiliary, so the dominant process must be Sensing or Intuition.

   a. An Introverted type with a P in the four type letters has a perception outer process (either Sensing or Intuition). For Introverts, the outer process is auxiliary; therefore, the dominant process would have to be Thinking or Feeling.

   c. Introverts with a J in their four letters could not have judgment processes (Thinking or Feeling) as their dominant, because these functions would be used in their outer world and the Introvert's dominant is used in the inner world.

11. a. A judgment process, either Thinking or Feeling. The J–P preference points directly to the dominant for Extraverts.

   b. For Extraverts to have Sensing or Intuition as their dominant, they would have to have a P in their type formula, because J–P points directly to the dominant for Extraverts, and both S and N are perception processes.

   c. Extraverts with J in their formula could not have a perception process (Sensing or Intuition) as their dominant function.

12. c. To help both Extravert and Introvert achieve balance, and to keep them from ignoring the less preferred world.

   a. The Introverts are less subject to superficiality than are Extraverts.

   b. Extraverts have fewer problems in putting their best foot forward than do Introverts.

13. b. The raw material needed as a basis for judgment. When the favorite process is a judgment one, perceptions provide the information on which to make choices; sound decisions cannot be made without adequate information.

a. Whether decisions are made quickly or slowly depends on other factors. For example, Extraverts are more likely to act quickly or impulsively, and Introverts after thoughtful consideration.

c. Although it is true that the auxiliary provides a second line of attack when the dominant does not work, the statement would not be restricted to the types with a dominant judgment process described in this question.

14. a. and b. Steadiness of purpose, and a means of evaluating the worth of their perceptions and the uses to be made of them. Both answers are correct. Perceiving types with insufficient judgment may spend too much time simply enjoying perceptions and too little time in using the information their perceptions provide.

c. Judgment processes are more likely to speed judgment, not suspend it.

15. c. Can make contributions toward greater effectiveness. Not only must the less-developed processes be heard, but they can be a source of richness and growth.

a. If the less-developed processes are suppressed, they are very likely to express themselves in embarrassing and detrimental ways.

b. The four mental processes are needed and used every day, for effective functioning. None can be ignored.

9

Introducing Type into Curriculum Reform

IN THIS CHAPTER, we shift from the use of type in one-to-one and small group relationships to more global applications. I am writing here to those who want to use type in curriculum work, to influence curriculum policy beyond the individual classroom, and to help more people bring their constructive energies into the process of reforming education through curriculum improvement.

The big question regarding curriculum is always what should be taught. Among all the limitless information and skills available to be put in the curriculum, what should we choose? And out of those chosen things, what should be required of all students—and at what stages of their schooling? These are huge questions. And we should ask ourselves how knowledge of type can help improve the quality of curriculum decisions.

Most of the chapter will be devoted to aspects of type not yet covered. But first we will revisit some ideas from previous chapters that have a bearing on curriculum work. Previously we looked at the four dimensions of type: E–I, S–N, T–F, and J–P. We considered their value for improving instruction. Their role in improving the curriculum is no less important, it is but much less obvious.

The Extraversion and Introversion Preferences

Of all the psychological concepts that have a place in curriculum making, none is more important or more neglected than the one represented in Jung's terms *extraversion* and *introversion*. Consider them in their largest meanings. It is only through introverting that we gain depth, and it is only through extraverting that we gain breadth. In reflection, we construct the meanings of our experiences. In extraverting, we test our mental constructions outwardly and become open to new experiences stimulated by the world outside ourselves. Our world is just as wide as our encounters with it; our understanding of it is just as deep as the quality of our reflection of those encounters.

Of course we want every student to develop breadth and depth. For that truly to happen, we must be aware that young people who prefer extraversion are likely to neglect the skills of introverting unless their environment prompts them to learn and use the skills. In schools, the curriculum must specifically include them. Young Extraverts may also settle for immature development of extraverting skills unless the curriculum leads them to higher development. They may settle for breadth that is ineffective because it is shallow. The reverse, of course, is true for young Introverts: a neglect of the skills of extraverting, and settling for depth that is ineffective because of its narrowness. It takes the world into account in very narrow ways.

The goals within the curriculum would be unrealistic if they expected the Extraverts to be as reflective and as concerned with depth as the Introverts. Likewise they would be unrealistic if they expected Extraverts to develop fewer but deeper interests, in imitation of Introverts. Development of the skills of the less preferred mode provides balance, but the balance scales will never be level. For Extraverts the curriculum goals should include skills of introverting sufficient enough to avoid shallowness. For Introverts the curriculum goals should include skills of extraverting so they learn to connect effectively with the world outside themselves.

Skills of Extraverting, Skills of Introverting

What kinds of skills should curriculum planners consider to help students develop both breadth and depth? First, planners should not suppose that Extraverts should learn the skills used in introverting by imitating Introverts, nor should Introverts learn the skills associated with Extraversion by following the Extravert's path. For example, the skills of social interaction, of presenting oneself or one's ideas in public, develop slowly and incrementally in the Introvert, with plenty of time given to planning, preparation, and rehearsal. The skills will form best when the topic of the extraverting activity is one the Introvert feels fluent in, keenly interested in, and well prepared to present.

As another example, the capacity to concentrate quietly for a long time that comes easily to the Introvert is hard work for the Extravert. Because they are always scanning the outside world for stimulation, Extraverts break away from scanning into sustained reflection only with discipline that takes effort to develop. The skills of reflection are best developed when the Extravert has a topic of strong interest that requires reflection to pursue it well. Strong interest is the springboard to skill development in both cases.

> **"The prevailing curriculum structure more nearly fits the Introvert's way of learning than the Extravert's."**

Curriculum Assumptions

The curriculum structure typical of today's school and colleges, I believe, favors the Introverted way of experiencing life. It puts more emphasis on the skills of reflection than the skills of action. It is built on the assumption that young people get their connection to the world of action outside the school or college. The curriculum structure is built on book learning, on reflective, vicarious experience rather than direct, active experience. When a particular curriculum departs from this pattern, it is because the curriculum developers consciously made the effort to depart.

The prevailing curriculum structure more nearly fits the Introvert's way of learning than the Extravert's. The Extravert's natural way to learn is to plunge into new opportunities; they pause briefly to reflect on the experience and to sort out its meaning and usefulness; then they get right back into action. If the curriculum were designed to honor the Extraverted way, then it would be framed by *action*. Books would be resources for the reflection part of the cycles of learning; they would not be mainly for *initiating* the learning cycle the way textbooks are currently used.

How might the curriculum be changed to accommodate Extraversion and Introversion differences? Whatever the skill, in whatever curriculum—mathematics, composition, social studies, et cetera—the curriculum planner should aim for designing themes and units that have both action and reflection throughout the entire study sequence. I am using "action" to mean the learners physically engage the world outside themselves—the people and objects that become part of the learning experience. The curriculums that do this best are ones that carry the classroom into the community and also bring the community events and resources into the classroom. The curriculum designer checks the plans to be certain that skills associated with Introversion and Extraversion are specifically provided with activities and guidelines that can be used in the coaching and practicing of these skills.

> **"A curriculum developed without attention to all four dimensions of type will certainly disadvantage some students while favoring others."**

Everyone who develops a curriculum works from assumptions about human nature. The basic realities of type differences need to be part of their view of human nature, important enough to get conscious attention as the curriculum is developed. A curriculum developed without attention to all four dimensions of type will certainly disadvantage some students while favoring others.

The Sensing and Intuition Preferences

The ideal curriculum for Sensing types puts them in direct personal contact with the physical realities of what is being studied—contacts that make use of all their senses. The ideal curriculum for Intuitive types intrigues and inspires them to pursue the curriculum's content; it engages their Intuition to explore the meanings and possibilities that seem to lie just ahead.

The best curriculums accomplish both at the same time. Some very elaborate curriculums, such as Man: A Course of Study, and some much more focused ones, such as a manipulative lab approach to mathematics, engage Sensing and Intuitive students equally well, with the same materials. They accomplish this because the curriculum developers gave first priority to engaging students in direct inquiry. Curriculums that emphasize direct inquiry have begun to appear in schools and colleges. Several dental and medical schools in the United States are experiencing good results from programs in which classroom book-driven instruction is paralleled from the beginning with hands-on clinic or lab inquiry. When developers and teachers understand the Sensing–Intuition contrast, I believe they will create curriculums that are much more relevant to the world beyond schooling.

When I taught high school social studies, long before I knew about psychological type, I noticed that some of us in the department emphasized facts and some emphasized general concepts—all using the same textbooks. I taught the facts of American history only to illustrate the general concepts I thought were important. That seemed to me the much better way, and I felt superior to those who "just taught facts," not knowing, of course, that I was merely exercising my Intuitive bias and stereotyping their "facts are facts" approach as nothing more than an accumulation of mental clutter.

As I look back now it seems to me that this group of bright and conscientious teachers was only moderately successful because we relied too much on the textbooks to initiate and guide the studies. Sensing-type students had to settle for the "facts" provided, most of them just statements or pictures in the book, because three-dimensional, concrete, personal facts were not available in the classroom. Intuitive-type students had abstract concepts to work with, but too few new direct experiences to inspire them, to spark their idealism and interest in life's possibilities. Had the teacher's guides helped us see the importance of keeping our students' senses and intuitions fully engaged, I believe we could have been much more effective. Now, when I see teachers launch units of study with concrete, direct activities and materials that provide personal experiences for their students, I see students light up, and I see the way I would like to have taught back then.

The Thinking and Feeling Preferences

With few exceptions today's curriculums favor the side of life experienced by Thinking types. Jung's view that both Thinking and Feeling judgment are *rational* processes is not generally accepted among educators. Most of us see Thinking as rational and Feeling as irrational. We want our curriculums to be rational, to encourage sound reasoning, so we design them to fit our ideas of what is objective, analytical, and logical. The subjective approach that is central to Feeling judgment is seen as secondary, perhaps even inferior. Type theory shows us that Feeling judgment is neither secondary nor inferior to Thinking judgment. It is an equal partner providing the other face of rationality: the personal side. The practical task we face is to help students distinguish between closures made by emotional reactions and those made by Feeling judgment, a kind of reasoning that treats emotions as important data to be brought into the rational processes.

What would a curriculum look like if it gave an equal place to a subjective approach? Perhaps the evolution of human knowledge could be seen through the subjective experiences of men and women who have pushed our understanding forward. Their biographies and autobiographies would be important tools for learning, as would videotapes and films that provide subjective insights. The scientist as an inquiring person would be studied as well as the scientific understanding he or she gave us.

Still more important in the curriculum would be opportunities for direct personal inquiry, as mentioned in the previous section. Inquiry that starts with strong personal interest, that reflects what individual students care about deeply, will automatically call on Feeling judgment, the mode of Judging preferred by half of our students. So as we construct curriculums and sort out the materials available, we can seek to select materials most likely to energize students of all type preferences, including those that emphasize direct personal inquiry based on strong personal interest and values.

The Judging and Perceiving Preferences

All curriculums need to provide structure for student learning activities. What kind of structure and how much structure are choices that can be better made with a knowledge of type preferences.

As shown in chapter 2, students who prefer to run their outer lives with a judgment process, the J types, learn best when they have a clear goal in mind and a definite plan that leads to the goal. They need a curriculum structure that lets them see a learning pathway at the beginning of each inquiry or plan: where to go and how to get there.

The J types differ in how they want the learning pathway to be planned. The SJ types tend to believe that the world they are learning about is a definite reality, requiring them to have a command of facts and skills that go with each responsibility they must take on as adults. They believe that the authors and teachers who plan and guide their learning should know the facts and skills needed and should plan the learning pathway for them to get them to the goals by the most direct means. Pathways they see as indirect or open-ended seem inefficient to the SJs and make them suspect their teachers don't know everything they are supposed to know. They want a structure decided in advance by competent authorities.

The NJ types, in contrast, tend to be suspicious of a "cut and dried" learning pathway, where their Intuition feels cramped. It is the nature of Intuition to see appealing possibilities and new ways of doing things. The NJ types would prefer to have a hand in choosing their own goals and in making plans that get them there. They want to build in a fresh approach or possibility that intrigues their Intuition.

Students who run their outer lives mainly with their perception preference, the P types, learn best when they can spontaneously follow an inquiry wherever it takes them. The perceptions that come to them, however they come, will tell them they are on a learning path that will pay off; they don't need a preset plan to tell them that. A general learning plan is fine for them so long as they can remain receptive and not feel bound into a path that seems to stifle the flow of perceptions. The *process* of finding out is just as satisfying for them as is reaching the goal.

The SP types seem to need a curriculum that encourages them to explore a hands-on, sensory-rich learning environment—for example, a hands-on science or natural history museum, or lab work with tangible materials and a learning guidebook in which to record observations. A curriculum well suited to SP types rewards them for doing what they thrive on: being keen observers of the details of the sensory world and finding out how it works. This kind of observation is a natural starting point for all their years of schooling, from beginning to read and write to the most advanced studies.

The NP types seem to do well in a curriculum that is structured to allow open-ended exploration, not requiring step-by-step processes but allowing for spontaneous, inductive means of solving problems. Such a structure ignites what they thrive on: the surge of energy from insights that Intuition gives them. The curriculum can help them learn to check and evaluate their Intuitive solutions carefully and can also help them recognize that they live in a J-oriented world that values schedules, completions, and products.

Using the Type Preferences in Developing Curriculum

How can any one curriculum accommodate the different type preferences that show up in any classroom? Some teachers do well teaching to all or most of the type preferences—whether or not they know about the theory of psychological types. They provide students with the structure and experiences suggested previously. In my experience, I have noted that teachers of the early grades generally have the same basic structure for all children, but some provide a variety of activities for learning besides the printed page and paper and pencil. These teachers regularly provide for physical, whole-body activity, inside and outside the classroom. They offer clear curriculum goals and make use of students' individual natural interests as means of reaching the goals.

The middle school teachers I have observed generally follow the same pattern, except that they give students more choices in ways of doing their work. Four examples from the middle grades are reported in chapter 3: the greenhouse project, the adopted grandparent program, the inner-city housing project, and the aluminum can project.

At the high school, college, and adult education levels the successful teachers also provide action, variety, and concrete experiences. However, at these levels, students are expected to take initiative, and for students who do not, the teachers prompt them. Generally speaking, the older the students, the more responsibility they have for seeing that their own needs are met in and out of the classroom.

I recommend that curriculum makers use the successes of such teachers as clues for how to use type differences in the classroom. In addition they should seek out other teachers who successfully teach to a variety of types and learn what is needed to build strong curriculums that work for all students. Curriculum diversity can enrich today's schooling, where I am saddened to see that talented teachers who know how to accommodate student diversity are being forced by the requirement of standardized testing to dramatically narrow their teaching approaches.

Curriculum Assumptions That Need to Be Changed

There are structural assumptions that underlie the school curriculum in the United States—what some call a "hidden curriculum." In this section, we will look at some of these assumptions to show how they hinder efforts to integrate the concepts of psychological type into the curriculum.

Structural Assumptions Underlying Curriculum Development

Behind the familiar curriculum work of formal education is a set of givens that are not often examined, but they must be if we are to have curriculum reform, and if type ideas are to become an integral part of curriculum making. These structural assumptions have remained essentially the same for more than a century. Key features of that structure include the following:

- Students are separated by age and by "achievement level."
- Teachers are separated from each other.
- Curriculum is separated into subjects.
- Subjects remain separate and are sequenced into time slots.
- A predetermined schedule regulates movement from subject to subject.
- A predetermined curriculum regulates what should be studied and in what order.
- Curriculum and instruction are geared to achievement of predetermined goals, and not to students' developmental processes or sequences.
- Instruction emphasizes correct answers to predetermined problems and tasks.

- Achievement is measured by predetermined paper-and-pencil tests.
- The tests compare individual students' achievement to norms of other students in the same grade level.
- Results on standardized achievement tests are used to provide accountability, student by student, school by school, district by district, and state by state.
- Predetermined rules, procedures, and behavior norms are the teacher's responsibility to monitor and maintain.
- Almost all classroom activity is in oral or written form rather than experiential and multisensory.
- Inside the classroom, the natural, informal social structure of students is discouraged.

> "So when we want to help a school, we need to help the faculty evaluate and change some features of the structure before or at the same time that we introduce type."

You may detect some biases of mine in the description of the structural assumptions. But these features of schools are truly the norm. They are not true of *all* schools and classrooms; but when departures are made from this structure, it is because someone made an intentional decision to follow a different drummer.

The structure fails much of the time, and for many students. It fails because it works against respect for individual differences in students and teachers. The use of type theory will make only superficial improvements in schools so long as schools adhere to this structure. So when we want to help a school, we need to help the faculty evaluate and change some features of the structure before or at the same time that we introduce type.

Achievement Versus Development

This threadbare structure still stands mainly because in American culture achievement is still seen as more important than development. If development were given priority, a new structure would emerge in schools and colleges.

First, we have to be clear about the distinction between *development* and *achievement*. The focus of formal education is almost totally on achievement. Children are supposed to know their ABC's by the end of kindergarten and be ready to start reading. Their achievement of this and everything else is compared to the achievement of all the other children. A child should be able to do certain things in kindergarten or else experience negative comparisons that are likely to make him or her feel shame and humiliation. Needless to say, these are not good motivators. The reason the system tolerates such consequences is its concern for holding children, teachers, and parents accountable. The system applies this pressure because it doesn't want any children to fall through the cracks; it wants everyone to move along. How ironic. A child's development *and* achievement are set back because the system doesn't adequately attend to *developmental* differences.

The structure I described previously downplays the importance of developmental differences. Never mind that a child knew how to read before kindergarten; or that another child had almost no exposure to printed material; or that yet another child does not know how to act in a group of peers, while another child is already socially adept. Children's achievement should be measured in the context of *their own development stages* and sequences. Those who affirm this conviction naturally reject certain features of the existing curriculum structure. I argue that we should reject all the structural features I named because they are all logically unsound when development is given priority.

Development-based curriculum has had its advocates, but they have not been successful in changing the existing structure. When the testing movement gained credibility, the concern for achievement became paramount and entrenched. But there is hope for a shift in emphasis. Many Americans are disillusioned with today's school systems, and many of them point to the achievement and testing treadmill as a major culprit. When achievement is viewed in the context of development and when curriculum and teaching both promote students' development, achievement happens naturally.

This fact presented itself to me vividly as an outcome of some data I obtained several years ago from 240 adults, mostly teachers, and later confirmed with many more people. I asked this of each person: "Describe a learning experience you have had, as an adult or as a child, in school or anywhere else, that you regard as a potent learning experience—where the ingredients for learning came together in an especially effective way for you. It need not be a big event in your life—small is fine—but it should be an example of what you experienced as effective and efficient learning."

I asked them to write a paragraph describing the episode, and a few sentences explaining what they thought were the ingredients that made the learning potent. Their responses covered a range of ages and diverse situations, from the impact of a second-grade teacher who enlisted the respondent to be a reading helper, to a flying instructor who let go of all the controls and said, "You've learned what to do. Now do it; get us back on the ground in one piece."

I analyzed their statements of ingredients to look for patterns, to see what common ingredients emerged. I found fifteen common factors that appeared in a majority of the statements. I put them into a list, showed it to the respondents, and asked them to mark the items that accurately represented for them the nature of the potent learning experience they had described. Most people marked ten or more of the items, and all fifteen were clearly supported. During discussions, we added two more to the list.

Here is the list. Before you read it, you may want to pause and think back to a potent learning experience of your own, and then see how many of the items you find to fit your experience.

The potent learning environment is one in which the following happen:

- The learner is moving toward a goal he or she strongly desires.
- A dramatic emphasis is given to needs.
- There is a social context that supports the learning.
- The learner feels a sense of community.
- The learner's personality strengths are engaged.
- Self-reflection is sponsored.
- Discovery, the *aha!* experience is fostered.
- The learner's patterns of thought are respected.
- There is a clear and present desire for learning.
- Immediate and practical application is encouraged.
- Sustained success occurs.
- The learner is aware of the interest and expectations of others.
- Feedback is clear, appropriate, and quick.

- The learner can synthesize prior experience.
- The learner's capacity to deal with his or her world is enhanced.
- The learner sees desired behaviors modeled.
- The learner is respected as a person.

Looking back over those responses, I have recognized one other ingredient that encompasses them all: The learning episodes the respondents chose to report were experiences that were developmentally right for them. What made them potent was the developmental fit. Perhaps the obverse is true: Learning experiences that don't match the person's developmental situation aren't potent.

The message in the responses seems clear to me. If curriculum workers took these features as criteria for planning learning environments, the result would be curriculums that had student development in the center of the planning, with achievement seen as a natural by-product of development. What they need to guide their planning are sound theories of development. There are various good theories of development available. Type development theory is to me one of the most promising.

Type Development

Let's review some key features of type development. In the theory of type development, individuals grow and flourish as they first build strength in their dominant process. Once the dominant is secure and trustworthy, people have energy freed up to develop strength in the other processes, starting with the auxiliary process. If we act on these principles, young people should be given continuous opportunities to specialize in activities that call on and strengthen their dominant processes. The curriculum that is aimed at having students "well-rounded"—reaching standard, general competencies expected of all students—is largely oblivious of what supports type development.

A recurring theme in this book, the importance of using a personality preference strength to strengthen a weakness, is based on the crucial role of the dominant mental process in a person's development. The conventional belief that teachers should identify students' deficits and teach directly to the deficits may often violate the principle of strengthening the student's dominant process. Ideally a teacher should always ask, "How can this student's dominant be engaged to energize the learning needed to meet the curriculum objectives?" And the curriculum should be planned to give teachers ideas and resources for addressing that question.

Teachers who know how to recognize the expression of type preferences in students' behavior can tell when students are using their dominant process confidently and effectively. Those students may then be ready to take on responsibilities that put their auxiliary function in the foreground. Some young people become ready for that in the elementary school years, some not until later. Recognizing and working with students' dominant and auxiliary processes is the subject of chapter 10.

> **"Believing that the types are developmental pathways, I have tried to work diligently to convince education leaders that curriculum decisions must take type development into account."**

It is time to insert another of Carl Jung's ideas: One's type implies a developmental pathway through life. The sixteen paths differ in just the ways that the types themselves differ. When a child is allowed and encouraged to stay on the path, the development that results is strong and healthy. If circumstances, including school life, push the child off the path, development is hindered; the child's energy goes into nonintegrated skills and defenses; the process of becoming one's own person is slowed or stalled; and in adult life this person may have neuroses that absorb much energy and require even more energy to overcome.

I believe this as strongly as I believe that psychological types are a fact. Believing that the types are developmental pathways, I have tried to work diligently to convince education leaders that curriculum decisions must take type development into account.

Taking Type Development into Account in Curriculum Work

What would it look like if curriculum took type development into account? Let's take for example an ESFJ boy. With Extraverted Feeling as his dominant process, he will thrive on opportunities to be a harmonizer, to do things for people that they value, and to take leadership in social situations. If school can provide him with situations that draw on his Extraverted Feeling, he will achieve—not just in categories his type favors, but across the wide spectrum of curriculum objectives. But his *sequence* of achievements, the order and timing of what he knows and can do, will be an ESFJ sequence, and therefore, different in many respects from that of other types.

How Many Pathways?

Taking sixteen types into account is an enormous job. Would we need sixteen different pathways? Where would we start? First we have to remind ourselves that curriculums are not built around individuals. By their nature, they are designed for students in general, not for particular students. They are abstract road maps, plans designed to get educators and students to the goals the society wants met. To make the maps, curriculum makers must base their work on theories of how to get from one educational point to another. So, consciously or unconsciously, they use theories and beliefs about human nature and how to structure and sequence learning experiences to best fit their view of human nature.

In the *ideal* world, we would have all curriculum makers be enthusiastic about type theory. They would know that psychological types are realities that can't be ignored. So they would make up sixteen different structure and sequence plans, taking into account the developmental pathway of each type. And they would write evaluation plans that do not expect all types to reach certain achievement goals in the same year of school. Of course, they would take into account other good theories of development, too.

Influencing the System

Now back to the real world! Having no magic wand to use on curriculum makers, we have to work out a strategy for influencing the existing system, taking into account the realities we face. I have created a global plan with four main steps that I think will work, although it may take a number of years to coalesce.

Step one is to support all movements aimed at decentralizing the curriculum process. I am not making a case for decentralizing everything—just the curriculum process. State agencies should not be making curriculum decisions. Of course, they must be responsive to the public and carry out their mandate to set up accountable goals for school systems. But the means for reaching the goals should be decided locally, with the state agency providing assistance but not mandates. The forces for decentralization are out there, and we can align ourselves with them. State legislators will listen to intelligent arguments from citizen groups such as school advisory committees. Nearly all of us can get on our local committees.

How does this first step fit our goal of promoting uses of type? We can influence individual schools to use type, perhaps even whole school districts. But state agencies typically rely on top-down regulation, and mandates from the top about using type would surely set up resistance and work against our purposes. So long as schools are free to use whatever means they wish in reaching the state's mandated goals, we have the opportunity to influence curriculum decisions.

Step two is to get entry into the culture of individual schools. The problem of making major changes in curriculum and instruction is, as the phrase goes, like redesigning a bicycle while riding it. Schools have to keep going. They don't have many stopping points at which new designs can be put in place and tried out. Users of type have all learned about the problems of introducing type to people who aren't ready for it, or as another phrase puts it, help that isn't perceived as help isn't helpful. So we learn to be more sensitive to the culture of a school, and we try to match our entry techniques to it. Chapter 12 deals with this topic in some detail. Whether we move directly or indirectly, our ultimate objective is to have the majority of staff convinced that types are real and need to be part of reaching mandated goals.

Step three is to convince school staff that student development, and not just achievement, should drive the curriculum. The more sensitive they are to the idea of types as developmental pathways, the easier this job will be. Our best ally to accomplish this is each teacher's own experience of his or her own type pathway. They know the surge of energy and satisfaction that comes from working on tasks that call on their type strengths, and they know the depression that comes from being denied access to the path.

In type workshops in which participants are often divided into eight or sixteen type-alike groups, they are encouraged to talk about characteristics they have in common. The insights from this activity are powerful. And when the type groups report to the whole workshop, most participants say the reality of the types became strikingly clear to them. If you have an opportunity to lead such groups, ask them to also describe their type's developmental pathway. This may be obscure to those who are not familiar with type, so you can instead ask "When you were a child, what kinds of responsibilities energized you? What can teachers do to promote such roles for students?"

If student development is driving the curriculum, a new view of accountability will emerge. Students won't be expected to reach the common goals at the same time or in the same sequence. Achievement testing based on a single sequence of achievement for everyone will likely be replaced by individual student portfolios, and competency testing will be done in many ways besides paper-and-pencil tests.

In the 1930s a large-scale experiment demonstrated the feasibility of such a change in student evaluation. Called the Eight-Year Study, it involved thirty high schools and 300 colleges. College admissions staff knew the reputations of the high schools in the study, and they agreed to accept any student from those schools solely on the recommendation of the school principal. No records of courses taken or grades were needed. This gave the schools freedom to experiment with their programs. Many of the schools continued to use fairly conventional courses and evaluation procedures. Others experimented in many ways, including the use of student portfolios instead of grades and standardized achievement tests. Data on all the students from the "experimental" schools were gathered during their four years at the participating colleges. Their academic results were as good as or better than their college classmates who had entered college through conventional college-prep curriculums. The leadership abilities of the students in the study were distinctly superior. When a subgroup of students from just the high schools that had the most experimental programs was considered separately, those students outperformed their college classmates in all categories. Unfortunately, the entry of the United States into World War II brought an end to this cooperative experiment, which was not revived after the war. Perhaps the time is right for another eight-year study.

Step four is to help the school staff put type theory into the curriculum process. Let me make an aside here: As most of us using type have found, the term *type theory* puts off many people. They take it to mean that type is just a theory, not a fact.

Jung, Briggs, and Myers had absolutely no doubts about the existence of psychological types. Nor do I. Types are a fact. They used the term *type theory* to mean a way of explaining the nature of types. They did not use the term *theory* to mean "speculation," as we might use it in saying "I have a theory about the conspiracy to kill John Kennedy." You can bypass the problem by substituting *type concepts* for *type theory*.

"To communicate to others the significance of Jung's view, I believe we should begin to talk about the types as sixteen kinds of mind, as sixteen different ways of processing human experience."

Kinds of Mind

For curriculum decision makers to be convinced that type concepts should be used in the curriculum process, they must first believe that type describes fundamentally different kinds of mind. To convince people of that, I believe we should begin to talk about the types with a little different language.

We have inherited a centuries-old view of what mind is. The assumption is that all humans, except perhaps those regarded as mentally defective, have the same basic mental equipment; we just differ in the amounts we possess of different traits—traits such as self-confidence, IQ, motor skills, social awareness, et cetera. Some people even put type preferences such as Extraversion and Intuition on the list. This could be called a unitary view of mind. Everyone has the same hardwiring, but we differ in our software.

What Jung has given us is a different view of mind. The concept of psychological types suggests that even our hardwiring is different, probably in sixteen different ways. To communicate to others the significance of Jung's view, I believe we should begin to talk about the types as sixteen kinds of mind, as sixteen different ways of processing human experience. Types should not be viewed as sixteen minor variations on a unitary model of mind, along with other variations, but as sixteen distinct ways of being in the world, sixteen ways of deciding what is important to know and to do.

Some have used the term *cognitive styles* in referring to the types, but this too suggests surface variations, not fundamental differences. Type differences *are* fundamental, and I believe they can be constructively proposed as sixteen forms of cognition. The practical effect of this proposition is to help us explore and better define sixteen developmental pathways. In situations where sixteen is too many to handle, the types can be sorted into groups. The groupings will differ depending on the learning situation. The function combinations—ST, SF, NF, and NT—often work well as a stand-in when considering patterns of mental processing. Even better, but bringing the number to eight, is grouping by cousin types. Cousin types are the two types that have the same dominant process in the same attitude, but a different auxiliary process. Cousin types can be easily seen in the *Descriptions of the Sixteen Types* in appendix A. On each page of the descriptions the cousins are above and below each other, for example, the two extraverted dominant Thinkers, EN**T**J and ES**T**J.

Engaging All the Types Through Their Strengths

Type development and other good theories of development need to be given priority in schools and colleges. When that is done, curriculum decisions will be driven by the progress of individuals, in their own developmental pathways and their own time frames. Curriculums are, of course, for groups and not individuals; but the curriculum can give the teacher recipes for learning activities in which all students participate successfully, irrespective of their own achievement levels.

When faculties are free to make the decisions, we can help them use type to design programs with activities geared to all the types. We want to see learning activities engaging all types more and more until they fill the curriculum. These activities should span the whole range of *responsibilities* that motivate the types: responsibilities in investigating, producing, troubleshooting, caretaking; responsibilities in creating, organizing, harmonizing, analyzing, managing, and more. As you read the descriptions of the sixteen types, you will see that the kinds of activity in these lists are associated with particular types. Some types, especially ESFJ and ENFJ, instinctively take on harmonizing responsibilities; others, particularly ISTJ and ISFJ, take on caretaking; and so on.

I would like to close the chapter with a story that suggests the kind of small steps it will take to achieve the goal of curriculum change. I had the opportunity to introduce type concepts at a special school for students ages 9 to 14 who had been designated learning disabled or emotionally handicapped. After I had given a type explanation and MBTI® results to the whole faculty, I met with small groups of teachers to help them learn to apply type to their work. These sophisticated teachers worked diligently to find good instruction techniques. As the teachers discussed the difficulties of teaching their students, I surmised that the developmental needs of these students were not being met in ways described earlier in this chapter.

I asked the first group of teachers to choose three or four students they all knew who were the most enigmatic and frustrating, and then one at a time we guessed their types, based on clues in their behavior. One student they guessed to have preferences for I, N, T, and P. His teachers said that he did not take his work seriously, was withdrawn, and could seldom be pulled into classroom activities. The teachers asked me what might help his situation. Based on my knowledge of an INTP's dominant introverted Thinking preference, I told them that many INTP boys I knew loved computers. Had they tried to reach him through the computer? Well, they said, he has one at home, apparently knows a lot about them, but here at school he never earns enough points to go to the computer lab. I suggested they try to start his engines by getting him assigned as assistant to the computer lab director. Their lack of response told me I hadn't sold them on the idea or hadn't made the point clear to them. Traditional structure one, Gordon zero.

So we discussed another child, a boy they guessed to be an E, N, T, and J. The teachers said his classroom behavior alternated between bullying and sulking, and he did not do his assignments. I asked them to read a brief description of the ENTJ type. Then I explained that Extraverted Thinking types want, above all else, to put logical order into their environments. I highlighted the statement that said ENTJs thrive on being in charge. When I asked what opportunities this ENTJ student had to be in charge of anything, his teacher said, "None. He can't even manage his own behavior, so how could he be made responsible for anything else?" I suggested she find something she could put him in charge of, and let me know the result—but I was not expecting any immediate action.

At the close of the day that teacher found me and excitedly told me, "You are not going to believe what happened with Duane! On the way back to my room this morning, I thought of something for him to be in charge of. We have a classroom library that students check out books from, and I don't do a very good job of managing it. I asked Duane if he would manage it, and he almost instantly became a different child. No bullying, no pouting, just cooperation and doing his work. And he figured out a good system for running the library."

Of course this small change was just an opening into the complex task of helping Duane get onto his path. But I believe the results convinced this teacher that understanding type was a worthwhile investment of her time and energy and also that some instructional problems are really *developmental* problems. Here was an example of the key principle of type development theory: to get a responsible behavior from someone acting irresponsibly, to entice their dominant into something constructive. Look again at the type descriptions. They clearly suggest responsibilities each type will *want* to undertake—will *need* to undertake to find psychological nourishment.

> **"The key principle of type development theory: to get a responsible behavior from someone acting irresponsibly, to entice their dominant into something constructive."**

The changes I have proposed in this chapter are big ones, but they are possible. Many small steps like the one taken by Duane's teacher can accumulate into big change. People who care about and use type concepts have seen major changes happen in their personal lives because of their understanding of type. Those personal events give them the conviction and energy to promote the uses of type in the world beyond themselves. People who care about type can begin to improve the curriculum structure; can affect curriculum policy, locally and statewide; can promote the priority of development over achievement; can help people see that the types are sixteen kinds of mind; can make concrete the idea of the developmental pathway; can demonstrate the leverage of the dominant process in influencing young people's lives; and in all these ways can help schools and colleges move toward genuine reform.

10

Developmental Needs & Type Concepts

PROMOTING ACHIEVEMENT of skills and knowledge is the first goal of our schools and colleges. Helping students develop as integrated persons is another goal. The realities of schooling are such that achievement gets virtually all the attention and development gets almost none. One reason for the imbalance is that teachers have many practical models to follow for promoting achievement, but very few models for helping students with development needs. Type concepts, unknown to many educators, are a practical resource that teachers can use to help individual students in their development.

This chapter is about helping students *individually* by looking at development through the lens of type. Understandably, teachers have little time for working with students singly, but when they can find time, their attention is usually on achievement matters, not development. When a student's achievement seems to be blocked, and usual academic assistance doesn't help, the student may be developmentally stuck. Type concepts often can shed light on the development problem. Teachers and others in helping roles who know type well usually find that thinking through the type dynamics of the student is an effective way to use their limited time.

Strengths and weaknesses in peoples' development, according to type concepts, come in patterns. By analyzing students in terms of type, you can get insights into their strengths and weaknesses and discern clues for determining how best to help them develop.

Observing and Analyzing Development Problems

Type preferences appear in some people when they are very young. And in those early years evidence of developmental problems can also be seen in their behavior. Knowledge of type preferences can help us understand what a behavior means. Also, type can often point to ways to facilitate development.

> "By analyzing students in terms of type, you can get insights into their strengths and weaknesses and discern clues for determining how best to help them develop."

Observing Type in Young Students

Let me illustrate by sharing an experience from a kindergarten class. A few days before Thanksgiving, the teacher set in front of each child a box of crayons and a piece of paper with a fanciful outline of a turkey on it. The turkey had big loopy feathers, and in each feather was a color name. The assignment was to color the turkey using the right color for each feather. The teacher said, "If you don't know your color words yet, it's OK. See up here? We have these color charts on the wall with their names on them. Look at one of the feathers and see the word in it. That same word will be on one of the charts and on one of your crayons. You can find the right crayon by looking on the side of the crayon. You see the word there? Look at different crayons until you find the one with the same word on it as the feather. The shape of the word will be the same. Then color that feather. Remember to color carefully and stay inside the lines. Then do the same thing for the next feather. And so on, until you finish."

In the next few minutes I watched several children, three in particular. The first was a boy. He didn't know the color names, so he began to compare the words on the crayons to the "Blue" he saw in the lower left feather on his sheet. When he found the matching crayon, he started to color the feather briskly. Before he finished the feather, his eye fell on another "Blue" three feathers away. He then spotted another. He stopped coloring the first feather, scanned the whole sheet, and put a blue mark on each feather that needed that crayon. After finishing the first feather, he quickly went to the second, and the next, each done a little faster and less neatly.

By the time he had finished all the blues and started on the orange feathers, the girl next to him was just finishing her first feather. She had laid down just as much crayon on the paper, just as many strokes, but all inside one feather. She was clearly getting a lot of sensual satisfaction from the smooth, careful strokes and the dense, neat layer of wax she had created.

I turned then to a third child, a girl, who had not yet touched crayon to paper. She sat with the blue crayon poised over a blue feather, looking distressed. I got down on her level and said, "Got a problem?" She nodded. "What's the problem?" "They're not the same," she said, pointing first to the feather, then to the crayon. "What's not the same?" "They're not the same." I looked more carefully at her pointing. She touched the front of each word, and I saw what she meant. On the feather was written "Blue," but the crayon and wall chart both were printed with the word "blue." "Ah, I see the problem. They are the same word; only sometimes the very first part of the word is shaped differently. If the rest of the word shape matches, go ahead and use that crayon." "OK?" "OK."

Moving around the room, I noticed that the boy who had all but finished his bird was getting real enjoyment out of his speed and his system, and neatness didn't interest him at all. The first girl was on her fourth feather, the first three looking like enamelware.

Then I returned to the second girl. Just one feather was colored. She had the red crayon poised over the right feather but had not touched crayon to paper. "Same problem?" I said. "Same problem." "OK. *Each* time the problem comes up, it is all right to use the crayon if the rest of the word matches."

The boy, with his eye drawn to the repetitive pattern of color names in the turkey and his desire to move through the task quickly, was showing an Intuitive way of handling this assignment. The sensory aspects of it did not much interest him. He may need some help to appreciate the Sensing experience of using crayon, but there was nothing in his behavior to suggest a development problem. If the teacher wants him to learn neatness, a different strategy is needed.

The first girl, surely showing a Sensing preference, was also doing what came naturally, with no development problem evident. The second girl, however, stuck on the shape of the words, was showing another aspect of the Sensing preference. Her concern over the exact physical appearance of the words is evidence of the Sensing preference for being grounded in physical realities. Her problem seemed to be a distrust of her Intuition. Her Intuition showed her the pattern similarities of the "Blue" and the "blue." But even after my explanation, she didn't trust her Intuition enough to make the small leap from the Blue–blue solution to using my instructions for all cases. Perhaps she was inordinately afraid of making mistakes and needed the teacher to show the importance of taking mental risks or to assure her that asking for help is a good thing.

In itself, this small incident doesn't give much evidence of a development problem. But it raises a red flag. If a child continues not to ask for help from the teacher when confused (and this child did not ask), and if the teacher does not see the situation as potentially serious, the problem may be exacerbated. The teacher who knows type can add this bit of data to his or her picture of the child and consider ways to help her and others in the class who may have a similar need.

Analyzing an Adolescent's Development Problems

Let's turn to an adolescent. Consider Lisa, for example, who was described in the introduction of this book. Reread the two paragraphs about Lisa. Now that you know something about type concepts, can you form a hypothesis about Lisa's type preferences? Extraversion seems obvious (talkative, gregarious). The friendliness and the desire to be helpful and popular strongly suggest a Feeling process at work. The other preferences are harder to detect in this brief description.

Here is a speculation. The easy rapport with others suggests a Sensing–Feeling combination. A preference for S and F is further suggested by her choosing to avoid complexities and her difficulty in getting an objective view of herself. Because she wants very much to be helpful and be accepted, but then misses the mark and annoys her friends, she may be a Judging type—so intent on ends that she neglects the means. Since her own motives seem to her to be so pure, the hurt and resentment she experiences from criticism further support the Feeling–Judging choice. So we can hypothesize Lisa's type to be ESFJ.

The first step in using type theory to help Lisa is to analyze her behavior, looking for clues to type preferences. Analysis of this kind draws on an understanding of the dynamics of a specific type—in this case ESFJ—and is a skill that people new to type should not expect of themselves. I present the process in this chapter because I want the book to be a useful resource for future reference as well as an introduction to type. I believe you'll find many ideas here you can put to use now regardless of your degree of familiarity with type. But however well we understand type concepts, it pays to always treat a guess about someone's type as a hypothesis to be tested and revised as needed.

Looking at Opposites

If Lisa is indeed an ESFJ, how does that identification help us think about her personal development needs? There are two fairly easy techniques for starting the process. First consider the type that is opposite hers: an INTP. In general, INTP's strengths are an ESFJ's blind spots, and vice versa. What an INTP does well naturally, an ESFJ probably does least well (see table 10.1), which contains the descriptions of the two types. As you read them see if you think Lisa's blind spots seem to be INTP strengths. When you examine the profile of the opposite type, you can better see the pattern and range of the strengths and weaknesses of the person you are trying to help, and you can begin to see avenues for helping their development.

The Zigzag Analysis

The second technique for analyzing strengths and weaknesses is to look at the person's "zigzag" process. *Zigzag* refers to a way of using the four mental processes—S, N, T, and F—in solving a problem. When the two kinds of perception are placed at the poles of one line, and the two kinds of judgment are placed on a second line, with arrows connecting all four, the problem-solving sequence looks like a "Z" or zigzag.

Isabel Myers believed that good problem solving could be viewed as a sequential use of the four processes—from S to N to T to F (see figure 10.1). When faced

Table 10.1

ESFJ	INTP
Practical HARMONIZERS and workers-with-people; sociable, orderly, opinioned; conscientious, realistic, and well tuned to the here and now. Having extraverted FEELING as their strongest mental process, they are at their best when responsible for winning peoples' cooperation through personal caring and practical help. They value:	Inquisitive ANALYZERS; reflective, independent, curious; more interested in organizing ideas than situations or people. Having introverted THINKING as their strongest mental process, they are at their best when following their intellectual curiosity, analyzing complexities to find the logical principles underlying them. They value:
• An active, sociable life, with many relationships • A concrete, present-day view of life • Making daily routines into gracious living • Staying closely tuned to people they care about so as to avoid interpersonal troubles • Talking through problems cooperatively, caringly • Approaching problems through rules, authority, standard procedures • Caring, compassion, and tactfulness • Helping organizations serve their members well • Responsiveness to others, and to traditions • Being prepared, reliable in tangible, daily work • Loyalty and faithfulness • Practical skillfulness grounded in experience • Structured learning in a humane setting • Appreciation	• A reserved outer life; an inner life of logical inquiry • Pursuing interests in depth, with total concentration • Work and play that are intriguing, not routine • Being freed of emotional issues while working • Working on problems that respond to detached intuitive analysis and theorizing • Approaching problems by reframing the obvious • Complex intellectual mysteries • Being absorbed in abstract mental work • Freedom from organizational constraints • Independence and nonconformance • Intellectual quickness, ingenuity, invention • Competence in the world of ideas • Inventing and theorizing • Spontaneous learning by following curiosity and inspirations

Figure 10.1

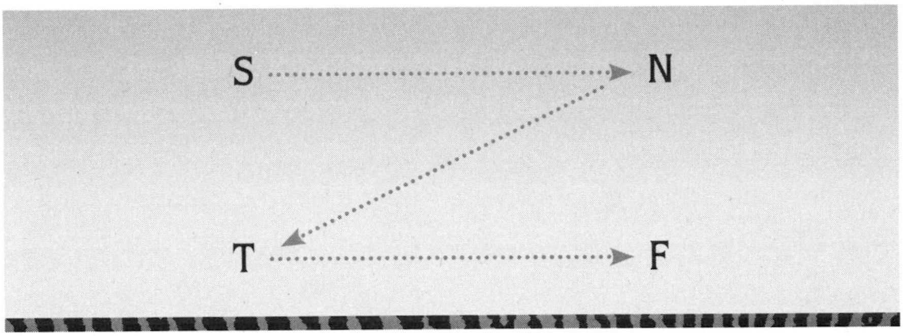

with a problem, we start constructively with Sensing to identify the facts, the given realities of the situation. The raw data by themselves do not settle the problem. The meaning of the data, their relationships to prior experience, are given by Intuition—so the arrow goes from S to N. Intuition also asks What are new ways to look at the problem and new possibilities in these data for finding a solution?

The arrow moves from N to T when we engage Thinking judgment to analyze and decide the logical consequences of acting upon each of the possibilities. And finally the possibilities are also weighed by Feeling judgment to assess how we care about the effects of each option. Using the Feeling preference, we test the human consequences, the harmony with basic personal values, or the values of others we care about and trust.

A mature settling of the problem involves the four processes in a balanced way. But, of course, each type plays favorites with the four processes, and balance is difficult to achieve.

In Lisa's situation, if she is an ESFJ, the imbalance favors Feeling, her dominant process, and Sensing, her auxiliary process (Remember, an EJ's favorite process is one of the two kinds of judgment—F in Lisa's case—and an Extravert uses the favorite process in the outside world.) So an ESFJ gives most attention to Feeling, second most attention to Sensing, and less to the other two processes. With these preferences added to the diagram, Lisa's zigzag would be as shown in figure 10.2.

Let's test the ESFJ hypothesis with the zigzag analysis. A person with F dominant, developmentally stuck as Lisa seems to be, would have the unbalancing power of her F pulling her mental processes too quickly through S and N, zipping past T, and coming to rest in a comfortable Feeling judgment; but the judgment, unfortunately, is based on too few raw data (S), and consideration of too few possibilities (N) that have been inadequately analyzed (T). That seems to be happening in Lisa's situation; she is regarded as flighty, and her work is described as trite and shallow. A mature ESFJ, on the other hand, has learned to use all four processes appropriately, even though the F will always exert the most influence in the zigzag.

Figure 10.2

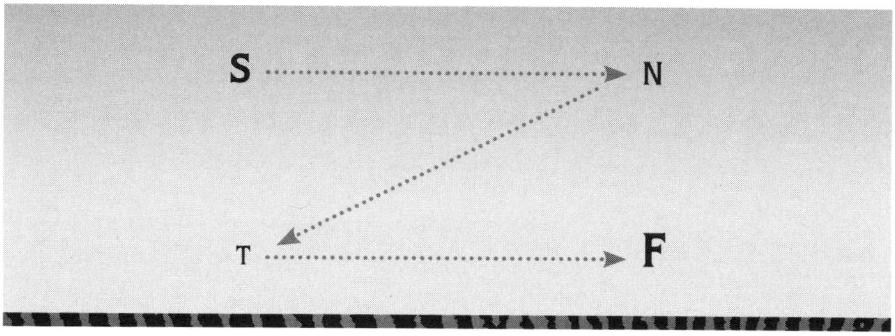

Using a Strength to Strengthen a Weakness

Let's consider a helping plan for Lisa. Lisa needs especially to give more time to her auxiliary Sensing, to gather better data, and then to develop her Intuition and Thinking. What can be done to help her? The first principle in a helping strategy is to use a strength to strengthen a weakness. The message or action of a teacher that will have the most influence with Lisa is one that will appeal to her Feeling process, her strongest process. Her EF combination means she has a very strong need to be accepted, to maintain harmonious relations with her friends. The need impels her to be very good at friendly talk and maintaining easy rapport. How can she use this strength to strengthen her weaknesses? Here are a few ideas:

1. Next time she is rebuffed by a friend, the teacher can ask her "What was your friend feeling when she criticized you? What happened just before? What were you feeling just before?"

   The objective is for her to tune more precisely into clues about her friends' feelings, to sharpen her Sensing perception and to stay longer in the Perceiving mode. The place to show her the value of improved perception is in an area of great importance to her: her status with her friends.

2. She is likely to do much better schoolwork when teamed with a classmate friend whose perception is better developed than her own, perhaps an ESP, a dominant S type. The guidelines for two-person teams in chapter 3 will be helpful in setting up such teams. Schoolwork that permits extraverting seems more likely to help Lisa develop her Sensing more fully; she probably needs dialogue to help her see what she is missing. And if the assignments she is given require objective judgment (T) and reflection (I), the teamwork dialogue should also stimulate her to do both Thinking and reflecting better than she would when working silently by herself.
3. Some exercises for listening skills—such as perception checking and paraphrasing—would appeal to her ESF nature and would strengthen her S.
4. She needs and will respond to honest praise much better than to criticism. She probably will receive and give attention to positive suggestions when they follow praise but not when they are couched in criticism.
5. Lisa probably would respond to values clarification activities that ask her to recognize values implicit in her behavior, prompt her to make value choices, and have her affirm her values to her schoolmates. To match Lisa's SJ preferences, the teacher should select valuing activities that are fairly concrete and not too vague and open-ended.
6. The teacher could assign tasks to Lisa that progressively require and reward greater amounts of commitment and risk taking. The natural step beyond value clarification is commitment and action on the priority values that have become clear.

Type Development Analysis

The process used for analyzing Lisa's situation can be applied to anyone. To begin using the zigzag, review the type descriptions in Appendix A, especially noting the dominant preferences. Each type's dominant and auxiliary suggest the bias you can expect to find in that type's use of the zigzag process.

Let's examine what type theory tells us about the natural bias in problem solving by considering three examples: ENFP, ISFJ, and ENTJ (figure 10.3).

Figure 10.3

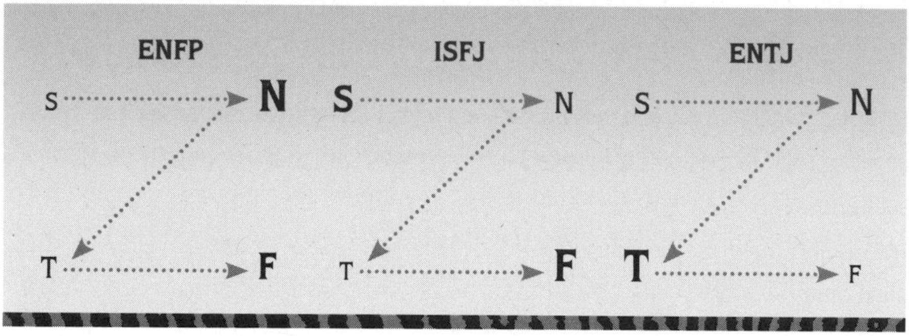

ENFP Natural Bias: Brainstorming and exploring possibilities are what ENFP sees as problem solving. The dominant extraverted N works like a radar screen, picking up all sorts of possibilities without regard to their relative merit. In the zigzag the tiny S is likely to be consulted just enough to show an ENFP something about the present situation that might need changing. Insights provided by N may be built on very few facts except that of personal excitement found in creating something new. The third process, T, is not seriously consulted, except perhaps to consider the language needed to persuade Thinking types who may otherwise be roadblocks. The auxiliary F is a cheerleader, picking the favorites among possibilities and strengthening commitment to them. The natural bias of ENFP is to let the possibilities and dreams of Intuition govern, with a little check-in from Feeling. The less preferred Thinking and Sensing may be overlooked or used solely to "sell" what Intuition wants, not to check it out.

An effective zigzag process for an ENFP begins when the auxiliary F reminds the dominant N about what's at stake: What do you care about deeply in this situation? Sort out the important values in your dream from the trivial likes and dislikes. Now stop long enough to find out all the relevant facts (S) and the logical flaws (T) that will wreck your dream (N) if you neglect them.

ISFJ Natural Bias: An ISFJ sees problem solving as adjusting day-to-day events to make life and work more satisfying—for oneself and others. The dominant introverted S carefully collects all the facts. In the zigzag the facts of the situation provided by the dominant S may loom so large and seem so solid that N shows few or no possibilities for constructive change in the status quo. Thinking may not be seriously consulted, except to consider the gloomy logical consequences of acting on N's "ill-founded" possibilities. Feeling closes the zigzag with the value judgment that things will be worse than they are now if one tinkers too much.

An effective zigzag process for an ISFJ begins when the auxiliary F recognizes a threat to basic values and prompts S into a partnership to sort out the meaningful facts and to consider unpleasant facts lest they disrupt the situation. As Sensing and Feeling begin to work together to establish the need to fix something, T is called on to look at unpleasant consequences if the problem is not solved, and N is asked to suggest new possibilities for Sensing and Feeling to take into account. The zigzag can then work effectively, and S can see the facts that will help make the change.

ENTJ Natural Bias: The natural, central features of problem solving for an ENTJ are to see problems and make decisions. The dominant Extraverted T drives toward the need to have things decided, organized, and settled in logical systems. Problems appear to the ENTJ as confusions that need logical analysis (T) to clear them up. ENTJ Thinking applies a cause-and-effect formula to the situation. As the zigzag suggests, ENTJ may attend to S and N only long enough to see a possible solution that stands the test of logic, and then is ready to act on it. Feeling is not likely to be consulted for human consequences or value implications. The desire for closure tends to block consideration of other appropriate facts and options for the fast-moving ENTJ.

An effective zigzag process for an ENTJ begins when the auxiliary N recognizes the complexities of a situation, highlights possibilities that can't be ignored, and thus slows down the decision process to allow S and N to provide more data. Intuition also provides hunches about how the decision might affect people and values that ENTJ wants to protect and support. Thinking closes the problem solving with the conviction that a logical conclusion has been reached.

Effective Use of the Zigzag for Any Type

Each type has its own type bias and its own effective way of using the sequence of mental processing suggested in the zigzag. The rule of thumb for finding the effective path for each type is to expect the auxiliary process to play a pivotal part.

The dominant process must lead the problem solving, but the auxiliary determines whether the problem solving has a balance of perception and judgment. The types with a dominant perception process (the IJ and EP types) need the judgment of their auxiliary to provide balance. The types with a dominant judgment process (the IP and EJ types) need the perception auxiliary to keep the dominant from closing the inquiry too soon, and to supply the facts and possibilities for a more considered judgment.

The Role of E–I in Problem Solving. Extraversion and Introversion also affect problem solving. Introversion puts emphasis on having the concepts and ideas clearly understood. Extraversion puts emphasis on finding out the influence of the environment on the problem, and on making sure there is an action plan after the decision has been reached.

The Role of J–P in Problem Solving. The Judging attitude provides energy toward closing options and making the decision. The Perceiving attitude provides energy toward gathering more information and finding new possibilities. If J moves without enough P, the decision may come too quickly, without adequate consideration of the necessary information. If P collects information and options past the time when these are useful in the situation, the decision may be delayed to the point that it is no longer timely.

Case Studies in Type Development Analysis

Following are four case studies—adapted from descriptions and analyses prepared by Anna Nuernberger—that you can use, if you wish, to test your ability to recognize type and to prescribe actions to help the students' development. If you want to try your hand at this process, read each of the descriptions (the text in the boxes), form a hypothesis as to what type formula best fits the student, and circle the appropriate letters. Then on a separate sheet, write a brief analysis of the kind that was done for Lisa, and identify several activities or teaching techniques you would recommend for helping the student. You can compare your analysis and recommendations with those that follow each box.

Jan: A Conscientious Student Who Gets Off Target

E or I   S or N   T or F   J or P

Jan is conscientious and hard working, seems to take her work very seriously, but sometimes accomplishes surprisingly little. At times her work is totally off target. She often is silent and seems remote and doesn't even try to make others understand what she's doing, or why. Most people have given up trying to understand her and leave her alone.

Jan's remoteness suggests Introversion and Thinking. Her conscientiousness and focus on work suggest Sensing and Judging. Her judgment seems poorly developed: she plods along without analyzing her work (Thinking judgment) or putting it in perspective (Intuition); and she does not tune in to other people's values, and may be unclear about her own priorities (Feeling judgment). Based on this limited data, we can hypothesize Jan to be an ISTJ who especially needs help in making better judgments.

Planning to help Jan: With the hypothesis that Jan's type is ISTJ, here are some suggestions the teacher could try.

1. If she is an S, she will be impressed only by specific, detailed suggestions. Advice not carefully worked out will seem like meddlesome interference to this independent type.
2. Her perseverance can lend stability to her work group. If she can see that the group may need her to help them keep on track, she may be more motivated to become an active group member.
3. Whenever possible, put her in charge of important routines and arrange for her to work out the policies with others. If she is an SJ, this responsibility will help her use her natural inclinations to strengthen weak areas. Within the division of labor, help her obtain jobs that are clearly defined.
4. Peers should be encouraged to explain their motives as logically as possible to her, and expect that she do the same.

5. Jan should be encouraged by small victories. Any small progress she makes in the developmental tasks described above should be given prompt recognition.

Dean: The Class Clown Who Doesn't Pay Attention

E or I S or N T or F J or P

Dean loves to entertain and can and does keep the group amused and distracted. Consequently, his own basic skills are poorly developed because he's usually on stage instead of at work. He seems to take nothing seriously, including himself. With no apparent effort he can read people and situations and instantly find fun in them.

Fun-loving, easy-going, and adaptable describes this Sensing, Feeling, Perceiving Extravert. Dean is probably an Extraverted Sensing type—ESFP—a type that often finds trouble with the academic system. Of all the types, ESFPs are most attuned to the present moment. Dean probably does his off-task socializing because academic work seems too remote and abstract to him, and it fails to hold his attention.

Planning to help Dean: With the hypothesis that Dean is an ESFP, here are some suggestions for working with him.

1. He may be cutting up to avoid having to read. If reading is troubling him, check him out on phonics. Because of this type's literal approach to reading printed symbols, Dean may need extra help in learning about the symbol-meaning connections. Getting to feel comfortable and competent in reading, especially in reading aloud, may be a turnaround for him.
2. ESFPs learn best by doing. The more sensory input they have, the greater chance they will learn. Whenever possible, lessons should be multisensory. If he is an ESFP, he may especially like a variety of media. Demonstrations, dramatizations, and pictures will mean far more to him than words or writing.
3. He is not likely to listen to a lot of talk. When giving him assignments, keep instructions simple and to the point. Don't expect him to read between the lines or come to conclusions without help.

4. Whenever possible, give him the responsibility of acting as arbitrator for conflicting factions. In that role he can direct his knack for easy rapport with people into the serious business of resolving problems, and improve his judgment skills in the process.

5. Planning and follow-through may be weak spots; Dean may work best with team members (probably EJ students) who will show him those skills in action.

6. Work that can be put into the form of play—be made playful—will appeal to him, and if he is given the responsibility for supervising the play plan, he will be able to work on his judgment skills.

7. "I hear, and I forget; I see, and I remember; I do, and I learn" is a truism for ESFPs. Dean will do best with activities that engage him and are satisfying to him in the present moment as opposed to skills "needed in the future."

John: The Tactless Bulldozer

E or I S or N T or F J or P

John is hasty in voicing conclusions, and he hurries on to new tasks before old ones are completed. Action for the sake of action seems to be his approach to everything. Although he often shows a lack of concern for the rights of others, he seems sincerely sorry when reproached about his transgressions. However, he seems to make the same blunders over and over, and his teacher wonders if there is any hope for him.

Because he is described as active and quick to voice conclusions, he is probably an Extravert. His rush to reach conclusions shows that he is probably a Judging type, but Js are more likely to finish what they begin. If his haste is due to an intolerance of ambiguity, he may be a Sensing type, but if his hurry to new activities is due to having more ideas and inspirations than he can control, he is probably an Intuitive. Neither his Thinking nor his Feeling judgments seem adequately developed, a real handicap for a J. John has a positive attitude toward work in general, a lot of energy, and a desire to accomplish things. His life field lists—forces in him that work for and against his personal effectiveness—would look like this:

John's Life Field

Forces for his effectiveness	*Forces against his effectiveness*
• Energy	• Jumps to conclusions
• Interest in activity	• Leaves work incomplete
• Quickness	• Behaves "blindly"
• Desire for accomplishments	• Seems purposeless
• Sincerity	• Behaves inconsiderately

With these data, it is difficult to see John's type. His forces against (1, 3, and 5) suggest a lack of perception, and (2 and 4) a lack of judgment. Clearly, his education has not been effective for him, possibly because his teachers are not able to teach to his type, and they don't understand him because of his contradictory signals and confusion about his own issues.

Planning to help John: John's teacher could best begin with a plan that takes into consideration the possibility that he is an EJ type and attempt to gather more data about his preferred processes. In the meantime, John will benefit from the following:

1. Learning activities that allow action and movement.
2. Activities that have specific standards, criteria, consequences, and products, which are made clear to him in the beginning. If he is a J, he is likely to take learning as serious business, and his "bulldozing" may come from frustration that others, including the teacher, are not taking a business-like attitude toward classroom work.
3. EJs generally thrive on being in charge of something, and John may act more responsibly if he can be given the responsibility of managing some classroom function(s).
4. Learning to state his own behavioral objectives when starting new learnings.

5. Being teamed with students who easily see the need for rational planning to reach goals.
6. Learning listening techniques, such as paraphrasing and summarizing what has been said.
7. Carefully outlining and planning each project in detailed sequence.

While trying out these ideas with John, the teacher should be watching for evidence of S, N, T, and F preferences. The four EJ types are different in the kinds of responsibilities they like to carry, and John's preferences may show themselves in his working with others.

Bob: Trying Hard But Fearing Failure

E or I S or N T or F J or P

Bob has little self-confidence. He almost never volunteers a response in class, except privately to the teacher, after class is over, because he isn't sure he's right. He often undertakes projects of such complexity that failure is almost certain, even though he is willing to work long and hard. It almost seems as though he were his own worst enemy and critic.

Shyness and a preference for complexity suggest Introversion and Intuition, and the long devotion to projects is characteristic of the Feeling types. Working long and hard without closure may indicate a Perceiving type. With the hypothesis that John is an Introverted Feeling type, INFP, here is Bob's zigzag (figure 10.4), followed by suggestions for helping him.

Figure 10.4

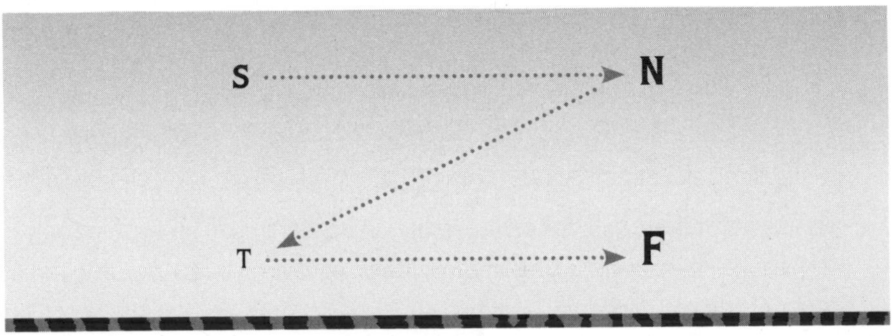

Planning to help Bob: For this INFP who is trying but fearing failure, self-confidence will come best from successful work on projects he deeply cares about, work that strongly engages his F values.

1. Busywork is not for INFPs. If we have surmised Bob's type accurately, then he must feel there is an important purpose for work he does. He will do well with a contract plan in which he can choose materials and activities for himself.
2. His confidence will be bolstered when he is shown evidence of benefits to others as a result of his own efforts, even though the results may fall short of his own expectations.
3. Teach him goal clarification techniques and show him how to break large "big picture" goals into small, component, sequential goals that can be evaluated and completed independently of each other.
4. Teach him evaluation techniques so that he can objectively assess his own work.
5. Teach him to check his plans with a dissimilar type who can tactfully question him about details and sequences.
6. He will likely benefit from uninterrupted periods of intense work on a single project and from frequent and sincere statements of appreciation and support.

Exercise: Analyzing Student Difficulties

Lisa, Jan, Dean, John, and Bob had at least one thing in common: their achievement of school objectives was being blocked by difficulties in their development—what teachers in earlier times called character development. If you have some students who can use a similar approach, use the following steps to outline a plan using type concepts:

1. Write a paragraph or two describing their basic traits.
2. Hypothesize a type for each, keeping in mind that you know them only in a small part of their lives and that their behaviors in the classroom may not present their true types.

3. Analyze their strengths and weaknesses based on type descriptions.

4. Analyze their zigzag patterns.

5. Make a list of things that could be done to help them in their development. The *Descriptions of the Sixteen Types* in Appendix A is a good resource for this. As you form your list, follow the principle of working from the person's strengths—using a strength to strengthen a weakness. The type descriptions highlight the personal characteristics that energize each type. Each person's development proceeds along a path built from the values and priorities identified there.

6. Reconsider your hypotheses of their types as you try the ideas. Continue to observe the students. If the interventions do not go well enough, see if other type preferences might be a better match to their behaviors. If you can, talk about them with someone knowledgeable about type.

Activities That Teach Use of Perception and Judgment

Many teachers have found that ideas for activities come to them when they scan a list of judgment and perception terms such as this one:

Judgment	Perception	Both Perception and Judgment
goal clarification	communicating	classifying
values clarification	observing	applying (concepts)
managing time	listening	finding relationships
choosing	smelling	designing (projects)
deciding	touching	interpreting
organizing	summarizing	evaluating
criticizing	imagining	hypothesizing
analyzing	collecting (data)	taking risks
empathizing	investigating	

How Type Development Concepts Contribute to Teaching Character Development

The task of helping young people to become integrated and worthwhile persons is infinitely complex. Type theory illuminates only a part of the task, although it is not a narrow viewpoint. At the heart of the theory is the fundamental concern for the development of two of education's broadest goals: keen perception and sound judgment. If people differ significantly in these mental processes (judgment and perception), educators need to recognize, honor, and use those differences. While the overall task may be infinitely complex, one part of it—the problem of getting in tune with students' different ways of processing experiences—is made much more clear and tangible through the use of type concepts.

> "At the heart of the theory is the fundamental concern for the development of two of education's broadest goals: the development of keen perception and sound judgment."

Your type is a developmental pathway. As you move through childhood and young adulthood, the path that offers most constructive growth is the path that permits active use of the type preferences. The life energy, however defined, goes into mastering the preferred perception and judgment processes. If life circumstances block the normal expression of type preferences, the energy may go into other preferences in order to comply with the demands of your environment, making the energy unavailable for the development of the dominant mental process, the foundation of your personality. In Jung's view, the person who in childhood is pushed off the development path that type provides is the person who in adult life must expend much energy and suffer much pain to find personal integration. This view is a major piece of his theory of mental health.

A teacher who wants to assist young people's personal development has little time and opportunity to provide that help. There are too many students and not enough time for teachers to learn about their individual development needs. This problem emphasizes the usefulness of type concepts. A teacher who can recognize type expressions has tools for quickly seeing developmental needs without having to probe too deeply into the student's personal life—that is, type gives the teacher a framework from which to hypothesize helping techniques that may fit the student.

I recommend that teachers begin using this approach with just a few students: the ones who seem clearly to have their academic progress blocked by development problems, such as Lisa and the others we looked at in this chapter. Taking them one at a time, we can consider the dynamics of their types. As a simple example, read the type description that the student has chosen, or that you have hypothesized, and highlight the words and phrases most revealing of that type's natural motivations and strengths. Then, once a day find something to say or do that acknowledges the student's strengths. It is through security in one's strengths that a person finds the energy and confidence to work on development needs and problems. With practice, this approach becomes less and less time consuming, almost second nature, and easy as well as rewarding.

EXERCISE

TYPE STRENGTHS and TROUBLE SPOTS

An important resource for helping such students is a colleague of the same type as the student. Here is a group discussion activity that works for me to demonstrate to teachers the value of using another teacher to help diagnose the problem of a student whose development is blocking achievement. The activity requires a group of twenty or more teachers of various types—ones who have responded to the MBTI® instrument and selected a best-fit type for themselves. Divide the teachers into eight groups, combining the cousin types (creation of a group with all sixteen types represented is unlikely except in a large group). Cousin types are the two that are above and below each other in Appendix A.

Ask participants in each subgroup to record on chart paper the key features of their types that they agree on, and at the bottom of the sheet report the contrasts. You can show a sample sheet with sections marked on the bottom for the contrasts; for example, ESTJ/ENTJ written at the top, and sections for S and N contrasts marked at the bottom eight or so inches of the chart. Of course, if only one type is represented in the group, such as ENTJ, there will be no contrast report at the bottom on the sheet.

Group Activity

Objective: Getting acquainted with key characteristics of the sixteen types, the strengths and potential trouble spots.

Instructions:

1. Do this activity with the participants. Begin by saying "We are arranged in groups by cousin types. If you have no partner(s), you can do this exercise on your own."
2. Ask the participants to answer these two questions:
   a. If we could use only a *few words and phrases* to tell the rest of the world about our type, which ones would we choose? Take ten minutes. List only the features you agree on. If you like, refer to your type description.
   b. If students of our type were performing below expectation in school, what reasons for the poor performance can we hypothesize out of our own experience? Take ten minutes, and list only the reasons you agree on.
3. Ask each group to choose someone to record the key words and phrases the group agrees on and the answers to 2b. Put the answers for a and 2b on separate sheets of chart paper.
4. Tell participants that they twenty minutes to complete the tasks and then the group as a whole will discuss the process and results.

Debriefing/discussing the group activity:

1. Give the groups twenty minutes to agree and produce their charts.
2. Have recorders, one at a time, give their charts to the leader, who puts them on the wall, with the recorder reading/reporting the group's work. Allow about two minutes for each report.
3. Call attention to interesting contrasts on charts as they are posted.
4. When all charts are posted, ask these questions:

   Was talking in your group a comfortable process? Why? Was understanding each other easy?

   As you listened to other groups' reports, what went through your mind?

   Are the differences between the groups real and important differences?

   The potential trouble spots noted by each group suggest the value of diagnosing the problems of a student by consulting a faculty member of the same type. Does that seem sensible to you?

EXERCISE

OBSERVATION AS A WAY TO IDENTIFY TYPE CHARACTERISTICS*

On the next eight pages are checklists you can use to infer students' types from their overt behavior. Even if you decide to use the Murphy-Meisgeier Type Indicator for Children® (MMTIC®) or MBTI instruments, the checklists are a useful supplement. Teachers who know type concepts and who know their students well can make reasonable guesses abut their types. Even if your guesses are not entirely correct, you will still understand your students better, after using this exercise. The checklists reflect the work of Isabel Myers and other students of type. However, only the Extravert–Introvert lists have been field tested as an observation instrument, although in a somewhat different form. These lists are not substitutes for the MBTI or the MMTIC instruments (which have reliability and validity data associated with them, and give students the opportunity to verify their types).

Instructions

Put a student's name at the top of the checklist (each list room for four names) and mark each box opposite a phrase that describes him or her. Comparing tallies of E and I, S and N, T and F, J and P can give you an estimation of the person's type.

*The author acknowledges with appreciation the contributions that Anna Nuernberger and Carolyn Mamchur made to this section.

STUDENT NAME				If your student is an **EXTRAVERT**, it is likely that he or she
				chooses to work with others, with large groups
				plunges into new experiences
				is relaxed and confident
				readily talks over events and ideas with others
				is interested in other people and their doings
				readily offers opinions
				shares personal experiences
				wants to experience things so as to understand them
				is enthusiastic about activities involving action
				asks questions to check on the expectations of the group or teacher
				has a relatively short attention span
				dislikes complicated procedures and gets impatient with slow jobs
				is interested in the results of the job, in getting it done and in how other people do it
				eagerly attends to interruptions
				acts quickly, sometimes without thinking
				likes to work by trial and error
				communicates well and greets people easily

STUDENT NAME					If your student is an **INTROVERT**, it is likely that he or she
					chooses to work alone or with one person
					holds back from new experiences
					chooses written assignments over oral presentations
					performs better in written work than in oral presentations
					pauses before answering, and shows discomfort with spontaneous questioning
					asks questions to allow understanding something before attempting to do it
					is hard to understand, quiet; seems "deep"
					is intense, bottling up emotions
					prefers setting his/her own standards when possible
					spends time in thought, before and after actions
					has a small number of carefully selected friends
					likes quiet space to work
					works intently on the task at hand
					works on one thing for a long time
					prefers jobs that can be done "inside the head"
					dislikes interruptions
					may spend too much time in thought and neglect to get into action

STUDENT NAME					If your student prefers **SENSING**, it is likely that he or she
					is realistic and practical
					is more observant than imaginative
					wants to have senses fully engaged and satisfied
					enjoys owning things and making them work
					prefers memorizing to finding reasons
					is aware of environment and changes moods as physical surroundings change
					learns best from an orderly sequence of details
					is interested in facts and what is really true
					keeps accurate track of details, makes lists
					is patient
					is good at checking, inspecting, and precise work
					likes to know the "right way" to solve problems
					likes an established routine
					enjoys using skills already learned more than learning new ones
					works steadily, not in fits and starts
					is impatient or frustrated with complicated situations
					seldom uses imagination or has inspirations

STUDENT NAME

					If your student prefers **INTUITION**, it is likely that he or she
					seems to like something new all the time
					is more imaginative than observant
					attends more to the whole concept than to details
					is aware only of events that relate to current interests
					becomes restless, impatient with routines
					is an initiator, promoter, inventor of ideas
					sees possibilities that others miss
					is quick with finding solutions
					doesn't always hear you out; anticipates your words
					likes to have and do things differently from others
					likes problems that require new ways of being solved
					dislikes precise work with many details
					enjoys learning a new skill more than using it
					works in bursts of energy, with slack periods in between
					jumps to conclusions; makes factual errors
					finds reading easy
					readily grasps meanings of words and symbols

STUDENT NAME					If your student prefers **THINKING**, it is likely that he or she
					wants logical reasons before accepting new ideas
					tries to be fair; is impersonal, impartial
					finds ideas and things more interesting than people
					is more truthful than tactful, if forced to choose
					is brief and businesslike
					takes very seriously facts, theories, and the discovery of truth
					takes seriously the solution of objective problems
					treats emotional relationships and ideals quite casually
					contributes intellectual criticism
					exposes wrongs in the habits and beliefs of others
					is offended by illogic in others
					holds firmly to a policy or conviction
					hurts other people's feelings without knowing it
					has a low need for harmony
					is upset by injustice
					seems not to know how his or her own actions affect other people's feelings

STUDENT NAME				If your student prefers **FEELING**, it is likely that he or she
				is personal, likes warm personal relationships
				is more interested in people than things or ideas
				is more tactful than truthful, if forced to choose
				is likely to agree with others in the group
				thinks as others think, believing them probably right
				finds it difficult to be brief and businesslike
				takes emotional relationships and ideals very seriously
				is offended by a lack of personal consideration in others
				is motivated by others
				may comply or conform to avoid disharmony
				permits feelings to override logic
				forecasts how others will feel
				arouses enthusiasm
				is upset by conflicts; values harmony
				dislikes telling people unpleasant things
				relates well to most people
				is sympathetic

STUDENT NAME				If your student is a **JUDGING** type, it is likely that he or she
				likes to have things decided and settled
				is more decisive than curious
				lives according to plans
				lives according to standards and customs not easily or lightly set aside
				tries to make situations conform to his or her standards, "the way they ought to be"
				makes definite choices from among the possibilities
				is uneasy with unplanned happenings
				bases friendship upon beliefs, standards, and tastes that are assumed to be shared
				has enduring friendships
				sets up "shoulds" and "oughts" and regularly judges self against these
				aims to be right
				is self-regimented, purposeful, and exacting
				is orderly, organized, and systematic
				likes assignments to be clear and definite
				has settled opinions; may be tolerant of routine procedures

STUDENT NAME

				If your student is a **PERCEIVING** type, it is likely that he or she
				is more curious than decisive
				lives according to the situation of the moment
				may not plan things, acts spontaneously
				is comfortable in handling the unplanned, unexpected, or incidental
				looks for new experiences, expects to be interested
				samples many more experiences than can be digested or used
				takes a "Live and let live" attitude
				bases friendships on propinquity and shared experience
				takes on friendships easily; may also neglect, drop, and resume them easily
				aims to miss nothing
				is flexible, adaptable, and tolerant
				wants to understand things more than manage them
				leaves things open
				has trouble making decisions
				starts too many projects and has difficulty in finishing them
				postpones unpleasant jobs
				welcomes new light on a thing, situation, or person

11

Are the Sixteen Types Sixteen Kinds of Mind?

THE CENTURIES-OLD view of mind passed down through many generations is that most humans have the same basic mental equipment; we just differ in the amounts we possess of different traits: IQ, abstract reasoning, social sensitivity, artistic gifts, attention span, assertiveness, curiosity, et cetera. Even the eight MBTI® preferences are often part of this list. This can be called a "unitary model of mind." Everyone has the same hard wiring, but we differ in our software. Jung's theory of psychological types seems to be at odds with the unitary view. Trait theory fits with the unitary view of mind; type theory appears to suggest something else. It suggests that even our hard wiring is different, probably in sixteen different ways. Perhaps we should begin seriously to regard the sixteen types as sixteen kinds of mind.

The types described by Jung and Myers are patterns they found in people's observable behaviors. Because the patterns were persistent, predictable, and meaningful in human interactions, and because they helped to explain large sets of behavior, Jung called the patterns "types." He distinguished types from traits (see chapter 2). Let's revisit this distinction, using Extraversion and Introversion as examples.

Types, Not Traits

Jung brought the terms *introversion* and *extraversion* to the study of human nature to designate two basic orientations in life. Everyone prefers one or the other, and the preferred one is our automatic, instinctual orientation. We are all capable of being in the other orientation, but it is not our automatic, initial response. He did not mean these type preferences to be treated as traits, as most people subsequently have done. Extraversion as a *trait* means extraversion as a strength or weakness. As a strength, it refers mainly to social skills; as a weakness, it refers mainly to the inability to move out of extraverting into introverting when appropriate. If extraversion and introversion were trait strengths, we could talk about *how much* of each one a person possessed. We might expect a mature, well-developed person to be highly skilled in both. However, when one examines Jung's work, it is clear this is not what Jung intended, and it is not what Myers intended to identify with the MBTI instrument. As *type* terms, extraversion and introversion are opposite orientations and not strengths or weaknesses. The MBTI assessment sorts people into types; it does not measure skills.

> **"In effect, type theory gives us sixteen distinct behavior patterns that can be considered as sixteen kinds of mind."**

In the MBTI model based on Jung's work, because Extraversion and Introversion are not traits or skills possessed in some quantity, they do not fit well into the view of mind that I referred to as the unitary model. As type preferences, they represent two *different kinds of mind*—the one tending to plunge into new experiences and the other pausing to reflect beforehand.

The same can be said for each of the other dimensions of type—S–N, T–F, and J–P; they do not represent traits but are different ways we process our experiences. We can expect certain traits to be more associated with one type preference than with its opposite; for example, among people who consider themselves shy, we can expect to find more Introverts than Extraverts. But we should not treat Introversion as another trait alongside of shyness.

Mind as Verb

In effect, type theory gives us sixteen distinct behavior patterns that can be considered as sixteen kinds of mind. The Myers-Briggs descriptions show us sixteen minds-in-action or, stated more accurately, sixteen kinds of mind-as-action. While the latter term sounds clumsy, I like it better because it emphasizes mind as verb rather than noun.

Mind as Thing Versus Mind as Process

The common assumption behind the unitary view of mind is that mind is a thing—a noun, a part of the human organism, an entity that causes us to attend, observe, reason, make judgments, and take action. Some regard mind as synonymous with brain. Expressions such as "Use your mind" and "A mind is a terrible thing to waste" reflect this view. If we regard mind as some kind of moving force or controller behind behavior, then mind is a mystery behind the scenes that can only be inferred from observed behaviors and can't be studied by direct observation.

If, in contrast, mind is a verb, and the terms we use to talk about mind are process or action words, then people's behaviors show us mind-as-action. Using mind as verb is a way of talking about the person being in purposive action: different ways and degrees of being *mindful*—for example, the person attending, observing, reflecting, caring, or reasoning. Mind is then a quality of the whole person, not a thing prompting the person to act in certain ways.

Jung's Mental Functions and Processes as Observable Qualities

I emphasize the noun–verb distinction because it bears directly on how we treat the idea of types. If we accept type preferences as real factors in our lives, then we have the choice of either treating Jung's functions as entities, as components of the mind/brain that prompt our behavior and can only be inferred but never directly observed or treating the functions as qualities/actions that can be *directly* observed in behavior and described. I support the latter viewpoint because it keeps us more open to growing in our understanding of type by reminding us to observe, observe, observe. It disciplines us to treat type concepts as a hypothesis that continually needs testing and validation.

It disciplines us to avoid treating the type preferences as forces assumed to be causing behaviors. In practical terms, treating mind as verb is the difference between saying such things as "You're a Thinking type, and that's keeping you from seeing when to show appreciation" (the unitary/trait/noun viewpoint) versus "Your difficulty in showing appreciation is certainly consistent with a preference of Thinking over Feeling" (the mind-as-action viewpoint). Another example is "Your Intuition is causing you to overlook some details" versus "You've overlooked some details; Intuitives have that tendency."

The mind-as-verb approach also helps us see and treat persons as persons, not just as types. Consider this contrast: "We need an ISTJ for this job. Pat's an ISTJ; let's bring him in" versus "This job seems to need ISTJ skills and interests. Who's got those skills? Pat?"

The Types as Kinds of Mind

So, accepting mind as verb, can we say the types are kinds of mind? Of different kinds of minding? Different ways of processing experience? If we say that "mind" is a term for the processing of experience—in all the many ways that are available—then it seems we can hypothesize the types as kinds of mind.

Those of us who use type concepts know that the types as Myers described them are ways of processing experience that are *essentially* different from each other. To me that makes them a worthy alternative to the prevailing view of mind. To emphasize that type is fundamental and not superficial in our psychological constitutions, I propose that type theory be sponsored as a challenge to the unitary model of mind.

Some people, who apparently accept the unitary model, refer to the types or Jung's function combinations as "cognitive styles." To me that term suggests stylistic variations on a common, unitary mind and is not, therefore, an adequate alternative to "kinds of mind."

What Jung and Myers have given us is, among other things, a pioneering theory in the field of cognitive psychology. Today, when some cognitive psychologists and educators are beginning to attack the unitary model of mind, the time is right for Jung's types to be proposed as a more constructive model. The challenge can be launched in all arenas, by the practitioner as well as the theorist.

How Can We Keep Track of Sixteen Different Kinds?

Being able to call to mind the main characteristics of each of the sixteen types is a skill that takes a while to develop. For me it took several years. Now, after nearly forty years using type concepts in my daily life, the process of improving my understanding of the types is just as active as it ever was.

Don't be discouraged by the fact that learning about the types is a long, slow process. Fortunately, there are ways to put type concepts to work bit by bit as we learn them. Long before the complexities of all the types emerge in our understanding, we can use the concepts without distorting them or making them trivial. Any of the type dimensions—E–I, S–N, T–F, and J–P—can be considered separately. If you have a basic grasp, say, of E and I, you can put it to work. For example, in a brief exchange with someone, guessing E or I may be useful as you decide whether you want to help the person process a thought aloud or allow time for the person to process the thought quietly inside.

> **"In Carl Jung's view of psychological make-up, all conscious mental activity can be sorted into four categories: Sensing, Intuition, Thinking, and Feeling."**

When using just E–I as an example, all the sixteen types are sorted into just *two* categories. That is the simplest way of using type ideas. However, it is more revealing and useful to sort the types into four categories, as noted in chapter 3 when the IS, ES, IN, and EN groupings were presented as a practical way of looking at classroom instruction. In this chapter we will concentrate on another four-way sort: ST, SF, NT, and NF.

Focusing on Jung's Four Function Pairs

In Carl Jung's view of psychological make up, *all* conscious mental activity can be sorted into the four MBTI categories: Sensing, Intuition, Thinking, and Feeling. Jung called these the "four mental functions." Myers referred to them as the mental processes. The other type preferences—E, I, J, and P—are *orientations* of the processes, not the processes themselves. E and I show a person's preferred way of being in the world, oriented toward outer events and people, or toward the inner world of ideas. J and P show the preference for orienting one's outer life in a planful or spontaneous way.

The previous chapters have shown that everyone uses all four mental processes or functions, but we have favorites. Each of us favors one of the perception processes and one of the judgment processes, making four combinations of preferred processes: ST, SF, NT, and NF. To help us with the problem of keeping track of sixteen types, we can use the four process combinations as four kinds of mind. Treating them as four kinds of mind is not inconsistent with Jung's theory. There is a strong practical reason for it as well: four patterns are much easier to remember and to manage than sixteen.

When we say that four types have a common mind-set—for example, the four NF types—we know we are bundling together a lot of differences. Those who use type concepts daily know we can expect an INFP to react differently than an ENFJ. Some differences can be accounted for by their orientation preferences: E, I, J, and P. We also know that a lot of differences can't be accounted for by type. But it is clear that we can expect a lot of commonality among people of the four NF types, and there is practical value in searching it out.

The idea of four kinds of mind was given an important boost by the work of Humphry Osmond, Miriam Siegler, and Richard Smoke (1977), which was reported in "Typology Revisited: A New Perspective," in *Psychological Perspectives*. I have used, with gratitude, their terms for the ST, NF, NT, and SF combinations. They called the ST combination Structural; the NF, Oceanic; the NT, Ethereal; and the SF, Expereal. The authors invented the term "expereal" to contrast with ethereal. They developed their insights without knowing about the work of Isabel Myers and the extensive research done with the MBTI assessment. The presentation here differs somewhat from theirs because it is based on Myers' work.

Four Kinds of Mind

Four types have the ST combination: ISTJ, ISTP, ESTP, and ESTJ. Similarly, four types have NF in common, four have NT, and four have SF. Following are explanatory descriptions of the four combinations of mental processes.

ST: The Structural Mind

What the ST types have in common is a Sensing way of experiencing life and a Thinking way of organizing experiences. They value what their senses experience that their Thinking can turn directly into objective reality. The best analogy for the structural mind is the computer as an elaborate filing system. STs want clean data that will be filed exactly where they want it, so it can be easily retrieved in the same form that they filed it. The ST process works best with unambiguous facts and specifics that can be clearly and correctly sorted into mental files. Of course, life doesn't present just unambiguous experiences that can be neatly classified. The ST solution to that problem is to simplify experience by reducing it to what will fit the filing categories. Mature STs recognize that this solution may oversimplify things, but they believe the reality they hold onto is the part most needed for future use; they will have the essential things ready for use when they are needed.

NF: The Oceanic Mind

NFs process experience in an entirely different way. To NFs, the unique, subtle, personal, and "ambiguous" features of experiences are what make them most valuable and interesting. In their view everything is ultimately connected to everything else; life is a seamless whole. To objectively sort and file experiences is to lose the subtle features that make possible the rich connections and relationships among things and people. NFs see the ST way of reducing experiences to distinct, objective categories as destroying the essentials rather than saving them.

Rather than being a filing system, the NF mind is like an ocean. Swimming around the edge of the ocean, just over the rim of consciousness, are all the bits of distinctive experiences that the NFs want to save for quick reference. When the conscious mind is through with the bits, they are allowed to swim away, over the rim, to find their own place. When a new problem is faced that requires recalling those bits of experience, they become available—not from a systematic file but from a process of letting associated memories come into consciousness, one pulling in another and another. Some that come are the exact ones sought, some are different. The NFs have faith that this process will preserve the best of experiences for future use; if the exact ones sought aren't found, others perhaps more interesting and just as useful will be retrieved and provide a creative solution to the new problem at hand.

NT: The Ethereal Mind

NTs have in common with NFs the global approach provided by Intuition. They have in common with STs the concern for objectivity that Thinking gives them.

Ideas in the form of mental models are the central feature of the NT mind. Before they launch themselves into the hurly-burly of life events, NTs want to have mental blueprints or maps to guide them, to provide an advance system of meanings by which they can stay oriented in daily life. Some NTs are bothered by the term "ethereal" as implying insubstantial. One suggested the term "conceptual mind." Osmond and his colleagues chose the term "ethereal" for the NTs to suggest their reliance on abstract constructs and principles, the etherlike material that is primary in their mental functioning. They also see NTs as tending to process everything in ways that makes "everything grist for the mental mill." Directly experiencing life, without first conceptualizing it, takes effort and feels awkward to NTs, who are keenly interested in objective data, not just facts as facts but as evidence to support one of their mental models.

SF: The Expereal Mind

The SFs have in common with STs the concreteness and matter-of-fact qualities that the Sensing function provides. With the NFs they share the personal, subjective approach of the Feeling function. "Expereal" is a term coined by Osmond and his colleagues to contrast with "ethereal" and to convey the central feature of SF mind: everything is validated in personal, practical, daily experience. Like the NTs, SFs believe in conducting their lives according to principles. But while the NTs seek out abstract principles first and then test them in life experiences, the SFs reverse the process. They take life events matter-of-factly; then when their experiences show them what works and what doesn't work, rules-of-thumb emerge—personal, practical guidelines that are credible as guiding principles because their own experience produced them.

SFs are immediately in touch with the tangible qualities of events, and they know directly the literal, personal meanings of what happens. In contrast, STs turn events into objects before they react to them personally. In even sharper contrast, the Intuitive function of the NFs and NTs probes for patterns behind the literal, direct, and sensory experience before it settles on the meaning and value of it.

In these four descriptions I have tried to use language that reaches beyond my own NT mind-set. My long-range goals for my own self-improvement include a big, never-ending task: finding phrases, anecdotes, and ways of framing ideas that bridge across type differences. Of course, none of us can ever leave our type behind and experience life through the mind-set of another type. Readers are welcome to write to me with suggestions for improvements of the language I have used to describe the types in this manner.

ST, SF, NF, NT Mental Priorities

While each of the sixteen types has a distinctive pattern of priorities and values associated with it, each of the four STs has some priorities in common, as do NFs, NTs, and SFs.

ST Priorities

- Conserving valued resources and protecting practices that work
- Finding situations where they can use and enjoy their technical skills
- Minimizing or eliminating ambiguity and uncertainty
- Getting roles defined in specific, objective ways
- Knowing exactly what output is expected of them
- Having or making objective rules
- Dealing with concrete, objective problems that are uncluttered with emotional issues

NF Priorities

- Finding situations where they can pursue their deep concern for broad, human value issues
- Finding situations that allow them freedom for creative expression
- Exploring the possibilities in relationships
- Finding situations that value their insights into complex interpersonal issues
- Making institutions responsive to people
- Promoting the ideals of harmonious relationships

NT Priorities

- Finding situations that need their objective curiosity and lead to intriguing possibilities
- Working at the abstract level of broad concepts and general ideas
- Analyzing complex, objective situations
- Working on problems that respond to their own new techniques and solutions
- Pursuing their own idealistic images of how things should be
- Having opportunities to independently produce innovative, ingenious solutions

SF Priorities

- Working in harmonious, familiar, predictable situations
- Maintaining the practical contacts that keep personal relationships warm and free from conflicts
- Enjoying the present moment, making the best of life's conditions
- Attending to the tangible needs of individuals
- Making a distinctly personal physical environment in which to live and work
- Being in situations where their keen attention to the here and now is useful and appreciated

ST, SF, NF, NT Interactions

As people use type on a daily basis, they begin to collect anecdotes and examples of type characteristics in action. Following are a few that typify the mind-set of the four function combinations and the results of their interactions with each other.

EXAMPLE 1. Three women, two NFs and an ST, were appointed to be a management team. Before they became managers, each was recognized as highly competent, and they had high regard for each other. One of the NFs headed the team. In their team meetings, the NFs talked effortlessly with each other, brainstorming various means of solving problems. The ST felt left out of the whirlwind style of dialogue, seldom talked, and often was unsure of exactly what had been decided. She concluded that she had previously misjudged the two NFs and now saw them as condescending and fickle. Over the weeks she came to doubt her own ability as a manager. The quantity and quality of her work declined, and she finally asked to be relieved of management responsibility—even though the team as a whole was regarded as very effective. This scenario shows us how the NF oceanic work style predominated to the point of handicapping the ST structural partner.

EXAMPLE 2. An SF single woman received Valentine letters from two male admirers—one an NF, the other she believed to be an ST. She showed the letters to an ST woman friend and asked her reaction. The friend said the NF's letter was insincere and flaky, and the ST's letter showed genuine caring. The critique of the letters was an ST projection, saying in effect, "If I had said those (ST) words, I would be expressing genuine caring."

EXAMPLE 3. An NF assistant principal, enthusiastically presented to her principal a plan for hosting representatives from each of the district's elementary schools so they could see an innovative program the fourth- and fifth-grade teams had developed. Expecting supporting, encouraging comments, she asked the ST principal what he thought. His response: "That's maybe fifty people. Where do we park the cars?" His ST pragmatism jumped out ahead of his human relations skills.

> "One of the main values of viewing the types through the four function combinations is the opportunity for discovering one's own biases."

Obviously, it is difficult to anticipate the viewpoint that is natural and automatic to a mind-set different from one's own. I believe the place for us to begin in bridging the differences is to first examine our own instinctual frame of mind.

Discovering the Biases of One's Mind-set

One of the main values of viewing the types through the four function combinations is the opportunity for discovering one's own biases. I do not mean bias in a negative sense, such as prejudice, but rather as a slant of mind, one's angle of seeing things. Whenever I have trouble understanding another person's point of view on something, or when my own perfectly clear ideas draw blank stares from people, I often turn to type differences for an explanation. Many times, the ST, NF, NT, and SF differences give me insights to clear up the problem. When you know people's types or can make a good guess about them, you will begin to see the four kinds of mind in their language and actions. Here are some examples I have observed.

Mind-sets in Organizational Problem Solving

Working with the school superintendent and the senior staff of a large school system, while teaching them about type, I sat in on a senior staff meeting. They knew the basics about people types, and I was to observe and to help them see type differences in action. The four kinds of mind were on display. When the superintendent turned the meeting to a discussion of a new performance appraisal plan for administrators, an ST began to identify specific ambiguities and misunderstandings her school principals were concerned about. She described flaws in the details of the plan. The man in charge of the new plan, an NT, responded that there could be no ambiguities because he drafted it carefully and he *himself* had explained it in detail at meetings attended by every administrator in the district. He said the flaws had already been found and the plan was crystal clear.

The ST began again to explain a particular complaint. Two other STs nodded and suggested refinements to the plan. The sole NF in the meeting said this seemed to be a communication problem that could be worked out better in another meeting specifically for that purpose. Two members had not yet spoken: an NT and an SF. When the superintendent asked for their views, the NT said he thought the plan was "conceptually sound, and ought to be workable." When the SF was asked about the plan, she said, "What plan? Until it's in place and running smoothly, there is no plan."

Later, going over this exchange with them, I tried to show them the examples of type in action: the NT with his blueprint that was "conceptually sound"; the STs with their concern for the small but crucial problems in the implementation; the NF with the suggestion for harmonizing the differences before going further; and the SF pointing out that the plan and its implementation are not separate and are nothing of importance until people use the performance appraisal system to their satisfaction in daily work. Each person's slant on the problem, when seen as a natural contribution of his or her type, could be taken as constructive, and all were needed to arrive at a workable solution.

Here is another, less complex example. An NF and an ST were partners in consulting work; the NF was the senior partner. They freely exchanged ideas with each other and planned their work carefully. After they had worked together for several months, the ST revealed that she had strongly considered breaking the partnership until she realized the NF really meant to act on only about 10 percent of the possibilities proposed at their meetings. The structural ST wanted to ground their planning in given facts and move step-by-step. The NF needed to be imaginative and to explore widely until a possibility jumped out and gave the inspiration for action. Both were grateful for their knowledge of type allowing them to have the patience needed to understand each other.

Whichever aspects of type are prominent in a meeting or relationship, groups whose members know about and constructively use type differences have a very big advantage. When type terms are part of the group's language, there is usually better listening, more good-natured humor, and a smoother flow of problem solving toward outcomes that all members can support.

EXERCISE

HIGHLIGHTING MIND-SET DIFFERENCES in an ORGANIZATION

How members view the priorities of their organization is often influenced by their kinds of mind. Successful uses of an exercise that shows the importance of the mind-set differences were reported by I. I. Mitroff and R. H. Kilman in a 1975 article in *Management Review* ("Stories Managers Tell: A New Tool for Organizational Problem Solving"). To teach problem-solving techniques to managers in large business organizations, the authors obtained the managers' type preferences and guided them through a three-step activity.

Step one required each person individually to write a short story about his or her idea of an ideal organization. The story could take any form. In step two the participants were divided into four groups—ST, NT, NF, and SF—and each group was asked to come up with a story that best expressed the *group's* concept of an ideal organization. There were no other instructions or constraints. At the conclusion of step two each group reported to the others the story its members agreed upon.

People who know type will find no surprises in the outcomes; the groups gave stories fully consistent with the theory. However, the study participants were routinely startled by the striking contrasts. I have had the same experience when using this exercise with groups. Following are brief versions of the patterns of stories reported by the authors.

An ideal organization of the STs was characterized by complete control, certainty, and specificity. Work roles were defined in detail, with clear hierarchical lines of authority, and were monitored with impartial, impersonal rules. The heroes of the ST stories were leaders who brought order and stability out of chaos and gave the organization a specific sense of direction.

The NT stories were centered on broad, global issues, with little if any attention to roles, rules, and lines of authority. Their ideal organization was guided by intellectual and theoretical concepts of good organization and was impersonally idealistic. They focused on big-picture economic issues and on new products and new horizons. The heroes of NT stories were broad conceptualizers who turned around a narrowly focused organization and steered it successfully toward new goals.

The NF stories also emphasized global, idealistic themes but focused on the personal and human goals of the organization. The ideal organization was organic and adaptive, serving the needs of humanity and its own members. If the NF groups drew a visual representation of the ideal organization, the diagram would show a circular or wheel-like structure in which there is no hierarchy, no clear lines of authority. The heroes in the NF stories gave the organization "a new sense of direction in the human or personal sense."

The SF stories focused on "the detailed human relations in their particular organization," the details of the interpersonal environment of the workplace, and not on theory or broad conceptual issues. Their attention was on "the human qualities of the specific people" in the organization and not on work roles or rules. The stories were realistic rather than idealistic. The heroes of the SF stories were people who "create a highly personal, warm human climate," who make you want to come to work to be with your work family.

The third step in the Mitroff–Kilmann exercise is coaching the participants in using the four points of view to solve problems within their organization. After they agree on a particular problem or issue to work on, the participants individually write their own view of the problem—objectives, issues, value assumptions, what an ideal resolution would look like, et cetera. Participants are then divided back into the four groups—ST, SF, NF, and NT—to develop a group statement that incorporated their individual statements. The actual problems looked strikingly different from the four perspectives, each of which had its special contribution to make to satisfactory solutions: ST, attention to day-to-day operational issues; NT, long-range strategic planning; NF, long-range human goals; and SF, day-by-day human relationships. The authors argued that failure to take into account all four viewpoints "can be disastrous to an organization."

This three-step exercise works with any organization, highlights the reality of the differences among the types, and demonstrates the value of the different viewpoints to the welfare of the whole group.

How Mind-set Influences Teaching

Looking at teaching and learning through the lenses of the four mind-sets is often more effective in highlighting issues than is the use of whole types or the E–I, S–N, T–F, and J–P dimensions separately.

Let me provide an example of bias in our mind-sets from a personal experience—conversations with a student of mine in a graduate seminar in education entitled Instruction: Theory and Research. This student was a biology instructor at a community college. During the seminar, participants had taken the MBTI instrument and learned the basics about type applications in education. After class, this student came to talk to me about an insight he had and to ask my advice. He had been having trouble with one class on human physiology. The trouble baffled him because he was highly regarded as a teacher and knew he was good. The students were conscientious and seemed bright enough to handle the material of the course, but "their eyes glaze over when I get about five minutes into my presentations." His insight was triggered by transparencies I had shown in class of type distribution of students in different college majors. One table showed the percentage of several thousand nursing students in the sixteen type categories. Seeing that SFs dominated the type table, and knowing that most of the students in his class were in a nursing program (and therefore had a high probability of being SF types), he wondered if type differences might be part of the problem. As an INTP, he realized that problem might stem from the NT–SF differences.

I asked him to demonstrate a recent presentation that he had observed was not working for his students. He sketched on the chalkboard a simple abstract model he used to start a lecture on the nervous system, to demonstrate how synapses work. Partway into the presentation he said, "This is where they glazed over." I reminded him of the contrast between NT *ethereal* and SF *expereal*, and he quickly realized how remote his model was from his students' personal experiences. I asked him to describe the kinds of direct experiences of the nervous system the nursing students were likely to have in their training. They would encounter patients with atrophied muscles, bedsores, cramps, and various other neurological issues. I suggested he begin a lecture on the nervous system using those practical experiences. He agreed to try, and we planned to meet the next week after class. A week later he came to me grinning with excitement and announced, "I've just invented a new kind of instruction for them. It works like a charm. I call it backward teaching!"

From his perspective as an NT instructor, the teaching was backward because it went *from* concrete, personal experience *toward* the abstract and impersonal principles underlying experience. What he was saying, of course, is that the sequence of learning that makes sense to him and is most helpful to him is turned around in the approach he devised for his SF students.

Guarding Against Mind-set Bias in Teaching

Following this situation and similar ones, I have thought of a general rule to use in planning instruction. When preparing a lesson, we must do more than just plan for ways to engage the E–I, S–N, T–F, and J–P differences. We also must consider how our own mind-set bias is likely to intrude and cause us to want to teach as we prefer to be taught. Consider the opposite of the NT–SF example: an SF teacher and an NT student. The NT student might be put off unless it is clear where the lesson fits into an abstract and impersonal perspective. The teacher, however, will feel most natural grounding the lesson in personal and concrete experience.

Consider an ST/NF difference. ST teachers go against their instincts when they don't begin a lesson with specific information about what is to be learned and the sequence that will be followed. NF students may see the teacher's efforts as lifeless, cut-and-dried, and feel frustrated by hearing about the details before understanding the big picture and what it means for them.

> **"To prevent mind-set bias in lesson planning, teachers will want to consciously consider learning-style issues at the beginning of planning and review for bias or missing perspectives before presenting the lesson."**

Similar challenges can be seen with the other combinations of mind-set differences. To prevent mind-set bias in lesson planning, teachers will want to consciously consider learning-style issues at the beginning of planning and review for bias or missing perspectives before presenting the lesson. Following is a review process that I have found helpful.

1. Have I provided a brief orientation to the new material, an advance organizer, that helps students see how it relates to their prior experiences? Intuitive students look for a familiar conceptual organizer, something that calls up the abstract frame of reference they need for processing the new material. Sensing students will want a familiar concrete organizer; they will want an anecdote, specific example, or sample that shows them the topic of the new material and alerts them to the categories of their memory bank to bring into awareness.
2. Have I planned for or allowed students to have choices in the way they study? Keeping in mind the range of natural interests of the types, have I provided access to diverse materials and experiences from which they can choose?
3. Do students have leeway to decide what kind of product they will present for evaluation? What sorts of abstract or concrete products will I as the teacher accept as evidence that they have accomplished the objectives? What kinds of choices make sense? Following are some examples.

Technical school. Two ST instructors at a technical school, who taught their elective courses with linear, self-checking, programmed materials, were concerned about the number of students who dropped their courses during the drop/add time period. Because psychological type was a regular feature at the school, the instructors discovered that nearly all the students who dropped were Intuitive types. By making a simple change in their instructional plan, they eliminated the problem. On the first day of classes, they told students to work with the programmed material for two or three sessions and then decide if that style of study suited them. Those who decided it didn't were free to choose or invent other means of learning the material, including working in small groups. All students were given the course objectives and shown the evaluation process; how they reached the objectives and prepared for the evaluation were up to each individual student. As you might suppose, some students chose to invent other ways to study, and nearly all of them turned out to be Intuitive types. The dropout rate was reduced but achievement levels remained the same—irrespective of the methods students chose.

College. An NT college instructor of physics, keenly interested in teaching and learning processes, spent many hours preparing a course format that offered more approaches to learning than the standard lecture and lab. He spent the most time preparing instructional modules, packets that guided students through various resources, including printed material, computer study aids, and lab work. After trials of the new system, he was disappointed to find that student achievement did not improve; some achieved very well, as before, but the new approach still left many students at levels lower than he wanted. With the help of an instructional resource person at his campus, he concluded that he had written the modules to fit his NT way of working, and they did not fit students of other types. He tackled the problem by enlisting Sensing-type graduate students to help him write a parallel set of modules. He admitted that the Sensing approach was painfully difficult for him to conceptualize. At the beginning of the next term, he offered parallel sets of modules for students: the original with the Intuitive slant and the new one with a Sensing approach. Students were told to sample the two sets by working through the first module of each and then deciding which suited them better. He made lecture sessions optional and set up small groups to work with graduate student mentors. Test scores went up significantly for all students.

High school. After learning about type differences, an SF business education teacher decided to teach her students how to build a portfolio to present samples of their work and other evidence of their skills to prospective employers. The contents and style of the portfolios varied dramatically, reflecting student differences in type, achievement, and tastes. By creating this assignment at the beginning of the course, she got to know her students and their learning styles and she provided students with a practical introduction to employer expectations.

Mind-set in Family Relationships

Nearly every household has a mix of kinds of mind among its members. Many television sitcoms show us the funny side of the mix. It isn't just the generation gap that interferes with communication. Messages are often not received with the meaning intended, and decisions made by one member may mystify the others. Understanding type differences helps demystify the miscommunications. Following are some examples that illustrate how knowing the ST, SF, NF, and NT differences can make problems more manageable.

Intuitive ideas, Sensing skills. Consider a family comprised of an NF and NT mother and father, both professionals, and an SF daughter, an only child, of middle school age. The daughter did well in school and received good grades, but she didn't show enough seriousness about her studies to suit her parents. When she was four, her parents perceived she had an interest in becoming a doctor. As a result, they decided to develop for her an academic path that would get her to medical school. The parents, in effect, wanted their daughter to devote her present life to achieving a future life that *they* could clearly visualize. The parents gave her plenty of reasons, both logical and personal, why she should be more future-oriented. However, an SF's instincts are to live fully in the present and let the future happen as it unfolds.

The daughter entered college on an academic scholarship. She discovered that medicine was not for her; the pre-med science courses convinced her of that. She went on to explore other majors. Her parents, pleased that their daughter was doing very well in college, got comfortable with not having a doctor in the family.

She decided on marketing as a major and ultimately landed a well-paying and exciting job in New York City.

NF parents, SF son. In another case the parents, both NFs, had the advantage of knowing about type for many years. Their SF son had just entered college. They recognized during his elementary school days that his Sensing mind saw the world differently and had different priorities from theirs. While he was bright, it was clear to them that he would not approach academic work as they had. They helped him be involved in many sensory-rich activities through the years that showed him how to manage academic work. His parents helped him find a college where residential groups form close relationships; his best friend has enrolled with him.

ST father, NT son. My ST father, a bank officer, wanted me to learn about budgeting and being responsible about money. Each Friday when I got my allowance, I was required to give him an itemized account of how I spent the previous week's allowance. He said he didn't care how I spent it, just that I kept track. I didn't think that keeping the record would help me be responsible about money. The requirement did not appeal to my NT mind at all. My SF mother, wanting no disharmony, persuaded me to accept my father's plan. So I agreed. The solution I worked out was that five minutes before suppertime each Friday, the time for getting my allowance, I sat down and made up a list of expenditures that I probably had made that week. I see now that both parents felt they were conveying to me some values that were high priorities in their mind-sets, and yet I was able to exercise my NT autonomy.

Thinking sisters, Feeling sister. Mind-set differences can, of course, strongly affect relationships between siblings. Three daughters, four years apart in age, were NT, NF, and NT, from oldest to youngest. As reported by the NF, now an adult, she felt squeezed into an NT sandwich. Day after day, her sisters talked NT—all sorts of abstract, impersonal subjects she felt were structured in a way to annoy her. Their talk seemed intellectual to her, and she decided she was not as bright as they were. As a highly successful professional later in life, who had learned about type, she came to see herself as the intellectual equal of her sisters, just with a different kind of intelligence.

Thoughts in Summary

A case can be made that the traditional concept of mind has practical limitations for us as we try to find useful ways to deal with human mental diversity. Treating the sixteen types as sixteen kinds of mind gives us a hypothesis to test. If the types represent truly *fundamental* differences in mind-set, then using the lenses of type to examine and deal with our human problems will yield better results than using the unitary model of mind as our basic assumption. If we are dissatisfied with our progress in solving problems of human understanding, perhaps some of our root assumptions about human nature need changing.

In this chapter I have argued for considering type differences not as style variations but as distinctly different ways of processing our experiences, different kinds of mind. That means we accept the type differences not as strengths or weaknesses to be shaped or improved but as given structures within which anyone can be helped to improve—in his or her type's own distinctive way.

When there are situations in which the sixteen types are too many variables to deal with, there are good reasons to sort them into four categories—the four mental process combinations—and deal with them as four kinds of mind. I hope the examples given in this chapter provide ideas you can develop and test in your own situation. I invite you to send me your reactions to my characterizations of the four kinds of mind, to help improve and extend the descriptions.

Finally, I propose that each of us look at our own mind-set bias to see how our preferred processes affect our interactions with people of other mind-sets. Once we see and understand our own slant on things, the door is opened to seeing the other person's mind-set and to learning how to engage it for mutual benefit.

12

Introducing Type Effectively into an Organization

What's the Problem?

THOSE OF US who know the power and value of type concepts in our own lives get a special joy when we can pass them on to others and see them light up with the new understanding. If we are part of an organization we want type to benefit everyone, to become part of the organizational culture. But influencing a whole organization is a different and more complex task than passing on something person to person.

When we are confident of our ability to ignite an interest in type in another person, it is easy to assume that our enthusiasm for type and our teaching skills will give us what's needed to energize an essential core of fellow enthusiasts in the organization, who will then spread type to everyone else. Our own enthusiasm for type lures us into expecting a chain reaction of interest. We expect type concepts to become a part of the language the members use in working with each other because they recognize the constructive qualities of type theory. But it is not realistic to expect this kind of contagion without more groundwork and planning.

What's Needed to Influence the Organizational Culture?

Some organizations *are* ready to learn about and apply type principles, and good teaching skills and enthusiasm will do the job. But most situations require more than that. What does it take to successfully influence an organization—beyond what is needed to effectively teach individuals?

That question is at the heart of the career of those who specialize in organizational development. Some of them have added the MBTI® assessment and a sound knowledge of type theory to their other skills and are sharing what they have learned through the Association for Psychological Type and various publications. In this chapter I share with you the approach I generally use. Included here are suggestions for:

- analyzing the organizational situations you encounter
- identifying the factors supporting, and those that would resist uses of, type concepts
- planning possible points and means of entry
- using type theory to help you plan
- making a specific plan that has a good chance of success

This chapter focuses on ways for you to introduce type into your own organization. Readers who would be introducing type as an outside consultant or trainer will find the chapter helpful, but it does not deal directly with consulting situations.

Every situation for introducing type is different, and each requires a specifically designed plan. What I present here is a *general strategy* for devising *situation-specific* plans.

Begin planning your approach by writing a description of your situation. You can write a formal proposal or make an outline or just put some notes down on a piece of paper. Regardless of how you proceed, it is important to put it in writing. Following are some questions that can help you organize your thoughts and plan a strategy.

Gather Information

The questions in this section ask you to gather detailed information about the situation and organization to which you propose to introduce type.

Q: *To what goal or ongoing effort of the organization can type be linked?*

I cannot overemphasize that type works best when leaders of the organization, or of a unit within the organization such as a work team, are *open to* and *looking for* tools to help them deal with problems or pursue particular goals. If they are not, then they are *not* ready to be introduced to type. You need to determine if they are ready to commit time and resources to improving individual effectiveness, teamwork, mission clarity, the quality of products and services, and other goals that can be enhanced by uses of type.

Even if *you know* that type knowledge is what the organization needs, your efforts may not influence organizational behavior unless the leaders are *actively inquiring* into means of improvement. They must view type as a possible means to help their situation. In most cases, learning about type and using the ideas will not be accepted as a goal of the organization just on the merits of type theory. The time and hard work it takes to learn and develop the skills of type can be justified in the members' minds to the extent that they are committed to the goal that type is supposed to help them reach.

Q: *How can you judge the readiness of the organization to use type?*

Even when you know that leaders and others are committed to improving organizational processes, they may not necessarily be ready for type. Do they seriously believe that individual differences need to be used more constructively? Are they committed to giving people time, training, and resources to work on developing their individual effectiveness? Are they ready to use a tool like type ethically, or is there a real risk that it might be used inappropriately? If it is hard for you to find positive answers to these questions, a direct introduction of type in the organization is not realistic. Perhaps a small-scale introduction is feasible; some means for that are given in the paragraphs that follow.

Q: *What happens when type is introduced in situations where people are not ready for it?*

I offer two contrasting cases from my experiences. In the first situation, the faculty of a large community college, after a long and difficult struggle, voted to approve a new constitution for the faculty senate. As a result the senate went from a low-profile advisory body to a position of proactive leadership in the college's instructional program. The senate's leadership team had to function as a team, deal with power struggles and personality clashes in the senate, and build new relationships with the college administration, including the president who had been on the job only a year. One of the team knew about type, saw its potential usefulness, and convinced the team to invite me to conduct a two-day retreat for the team on uses of type in their specific situation. The members were highly committed, had a very clear purpose for using type, and the retreat as well as the long-term results were positive. They clarified their goals, built a plan of action, and, in subsequent months, worked successfully through the plan.

> "An important step in introducing type into an organization is to find out the goal that the knowledge of type is intended to serve and the members' clarity about the goal and their commitment to achieving it."

In a contrasting situation, the superintendent of a large school district invited me to introduce type to his senior staff and to the school board members. The superintendent said the purpose was to better understand each other in order to accomplish more collaborative decision making. Because he was very interested in type and quite comfortable in openly discussing his type with the cabinet and board members, I made the mistake of assuming that he and the others were open to the conditions of collaboration, such as trusting relationships, straight talk, and respect for differences. Unfortunately that turned out to be a poor assumption on my part. There were three meetings: first the superintendent and his cabinet; then the superintendent and the board members; and finally a combined group. All meetings seemed to go well, but I learned in debriefing the third meeting that there was no consensus about a purpose for this work, that there was suspicion about hidden agendas, and that learning about type was not seen as being a means to a common goal or in service to a commitment. In that situation, some months later, I learned that their understanding of type did not affect their work or radiate beyond the team and into the organization.

An important step in introducing type into an organization is to find out the goal that the knowledge of type is intended to serve and the members' clarity about the goal and their commitment to achieving it. In the absence of these, type knowledge is likely to be just a curiosity that some will appreciate and others will forget. And the organization will not be broadly affected.

Q: ***What is my position of influence in the organization?***

Ask yourself who in the organization listens to you and regards your ideas as credible enough to be given serious consideration. Who is in your circle of influence, and are they people who have credibility with those outside your circle?

Your answers, carefully thought out, will suggest the pathways for spreading type ideas. The circle is your base for introducing type. In some organizations, unfamiliarity with psychological theories, including type, may cause such ideas to be met with suspicion or negation. Your credibility will have to carry type through the initial stages of introduction until the base group members see for themselves the value of type and are willing to commit to supporting the next step of its extension into the organization.

If you are a top administrator or a high-level resource person who is expected to bring new ideas into the organization, you have a different set of opportunities and constraints than do teachers or other employees who may not have those expectations attached to their jobs. The questions that follow apply to people at lower levels in an organization, although some may apply to the top leaders as well.

Q: *What are your purposes and motives in this situation?*

It pays to examine carefully your motives in introducing change to an organization. Do you have purposes other than the obvious one of using type to improve the ways you and others work? Do you have other motives that you may not have acknowledged? For instance, are you hoping to become more visible as a leader or potential leader?

The answers to these questions are for your personal consideration to clarify what is energizing you in your plan for introducing type. Being clear about your purposes will help you make better judgments about the plan and the situations that come up as you act on the plan. If your personal reasons do not mesh with the organization's objectives and active commitments, do not try introducing type. If type is not received well, the organization may decline future efforts to introduce type.

Q: *Who is the client?*

One way of looking at your role in introducing type into your organization is to consider yourself as a change agent. You are proposing that people change some aspects of their ways of thinking and relating to each other. I use the term "change agent" to mean that, with respect to type, *you* are the one introducing the change, whether or not you are the person who orchestrates and directs a change process.

Whatever your role in the change process, you have to have a client: a person or group that, in effect, authorizes you to bring a proposal for a change into the organization. Tacitly or explicitly, you negotiate with the client to find out what the client wants. If you introduce type to co-workers without considering this client relationship you may find that you have no support, and they may see your ideas as an unwanted intrusion. If you try to force the information on the group or if they do not view type as helpful to the situation, your efforts to introduce type will not be seen as helpful. In other words, you need to be sure the people who will be responsible for nurturing the change in the organization welcome type ideas.

However, keep in mind that sometimes the welcome mat doesn't come out until after a group has experienced an initial orientation to type, such as taking the MBTI® assessment and receiving feedback. If the opportunity is not right for introducing type widely within your organization, you can begin, if you are qualified to give the instrument, by introducing type to people within your circle of influence, and in that way you can develop a core group who are familiar with type concepts and applications.

It is not my intent to dampen your initial attempt to introduce type into your organization. However, I am urging careful planning so that your first effort is successful, which will sustain your enthusiasm and your organization's responsiveness.

If you do not have a client in the sense described here, then you start with yourself as your own client. That is, you apply type ideas in your own work and invite others to observe you using type. Invite those who believe you to be competent and credible in other respects. Invite those who themselves are credible, are informal status leaders among co-workers. I am suggesting that your invitations to them be informal, casual opportunities to see how you use type. If you are a teacher, show them specific ways type helps you in your teaching—for example, in better understanding and working with problematic students. These people can then become a client group and help you plan the next steps in introducing type.

Q: ***Can you find members who share the values implicit in type theory?***

Many of us are attracted to type theory because of the way it allows us to view human differences. By showing the complementary strengths and blind spots of the types, and showing that all types are valuable, Myers provided basic guidelines for the "constructive use of differences." Implied in the theory are values such as the worthiness and dignity of individuals despite their differences; the importance of collaboration for best results; and the necessity of trust, mutual support, and openness that allow the collaboration to happen. People who hold these values and try to practice them are the ones most likely to be ready for learning about and using type. They will see type as a practical tool for advancing the values.

Q: *When and how should you involve the organization's leadership?*

You will want to eventually involve the top person of the organization when you feel your ideas are formed and that person is ready to see type as credible and feasible for the organization. And because it is true that people are likely to support a change they help to design, the sooner you involve leaders in the organization, the more quickly and smoothly the process is likely to be.

Leaders will also want to be able to trust that introducing type into the organization will contribute to their success. They know that most innovations fizzle out, so they may be skeptical until they can see clearly the likelihood of success. No leader wants to be seen advocating an idea that may be rejected or ignored.

Although type may have taken you by storm, organizations have a tendency to resist change, and the process may be slow for many reasons. Such resistance has a purpose: stabilizing an organization. If you are prepared to anticipate the resisting force, it can often be converted into the supporting force.

And remember that the process will move more slowly for another reason that I mentioned in chapter 2: there is a natural progression in the absorption of type concepts that takes time.

Q: *How does type fit into your organizational culture?*

Some organizations are open to new ideas, with leaders actively looking for them. Some are quick to attend to new ideas but resist using them, perhaps because most members do not want to make changes in their practices. Some leaders are slow to consider new ways but, when convinced of their value, will give solid support for change.

One way of looking at these organizational differences was developed by Earle Page (1985) in a training handout called "Organizational Tendencies." Page observed that the organization's culture was strongly influenced by the type preferences of its leaders, either the current or founding leaders, or both. In addition an organization tends to attract and hold members who fit well in the culture. He saw the energy of an organization being distributed into four categories corresponding to the type preference combinations of Extraversion or Introversion, and Sensing or Intuition: IS, IN, EN, and ES. Although an organization needs the perspective of all four tendencies, it is usually steered by one of them.

IS energy is reflective and always practical. It is directed toward conserving what has proven to work well enough. Drawing strength from continuity, from protecting and enjoying the proven, it resists novel and unproven ideas, expecting them to be more disruptive than beneficial.

IN energy is reflective and engrossed in possibilities. It directs the organization to question the tried and true, take the long view, and imagine new ideas. Focused on anticipating the future, it assumes that a better way can and must be found.

EN energy pushes toward action on fresh ideas. It is focused on vitalizing the organization to take risks in trying new ways. Drawing strength from surges of enthusiasm for innovation, the EN viewpoint assumes organizations are at their best when pursuing important changes.

ES energy is directed toward action on life's practical realities. It steers the organization to get on with its obvious responsibilities. The emphasis is on staying on track, doing what is needed, and getting results.

All four perspectives or energies may be active in the organization. If they are recognized and valued for their positive characteristics and used in appropriate ways, the tension among them will be constructive. If not, then the tension will be seen as negative, and adherents of each viewpoint will see the others as having excessive influence and squandering the organization's resources. Page's exercise, "Organizational Tendencies" is very helpful in raising group members' awareness of these competing energies within the organization.

One of the four is likely to be a major shaper of your organization's culture, with the others playing a lesser role. Whichever is dominant will have a bearing on your approach to introducing type. The credibility of type will be an issue with all four, but for different reasons. If IS is dominant, and the organization is perceived as working well, you will need to show upfront that type can continue and protect well-accepted values and ways of working. That is quite a challenge, considering that uses of type are usually promoted as new ways of communicating and working, meant to replace the familiar. But if the IS organization is experiencing pain in areas where type could be helpful, it may well be open to considering practical new tools. In either case, in the IS organization, as you plan your credibility base, draw into it some status leaders who are IS stalwarts, and let them help you pace the introduction of type.

If your organization is energized around IN or EN values, change and newness are probably welcome, but the credibility of type is an issue in another way. IN and EN leaders are likely to have given considerable thought to the ideas they see as the guiding principles of the organization. For type to become one of those ideas, the leaders will need to see type as consistent with their visions for their organizations.

In contrast, if ES leaders are to see type as credible, they must believe that it is *clearly practical* and will help the organization get better results on its accepted objectives.

Keep in mind that the best of the values and skills of IS, IN, EN, or ES may not be steering the organization. The blind spots associated with each are also important to consider, Page counseled. *If not balanced by* other perspectives, the IS influence "may dry up the organization, narrowing leadership and productivity"; the IN influence may weaken the organization by pulling too much energy into "irrelevant ideas and alternatives"; the EN efforts for change may fail to see practical limits and exhaust the organization's resources; and the ES view may keep the leaders from seeing the necessity of change and keep the organization stuck in a rut. Observing some of the negative tendencies in your organization may help you size up the situation for introducing type.

It is also useful to consider the organization's "type" culture in terms of the day-to-day work of the organization. Does the work mostly call upon and reward introverted or extraverted behavior? Does the work attract and hold the interest of Introverts more than Extraverts, or vice versa?

Similarly, consider the other preferences: Sensing and Intuition, Thinking and Feeling, and Judging and Perceiving. Combining the four preferences can give you a hypothesis of the modal type of the organization. Read the type description of that type, and you will be able to discover some clues about the approach to introducing type that will be most appealing.

Q: *What are your assumptions about the specific influential people in this situation?*

At this point in your analysis, you have a fairly clear idea about which people are most influential in the situation: those who most affect the plan you are forming for introducing type. As you begin to see the roles you expect them to play in the plan, you will want to review your assumptions about the ways they will act and why they will act that way. If you are assuming a key person will act in a certain way and he or she doesn't, your plan may be upset. Try to test your assumptions ahead of time. Often you can ask people directly about how they will act by simply asking, for instance, "For this to work, here is what I will need . . . . " Talk it out whenever you can. Go over your assumptions with someone you trust who can give you a different perspective.

Deciding on Possible Entry Points

Your answers to the previous questions should give you a fairly complete estimate of the situation for introducing type. They may also suggest possible points of entry—that is, where, with whom, and how to start introducing type. In a school organization, typical points of entry are with people responsible for curriculum planning and instructional resources; with the leadership team, focusing on teamwork and management; with the counseling program; as part of a staff development program; with groups working on changing the organization, such as a school improvement team; or teacher by teacher, classroom by classroom. Your own position in the organization may indicate the point of entry. In each case, except perhaps the latter, you will need to have the leadership endorse and support the entry plan. You may be in a position that allows you only to plant the seeds of type with some person who then takes responsibility for the entry process, perhaps with you serving as a helper.

Analyzing the Forces For and Against

Whatever the point of entry being considered, the specific situation of the entry needs to be analyzed. The "force field" technique for analyzing a situation is useful in cases like this. There are three basic steps in force field analysis:

1. **Make a goal statement.** There are forces working for and forces working against the desired goal. For a successful analysis of the forces, you need a clearly focused goal statement. You can start with a fairly general goal, such as "the introduction of type so that it is accepted, used, and disseminated from the point of entry." Then the task is to decide what forces at this possible point of entry are working for and against the reaching of the goal.

2. **List the forces.** Begin the force field analysis with two lists, side by side, of forces for and against. For example, in the case of a community college senate leadership team, I asked questions about the situation until I had a fairly clear picture of forces for and forces against the constructive use of type. Because I was not a member of the organization, my interest was to plant the seeds, and I wanted to know whether the conditions were favorable for them to grow. When you are a member of the organization and want to assess the rightness of a possible entry point, your questions to yourself will be to estimate which people and conditions in the situation will be favorable and unfavorable to the use of type.

3. **Consider the strength of the forces.** The next step in force field analysis is to weigh the relative strength of each force in the equation: which favorable forces can you strengthen and how, and which unfavorable ones can you weaken and how? Can you do this with the resources at hand? The situation, as it is, is an equilibrium of the forces; to get energy into accomplishing my goal—the acceptance of type through this entry point—I had to change the balance of forces, change the status quo that did not then include uses of type.

An Example of Analyzing the Forces

Consider the situation of a young high school teacher who was eager to extend uses of type in his school. The school had a good record of serving the academically oriented, college-bound students. However it did not have a similar record with students not heading to college. As a vocational education teacher, he taught mainly the latter students. The principal put him on a committee of teachers charged with the task of finding out what was needed to better serve the students who were likely to enter the workforce after graduation, if they made it to graduation. The committee members were given time during the school day to do their work. The young teacher saw this committee work as an entry point for introducing type. Following is part of the force field analysis he did. His goal statement was "to have the committee support type as a way of looking at learning needs of students and improving their instruction."

His list of favorable forces:

- Committee appreciates my energy and ideas.
- Committee has agreed to consider type.
- Principal knows about type and supports its use.
- Type data about SP types being disadvantaged by the standard academic programs should help us see ways to improve instruction.
- Some teachers of academic subjects, and all of the administrators, are concerned about the students who aren't college-bound.
- Nearly all the teachers are interested in improving instruction.
- Other committee members are well known and respected by the faculty.
- We have funds to give the MBTI assessment to students and faculty.

His list of unfavorable forces:

- Committee members don't know about type, nor do most others on the faculty.
- I am one of the younger teachers and not well known.
- Teachers usually resist changing the curriculum and their ways of teaching.
- Committee has no idea of how much support its recommendations will receive.

- Teachers mostly ignored learning styles work (not type) we did on an in-service day two years ago.

He went through his lists to see what favorable forces could be strengthened and what unfavorable ones could be weakened. For our purposes, we don't need the details of his analysis, so following is a summary:

1. The committee is a good point of entry, because the other members are open to ideas and I have credibility with them.

2. I will need to go step-by-step, first introducing type to the committee, then getting their approval to collect some type data on students.

3. Although most faculty members do not know me well, the ninth-grade teachers do. I probably can get their okay and the principal's approval to administer the MBTI assessment to all freshmen and to have the teachers of ninth-graders take it, too. I expect to get some data that will show the committee the value of using type in their work and including it in their recommendations to the faculty.

4. Because two committee members are department heads, the next step would be for the committee to try out ideas, including type, on all the department heads.

These conclusions were the basis for his entry plan. After the committee members took the Indicator and participated in an orientation to type, they supported gathering data on the freshman class and teachers. Administering the Indicator to the ninth-graders and their teachers did provide some data of importance. Most interesting was the fact that more than one-third of the students reported as SP types, while only three of their teachers (less than 10 percent) reported as SPs. These entry activities opened the door for a wider introduction of type into the school.

Once an entry has been made, as in this case, the situation usually needs a revised force field analysis because the forces change. In addition, the goal statement may need to be changed as the goal is pursued into the next phase of introducing type into the organization.

Deciding on Strategy: The Long View

All of the analysis you have done to this point suggests a strategy, a big-picture plan. *Strategy* is a military term. It is distinguished from *tactic*, a plan for action within the strategy. A tactic is consistent with the strategy and is one part of carrying out the strategy.

Write out your strategy. It can begin with summary statements from the analysis you have done and with your ideas for entry. When you have it written fully, I suggest you try to boil it down to a few phrases or sentences. As your plan progresses and you bring others into the planning of next steps, the strategy statement in its brief form (perhaps amended by the base group) will serve to keep everyone's eye on the target. The young high school teacher had a beginning strategy, through the committee and the department heads.

Deciding on Tactics: An Action Plan

An action plan deals with details: who will do what, when, and how. This is the aspect of planning most of us know well, even though we often neglect to plan the details well. I have nothing fresh to add to this technique of planning except some details about introducing type to people.

Essential Details: Creating Appropriate Conditions for Introducing Type

I suggest you use the following questions as a checklist whenever you are planning to administer the MBTI assessment and/or explain type to people. Some of the details concern ethical issues. The last section of this chapter deals specifically with guidelines for the ethics of using type. Administering the Indicator and interpreting the results should be done by a qualified person, one who understands type and the limits and appropriate uses of psychological tests. If you are not qualified, read the epilogue following this chapter. It includes more information about this and suggestions for locating a qualified person. If you do get someone else, review the following guidelines to be sure the program is presented in a manner that best suits your group:

1. **The people taking the MBTI assessment:**

   a. What do they see as their purpose for taking it? Watch for hidden agendas and misunderstandings. Don't rely just on reasons and reported perceptions given to you by an intermediary whose motives you don't know.

   b. What is their view of the potential value of it? You may need to clarify their understanding.

   c. What do they see as their options for taking or not taking the instrument? What do they see as the consequences of not taking it?

   d. What uses do they see for the reports, and what level of control do they have over the results?

   e. What do they see as the leaders' expectations of them that are implied in introducing type to members of the organization? The ethics guidelines that follow this section will help you form specific answers to all of these questions.

2. **The formats and approaches:** How shall I fit the administration of the MBTI assessment and the type explanation to the people? You will want to anticipate the dynamics of the group and fit the introduction to the members. Design the explanation session around their purpose for taking the Indicator. For example, if work-team dynamics is the theme, then the session should give the team members opportunities to practice using type in team dialogue, and they will need to discuss their types with each other. When type is introduced *appropriately* into the team-building process, team members report that type concepts provide a concrete, objective way for them to talk about their personality differences in teamwork—their differences in perception, decision style, pace, priorities, et cetera—without getting personal, that is, without feeling that the mention of differences constitutes a personal attack.

   If the purpose of introducing type is to examine learning and teaching styles, there are many activities in this book that can be used. Whatever the purpose they understood was being served by learning about type, it is important that participants in the session have opportunities to practice using type for that purpose.

3. **Administration and scoring of the Indicator:** What options fit your situation? Whether it is administered in a group session or individually, during work hours, or filled out at home, it is important to follow the guidelines for administration and scoring given in the *MBTI® Manual*.

4. **Resources and follow-up support:** What materials will the participants need to have during the type explanation session, to take home as a reference, and to have available in a resource library within your organization? What resource people may be needed to help them learn type -related skills and to explore type beyond your knowledge? Their continued and constructive uses of type will depend on such follow-up support.

At a minimum they will need a sheet of words and phrases that characterize the type preferences, a report of their MBTI results, a copy of the *Descriptions of the Sixteen Types* booklet, and perhaps other full descriptions of the sixteen types. That is their basic set for any explanation session and for taking home. In addition, they should have handouts related to their purpose for taking the Indicator. Publications for the resource library can be found in the catalogs available from CPP (www.CPP.com) and CAPT (www.CAPT.org).

Ethical Guidelines for Using the MBTI® Instrument

Since 1975 when the MBTI instrument was first published for general use, millions of people have taken it and have been introduced to the concepts behind it. Conscientious practitioners kept track of the successes and pitfalls they experienced in administering the Indicator and guiding people in uses of its concepts. They began to shape an informal code of ethical practices for using the Indicator, and some of the practitioners formalized the code into guidelines when they formed the Association for Psychological Type in 1979. Adhere to these guidelines as you shepherd your plan.

The Ethical Principles

Following are the most basic principles for using the MBTI assessment I extracted from the ethical guidelines adopted by the APTi membership:

Voluntary. The client has the choice of taking the Indicator or not. Even subtle pressure should be avoided. In situations where the success of using it depends on every member trying out the ideas of type, as in teams or families, you can offer the instrument to all members, score it for those who choose to take it, and then provide a group type explanation to all, including anyone who didn't take it. After the explanation and during introductory activities, those who didn't take it nearly always are willing to hypothesize a type for themselves and ask to take the MBTI assessment.

Confidential. The practitioner gives the MBTI results directly to the person and not to anyone else. An individual's type does not go to the boss or into a personnel file unless he or she offers to give the information. People usually are comfortable talking about their type, but the MBTI outcome is theirs to reveal or not.

Enhance, not restrict. MBTI results and type concepts are used only to enhance someone's understanding and opportunities, not to restrict their options. The career counselor, for example, does not counsel a client away from a particular occupation because his or her type is rare in that occupation but, rather, provides the information in the context of discussing the opportunities and challenges of the that career in relation to the strengths of the client's type.

Person-to-person explanation. The MBTI respondent always gets a personal explanation of type from the practitioner. He or she always has an opportunity for dialogue about the results and for exploring the ideas to find a best-fit type. For that reason they never get their results through the mail or secondhand.

Full type description. The respondent always gets a full type description to accompany the MBTI scored results. I always give them a resource booklet such as *Descriptions of the Sixteen Types or* Myers' *Introduction to Type®* that includes not only a full description of their reported type but also all the other types—which some may want to explore to find a better fit. Respondents need good resource materials in their hands when they are later considering type or explaining it to family or colleagues.

What's indicated, what's not. In explaining MBTI results and the type concepts, the practitioner needs to distinguish between what the Indicator does and does not indicate: type characteristics are tendencies, not imperatives; they are preferences, not abilities or achievement potential; and they represent one view of personality, not a panacea. And the MBTI assessment indicates types, not stereotypes.

Finally, before you start to introduce type into your organization, revisit chapter 5, "Type Is a Four-Letter Word." It will help you spot pitfalls you will want to avoid.

EPILOGUE: NEXT STEPS

THE COMMUNITY OF people who use the Myers-Briggs Type Indicator® assessment has expanded rapidly since the first edition of *People Types & Tiger Stripes* was published in 1979. Many of them stay in contact with each other and with new ideas about type through the Association for Psychological Type International (APTi), a membership organization formed that same year. APTi membership is open to all persons interested in type (go to www.aptinternational.org).

APTi has developed a number of ways of spreading knowledge about type. It helps create local chapters whose members meet to "talk type." It sponsors regional conferences and, in the odd-numbered years, an international conference. APTi members join one or more interest areas: Careers and Occupations, Counseling and Psychotherapy, Education, Multicultural and International Issues, Management and Organizational Development, Psychological Theory and Research, and Religion and Spirituality. APTi members exchange ideas through APTi's quarterly newsletter, *Bulletin of Psychological Type*. There is also the *Journal of Psychological Type*®, now an e-journal published by CAPT (www.capt.org) that focuses on research involving psychological type.

In 1985 APTi initiated a training program designed to provide participants with the basic knowledge needed for ethical use of the MBTI® assessment. Minimum requirements to purchase the Indicator are established by its publisher, CPP, Inc., and include professional use of the instrument and completion of course work in psychological tests and measurement (or equivalent documented training in tests and measurement). Information about how to qualify to purchase and use the Myers-Briggs Type Indicator instrument can be found at www.capt.org and www.cpp.com.

The Myers and Briggs Foundation website, (www.myersbriggs.org) is another helpful resource. The foundation was established to extend the work of Katharine Briggs and Isabel Myers through research, and to support sound and ethical uses of the MBTI assessment.

The resources for learning about and supporting your uses of type are too numerous to mention, and the list is growing rapidly. When the first edition of *People Types & Tiger Stripes* was published in 1979, it was the first book about applications of the MBTI® assessment besides the *MBTI® Manual* and Myers' booklet *Introduction to Type*. Now, the CAPT catalog, for example, lists more than 200 books, not to mention trainer's materials and audiovisual resources—over a very wide range of applications.

If you are involved with the education of children in the elementary and middle school grades, you will want to become familiar with the Murphy-Meisgeier Type Indicator for Children® (MMTIC®) assessment and related materials, now published by the Center for Applications of Psychological Type. CAPT also publishes a booklet that provides descriptions of the sixteen types for young people, which may assist you on your journey to the understanding and use of type.

Best wishes for your explorations into type. You can contact me through CAPT.

A

APPENDIX

Descriptions of the Sixteen Types*

What the MBTI® Instrument Reports

- The Myers-Briggs Type Indicator® (MBTI®) instrument identifies people's preferences among sets of mental processes.
- Each MBTI item you answered is counted on one of four scales.
- Each scale is made up of a pair of opposites, with a range of preferences between them.
- Your answers on each scale add up to a preference score, to estimate how much you prefer one of each pair over the other.
- The preferences combine sixteen ways, representing sixteen types of mental processing. Each type has a distinctive way of attending to the world and making decisions. Everyone has interests in all categories, but favors one from each pair. The MBTI instrument sorts people according to these preference clarity categories:

Extraversion or Introversion Sensing or Intuition Thinking or Feeling Judging or Perceiving	slight | moderate | clear | very clear

- Everyone uses all eight categories, but each person has preferences among them and uses those more. It is a lot like handedness—everyone uses both hands but favors and is better at using one of them.
- Each different combination of preferences represents a type—what the psychology pioneer Carl Jung called psychological types. There are sixteen combinations to represent the sixteen types.
- A type is not a pigeonhole or stereotype; it is a particular way that mental energy is organized.
- Your results from the MBTI instrument will indicate one of the sixteen type descriptions for you to consider.

---

*The material in this appendix is adapted from *Descriptions of the Sixteen Types* by Gordon D. Lawrence (CAPT). Used with permission.

Words to Help Understanding of the Type Concepts

EXTRAVERSION (E)

When I prefer Extraversion, I am . . .

- Oriented to the outer world
- Focusing on people and things
- Active
- Using trial and error with confidence
- Scanning the environment for stimulation

INTROVERSION (I)

When I prefer Introversion, I am . . .

- Oriented to the inner world
- Focusing on ideas, inner impressions
- Reflective
- Considering deeply before acting
- Finding stimulation inwardly

SENSING PERCEPTION (S)

When using my Sensing, I am . . .

- Perceiving with the five senses
- Attending to practical and factual details
- In touch with the physical realities
- Attending to the present moment
- Confining attention to what is said and done
- Seeing "little things" in everyday life
- Attending to step-by-step experience
- Letting "the eyes tell the mind"

INTUITION PERCEPTION (N)

When using my Intuition, I am . . .

- Perceiving with memory and associations
- Seeing patterns and meanings
- Seeing possibilities
- Projecting possibilities for the future
- Imagining; "reading between the lines"
- Looking for the big picture
- Having hunches; "ideas out of nowhere"
- Letting "the mind tell the eyes"

THINKING JUDGMENT (T)

When reasoning with Thinking, I am . . .

- Using logical analysis
- Using objective and impersonal criteria
- Drawing cause-and-effect relationships
- Being firm-minded
- Prizing logical order
- Being skeptical

FEELING JUDGMENT (F)

When reasoning with Feeling, I am . . .

- Applying personal priorities
- Weighing human values and motives, my own and others
- Appreciating
- Valuing warmth in relationships
- Prizing harmony; trusting

JUDGING (J)

When I take a Judging attitude, I am . . .

- Using thinking or feeling judgment outwardly
- Deciding and planning
- Organizing and scheduling
- Controlling and regulating
- Goal oriented
- Wanting closure, even when data are incomplete

PERCEIVING (P)

When I take a Perceiving attitude, I am . . .

- Using Sensing or Intuitive perception outwardly
- Taking in information
- Adapting and changing
- Curious and interested
- Open-minded
- Resisting closure to obtain more data

Descriptions of the Sixteen Types Reported by the MBTI® Instrument

Using these descriptions and other resources, decide if the indicated description fits you. If it does, the resources will help you see many uses of this knowledge. If the description does not seem to be a good fit, look for another description that is a better fit. The person explaining your MBTI results can direct you to the other resources. The MBTI instrument is a tool to help you start examining the types. While it was developed with great care, and is accurate for most people, you are the one to decide which type is the best fit for you. You may want to read all of the descriptions as you decide.

How to Read the Descriptions

The descriptions are grouped in two ways. The types who prefer Extraversion are on the left side of each page, and the types who prefer Introversion are on the right. The types with Thinking as the strongest mental process are grouped together and across from those with Feeling as the strongest mental process (pages 256 and 257). The Sensing types are across from the Intuitive types (pages 258 and 259). The strongest mental process in each case is indicated by the larger letter in the four-letter type designation, such as ISFP.

The descriptions are arranged with opposite types across from each other on the same page. For example, ENTJ is across from ISFP, the type that is opposite in all four dimensions. As you read the phrases listed for each type, you should not assume that a positive value listed for one type implies a negative trait for the opposite type. For example, when we read that ENTJs value efficiency, we must not infer that ISFPs are inefficient. Similarly, because ISFPs value compassion does not mean that ENTJs are cold-hearted. Opposite types are across from each other to help you decide your best fit type.The contrasts shown by the opposites help to clarify what is given priority in our mental processing. What has high priority for ISFP is not given high priority by ENTJ, and vice versa. The descriptions emphasize the values and priorities of the types more than they tell what behaviors are associated with each of the types. The values are emphasized because they are the motivational energy behind the behaviors.

ENTJ

Intuitive, innovative ORGANIZERS; analytical, systematic, confident; push to get action on new ideas and challenges. Having Extraverted THINKING as their strongest mental process, ENTJs are at their best when they can take charge and set things in logical order. They value:

- Analyzing abstract problems, complex situations
- Foresight; pursuing a vision
- Changing, organizing things to fit their vision
- Putting theory into practice, ideas into action
- Working to a plan and schedule
- Initiating, then delegating
- Efficiency; removing obstacles and confusion
- Probing new possibilities
- Holding self and others to high standards
- Having things settled and closed
- Tough-mindedness, directness, task-focused behavior
- Objective principles; fairness, justice
- Assertive, direct action
- Intellectual resourcefulness
- Driving toward broad goals along a logical path
- Designing structures and strategies
- Seeking out logical flaws

ESTJ

Fact-minded practical ORGANIZERS; assertive, analytical, systematic; push to get things done, working smoothly and efficiently. Having Extraverted THINKING as their strongest mental process, they are at their best when they can take charge and set things in logical order. They value:

- Results; doing, acting
- Planned, organized work and play
- Common sense practicality
- Consistency; standard procedures
- Concrete, present-day usefulness
- Deciding quickly and logically
- Having things settled and closed
- Rules, objective standards, fairness by the rules
- Task-focused behavior
- Directness, tough-mindedness
- Orderliness; no loose ends
- Systematic structure; efficiency
- Categorizing aspects of their life
- Scheduling and monitoring
- Protecting what works

ISFP

Observant, loyal HELPERS; reflective, realistic, empathic, patient with details. Shunning disagreements, they are gentle, reserved and modest. Having Introverted FEELING as their strongest mental process, they are at their best when responding to the needs of others. They value:

- Personal loyalty; a close, loyal friend
- Finding delight in the moment
- Seeing what needs doing to improve the moment
- Freedom from organizational constraints
- Working individually
- Peacemaking behind the scenes
- Attentiveness to feelings
- Harmonious, cooperative work settings
- Spontaneous, hands-on exploration
- Gentle, respectful interactions
- Deeply held personal beliefs
- Reserved, reflective behavior
- Practical, useful skills and know-how
- Having their work life be fully consistent with deeply held values
- Showing and receiving appreciation

INFP

Imaginative, independent HELPERS; reflective, inquisitive, empathic, loyal to ideals: more tuned to possibilities than practicalities. Having Introverted FEELING as their strongest mental process, they are at their best when their inner ideals find expression in their helping of people. They value:

- Harmony in the inner life of ideas
- Harmonious work settings; working individually
- Seeing the big picture possibilities
- Creativity; curiosity, exploring
- Helping people find their potential
- Giving ample time to reflect on decisions
- Adaptability and openness
- Compassion and caring; attention to feelings
- Work that lets them express their idealism
- Gentle, respectful interactions
- An inner compass; being unique
- Showing appreciation and being appreciated
- Ideas, language, and writing
- A close, loyal friend
- Perfecting what is important

ESFJ

Practical HARMONIZERS, workers with people; sociable, orderly, opinioned; conscientious, realistic and well tuned to the here and now. Having Extraverted FEELING as their strongest mental process, they are at their best when responsible for winning people's cooperation with personal caring and practical help. They value:

- An active, sociable life, with many relationships
- A concrete, present-day view of life
- Making daily routines into gracious living
- Staying closely tuned to people they care about so as to avoid interpersonal troubles
- Talking out problems cooperatively, caringly
- Approaching problems through rules, authority, standard procedures
- Caring, compassion, and tactfulness
- Helping organizations serve their members well
- Responsiveness to others and to traditions
- Being prepared, reliability in tangible, daily work
- Loyalty and faithfulness
- Practical skillfulness grounded in experience
- Structured learning in a humane setting
- Appreciation

ENFJ

Imaginative HARMONIZERS, workers with people; expressive, orderly, opinioned, conscientious; curious about new ideas and possibilities. Having Extraverted FEELING as their strongest mental process, they are at their best when responsible for winning people's cooperation with caring insight into their needs. They value:

- Having a wide circle of relationships
- Having a positive, enthusiastic view of life
- Seeing subtleties in people and interactions
- Understanding others' needs and concerns
- An active, energizing social life
- Seeing possibilities in people
- Thorough follow-through on important projects
- Working on several projects at once
- Caring and imaginative problem solving
- Maintaining relationships to make things work
- Shaping organizations to better serve members
- Sociability and responsiveness
- Structured learning in a humane setting
- Caring, compassion, and tactfulness
- Appreciation as the natural means of encouraging improvements

INTP

Inquisitive ANALYZERS; reflective, independent, curious; more interested in organizing ideas than situations or people. Having Introverted THINKING as their strongest mental process, they are at their best when following their intellectual curiosity, analyzing complexities to find the underlying logical principles. They value:

- A reserved outer life; an inner life of logical inquiry
- Pursuing interests in depth, with concentration
- Work and play that is intriguing, not routine
- Being free of emotional issues when working
- Working on problems that respond to detached intuitive analysis and theorizing
- Approaching problems by reframing the obvious
- Complex intellectual mysteries
- Being absorbed in abstract, mental work
- Freedom from organizational constraints
- Independence and nonconformance
- Intellectual quickness, ingenuity, invention
- Competence in the world of ideas
- Spontaneous learning by following curiosity and inspirations

ISTP

Practical ANALYZERS; value exactness; more interested in organizing data than situations or people; reflective, cool and curious observers of life. Having Introverted THINKING as their strongest mental process, they are at their best when analyzing experience to find the logical order and underlying properties of things. They value:

- A reserved outer life
- Having a concrete, present-day view of life
- Clear, exact facts (a large storehouse of them)
- Looking for efficient, least-effort solutions based on experience
- Knowing how mechanical things work
- Pursuing interests in depth, such as hobbies
- Collecting things of interest
- Working on problems that respond to detached, sequential analysis and adaptability
- Freedom from organizational constraints
- Independence and self-management
- Spontaneous hands-on learning experience
- Having useful technical expertise
- Critical analysis as a means to improving things

ESTP

REALISTIC ADAPTERS in the world of material things; good-natured, easygoing; oriented to practical, firsthand experience; highly observant of details of things. Having Extraverted SENSING as their strongest mental process, they are at their best when free to act on impulses, or responding to concrete problems that need solving. They value:

- A life of outward, playful action in the moment
- Being a troubleshooter
- Finding ways to use the existing system
- Clear, concrete, exact facts
- Knowing the way mechanical things work
- Being direct, to the point
- Learning through spontaneous, hands-on action
- Practical action, more than words
- Plunging into new adventures
- Responding to practical needs as they arise
- Seeing the expedient thing and acting on it
- Pursuing immediately useful skills
- Finding fun in their work and sparking others to have fun
- Looking for efficient, least-effort solutions
- Being caught up in enthusiasms

ESFP

REALISTIC ADAPTERS in human relationships; friendly and easy with people, highly observant of their feelings and needs; oriented to practical, firsthand experience. Extraverted SENSING being their strongest mental process, they are at their best when free to act on impulses, responding to needs of the here and now. They value:

- An energetic, sociable life, full of friends and fun
- Performing, entertaining, sharing
- Immediately useful skills; practical know-how
- Learning through spontaneous, hands-on action
- Trust and generosity; openness
- Patterning themselves after those they admire
- Concrete, practical knowledge; resourcefulness
- Caring, kindness, support, appreciation
- Freedom from irrelevant rules
- Handling immediate, practical problems and crises
- Seeing tangible realities; least-effort solutions
- Showing and receiving appreciation
- Making the most of the moment; adaptability
- Being caught up in enthusiasms
- Easing and brightening work and play

INFJ

People-oriented INNOVATORS of ideas; serious, quietly forceful and persevering; concerned with work that will help the world and inspire others. Having Introverted INTUITION as their strongest mental process, they are at their best when caught up in inspiration, envisioning and creating ways to empower self and others to lead more meaningful lives. They value:

- A reserved outer life; spontaneous inner life
- Planning ways to help people improve
- Seeing complexities, hidden meanings
- Understanding others' needs and concerns
- Imaginative ways of saying things
- Planful, independent, academic learning
- Reading, writing, imagining; academic theories
- Being restrained in outward actions; planful
- Aligning their work with their ideals
- Pursuing and clarifying their ideals
- Taking the long view
- Bringing out the best in others through appreciation
- Finding harmonious solutions to problems
- Being inspired and inspiring others

INTJ

Logical, critical, decisive INNOVATORS of ideas; serious, intent, very independent, concerned with organization; determined, often stubborn. With Introverted INTUITION as their strongest mental process, they are at their best when inspiration turns insights into ideas and plans for improving human knowledge and systems. They value:

- A restrained, organized outer life; a spontaneous, intuitive inner life
- Conceptual skills, theorizing
- Planful, independent, academic learning
- Skepticism; critical analysis; objective principles
- Originality, independence of mind
- Intellectual quickness, ingenuity
- Nonemotional tough-mindedness
- Freedom from interference in projects
- Working to a plan and schedule
- Seeing complexities, hidden meanings
- Improving things by finding flaws
- Probing new possibilities; taking the long view
- Pursuing a vision; foresight; conceptualizing
- Getting insights to reframe problems

ENTP

Inventive, analytical PLANNERS OF CHANGE; enthusiastic and independent; pursue inspiration with impulsive energy; seek to understand and inspire. Extraverted INTUITION being their strongest mental process, they are at their best when caught up in the enthusiasm of a new project and promoting its benefits. They value:

- Conceiving of new things and initiating change
- The surge of inspirations; the pull of emerging possibilities
- Analyzing complexities
- Following their insights, wherever they lead
- Finding meanings behind the facts
- Autonomy, elbow room, openness
- Ingenuity, originality, a fresh perspective
- Mental models and concepts that explain life
- Fair treatment
- Flexibility, adaptability
- Learning through action, variety, and discovery
- Exploring theories and meanings behind events
- Improvising, looking for novel ways
- Work made light by inspiration

ENFP

Warmly enthusiastic PLANNERS OF CHANGE; imaginative, individualistic; pursue inspiration with impulsive energy; seek to understand and inspire others. With Extraverted INTUITION as the strongest mental process, they are at their best when caught in the enthusiasm of a project, sparking others to see its benefits. They value:

- The surge of inspirations; the pull of emerging possibilities
- A life of variety, people, warm relationships
- Following their insights wherever they lead
- Finding meanings behind the facts
- Creativity, originality, a fresh perspective
- An optimistic, positive, enthusiastic view of life
- Flexibility and openness
- Exploring, devising, and trying out new things
- Open-ended opportunities and options
- Freedom from the requirement of being practical
- Learning through action, variety, and discovery
- A belief that any obstacles can be overcome
- A focus on people's potentials
- Brainstorming to solve problems
- Work made light and playful by inspiration

ISFJ

Sympathetic MANAGERS OF FACTS AND DETAILS, concerned with people's welfare; stable, conservative, dependable, painstaking, systematic. Having Introverted SENSING as their strongest mental process, they are at their best when using their sensible intelligence and practical skills to help others in tangible ways. They value:

- Preserving; enjoying the things of proven value
- Steady, sequential work yielding reliable results
- A controlled, orderly outer life
- Patient, persistent attention to basic needs
- Following a sensible path, based on experience
- A rich memory for concrete facts
- Loyalty, strong relationships
- Consistency, familiarity, the tried and true
- Firsthand experience of what is important
- Compassion, kindness, caring
- Working to a plan and schedule
- Learning through planned, sequential teaching
- Set routines, common-sense options
- Rules, authority, set procedures
- Hard work, perseverance

ISTJ

Analytical MANAGER OF FACTS AND DETAILS; dependable, conservative, systematic, painstaking, decisive, stable. Having Introverted SENSING as their strongest mental process, they are at their best when charged with organizing and maintaining data and material important to others and to themselves. They value:

- Steady, systematic work that yields reliable results
- A controlled outer life grounded in the present
- Following a sensible path, based on experience
- Concrete, exact, immediately useful facts, skills
- Consistency, familiarity, the tried and true
- A concrete, present-day view of life
- Working to a plan and schedule
- Preserving and enjoying things of proven value
- Proven systems, common-sense options
- Freedom from emotionality in deciding things
- Learning through planned, sequential teaching
- Skepticism; wanting to read the fine print first
- A focus on hard work, perseverance
- Quiet, logical, detached problem solving
- Serious and focused work and play

B

APPENDIX

The Four Columns: Combinations of Perception and Judgment

(Sensing plus Thinking)	(Sensing plus Feeling)
ST	**SF**
Practical and matter-of-fact	Sympathetic and friendly
Like using abilities in: Technical skills with facts and objects	**Like using abilities in:** Practical help and services for people
For example: • Applied Sciences • Business • Production • Construction and more	**For example:** • Patient Care • Community Service • Sales • Teaching and more
(Intuition plus Thinking)	**(Intuition plus Feeling)**
NT	**NF**
Logical and ingenious	Enthusiastic and insightful
Like using abilities in: Theoretical and technical developments	**Like using abilities in:** Understanding and communicating with people
For example: • Physical Sciences • Research • Management • Forecasts, Analysis, • and more	**For example:** • Behavioral Sciences • Research • Literature and Art • Teaching and more

REFERENCES

DeNovellis, R. and G. Lawrence. 1983. Correlations of Teacher Personality Variables (Myers-Briggs) and Classroom Observation Data. *Research in Psychological Type* 6: 37–46.

Hammer, A. L. 1985. Typing or Stereotyping? Unconscious Bias in Applications of Psychological Type Theory. *Journal of Psychological Type* 10: 14–19.

Hoffman, J. and M. Betkouski. 1981. A Summary of Myers-Briggs Type Indicator Research Applications in Education. *Research in Psychological Type* 3: 3–41.

Jung, C. G. 1921/1971. *Psychological Types.* Princeton: Princeton University Press.

Lawrence, G. D. (1984). A Synthesis of Learning Style Research Involving the MBTI. *Journal of Psychological Type,* 8: 2–15.

Lawrence, G. D. (1997). *Looking at Type and Learning Styles.* Gainesville, FL: Center for Applications of Psychological Type.

McCaulley, M. H. and F. L. Natter. 1974. Psychological (Myers-Briggs) Type Differences in Education. In F. L. Natter and S. A. Rollin (eds.), The Governor's Task Force on Disruptive Youth: Phase II Report (pp. 92–212). Tallahassee, FL: Office of the Governor.

McCaulley, M. H. 1978. *Application of the Myers-Briggs Type Indicator to Medicine and Other Health Professions.* HRA Contract 231-76-0051, DHEW. Gainesville, FL: Center for Applications of Psychological Type.

Mitroff, I. I. and Kilmann, R. H. (1975). Stories Managers Tell: A New Tool for Organizational Problem-Solving. *Management Review,* 64(7): 18–28.

Myers, I. B.1962/1975. *Manual: The Myers-Briggs Type Indicator.* Palo Alto, CA: Consulting Psychologists Press.

Myers, I. B., McCaulley, M. H., Quenk, N. L. & Hammer, A. L. (1998). MBTI Manual: A guide to the development and use of the Myers-Briggs Type Indicator (3rd ed.). Palo Alto, CA: Consulting Psychologists Press.

Myers, I. B. and M. H. McCaulley. *1985. Manual: A Guide to the Development and Use of the Myers-Briggs Type Indicator,* 2nd ed. Palo Alto, CA: Consulting Psychologists Press.

Myers, I. B. with P. B. Myers. 1980. *Gifts Differing.* Palo Alto, CA: Consulting Psychologists Press.

Osmond, H., M. Siegler, and R.Smoke. (1977, Fall). Typology Revisited: A New Perspective. *Psychological Perspectives* 8(2): 206–219.

Page, E. C. 1985. *Organizational Tendencies.* (Training handout). Gainesville, FL: Center for Applications of Psychological Type.

Thompson, L. L. 1984. An Investigation of the Relationship of the Personality Theory of C. G. Jung and Teachers' Self-Reported Perceptions and Decisions. Doctoral dissertation, Ohio State University.

Wiggins, J. S. (1989). Review of the Myers-Briggs Type Indicator. In The Tenth Mental Measurements Yearbook, J. C. Conoley and J. J. Kramer (eds.), pp. 536-538. Lincoln, NE: Buros Institute of Mental Measurements, University of Nebraska-Lincoln.

Zemke, R. 1992. Second Thoughts about the MBTI. *Training* 29 (4):43–47.

Further Reading

Allen, M., C. Hayman, and K. Abella. 2009. *Discovering Type with Teens: A Comprehensive Leader's Guide with Materials for Presenting the Myers-Briggs Type Indicator® Instrument to Young People.* Gainesville, FL: Center for Applications of Psychological Type.

Kise, J. A. G. 2006. *Differentiated Coaching: A Framework for Helping Teachers Change.* Thousand Oaks, CA: Corwin Press.

Kise, J. A. G. 2007. *Differentiation Through Personality Types: A Framework for Instruction, Assessment, and Classroom Management.* Thousand Oaks, CA: Corwin Press.

Kise, J. A. G., and B. Russell. 2008. *Differentiated School Leadership: Effective Collaboration, Communication, and Change Through Personality* Type. Thousand Oaks, CA: Corwin Press.

Lawrence, G. D. and C. R. Martin, 2001. *Building People, Building Programs: A Practitioner's Guide for Introducing the MBTI To Individuals and Organizations.* Gainesville, FL: Center for Applications of Psychological Type.

Murphy, E. and C. Meisgeier 2008. *MMTIC® Manual: A Guide to the Development and Use of the Murphy-Meisgeier Type Indicator for Children®*. Gainesville, FL: Center for Applications of Psychological Type.

Myers, I. B., M. H. McCaulley, N. L. Quenk, and A. L. Hammer. 1998. *MBTI Manual: A Guide to the Development and Use of the Myers-Briggs Type Indicator* (3rd ed.). Mountain View, CA: Consulting Psychologists Press.

VanSant, S. and D. Payne, 2009. *Great Minds Don't Think Alike: Success for Students through the Application of Psychological Type in Schools.* Gainesville, FL: Center for Applications of Psychological Type.

INDEX

A

B

C

D

E

K

L

M

O

P

Q

S

T

Z

GORDON LAWRENCE, PH.D., is renowned for developing practical uses of the Myers-Briggs Type Indicator® instrument since the early 1970s. He helped organize the first-ever conference of MBTI® users in 1975 and helped to found the Association for Psychological Type four years later. When the first edition of *People Types and Tiger Stripes* appeared in 1979, it was the first book about uses of the MBTI instrument other than the *MBTI® Manual*. Through workshops and teaching he introduced the MBTI instrument and psychological type concepts to thousands of people. In addition to many articles about type, he wrote *Descriptions of the Sixteen Types* (CAPT 1995) and *Looking at Type® and Learning Styles* (CAPT1997). He coauthored with Charles Martin, Ph.D., *Building People, Building Programs: A Practitioner's Guide for Introducing the MBTI® to Individuals and Organizations* (CAPT 2001).

Dr. Lawrence was the third president of the Association for Psychological Type (APT), and he directed the development of the APT MBTI training program to qualify people to purchase and use the MBTI instrument. He used the MBTI assessment extensively in research, teaching, and consulting during the twenty years that he was professor of instructional leadership at the University of Florida. He served on the board of directors of the Center for Applications of Psychological Type in Gainesville, Florida, from its founding in 1975 by Isabel Myers, the developer of the MBTI instrument, and Mary McCaulley, Ph.D.

discovering type with teens!
discovering type with teens!
A comprehensive leader's guide with materials for presenting psychological type to young people.
MOLLIE ALLEN • CLAIRE HAYMAN • KAY ABELLA